I0822177

A Child of the Revolution

A Child of the Revolution

William Henry Harrison and His World, 1773–1798

Hendrik Booraem V

The Kent State University Press
Kent, Ohio

For R. D. B.

Library of Congress Catalog Card Number 2012013501
ISBN 978-1-60635-115-4
Manufactured in the United States of America

Library of Congress Cataloging-in-Publication Data
Booraem, Hendrik, 1939–
A child of the revolution : William Henry Harrison and his world, 1773–1798 / Hendrik Booraem V.
p. cm.
Includes bibliographical references and index.
ISBN 978-1-60635-115-4 (hardcover : alk. paper) ∞
1. Harrison, William Henry, 1773–1841—Childhood and youth.
2. Harrison, William Henry, 1773–1841—Career in the military.
3. United States. Army—Military life—History—18th century.
4. United States—History—1783–1815.
5. Presidents—United States—Biography. I. Title.
e392.b69 2012
973.3092—dc23
[B]
2012013501

12 13 14 15 16 5 4 3 2 1

Contents

A child of the Revolution, my attachment to liberty was imbibed in my earliest youth.

—*Harrison to Luther Bradish, 20 February 1836*

'Twas in truth an hour
Of universal ferment; mildest men
Were agitated; and commotions, strife
Of passion and opinion, filled the walls
Of peaceful houses with unquiet sounds.
The soil of common life was at that time
Too hot to tread upon.

—*Wordsworth,* The Prelude

But man in general was not born to remain in a state of childhood; nature marks a time when he emerges from infancy, and this critical moment, though short, is attended with a long train of consequences. . . . As the roaring of the sea precedes the tempest, so the murmur of rising passions portends this stormy revolution.

—*Rousseau,* Emile

Preface

Of the two subjects in this book's subtitle, *William Henry Harrison and His World, 1773–1798*, the *world* is the dominant one—the exciting world of the new United States after the fighting had stopped, stirring with high ideals and noble dreams but also with disruptive social and political currents of all kinds, a world in which men and women cherished distant goals while struggling to keep their own lives afloat. The balance could hardly be otherwise: Harrison was a boy or very young man in these years, not yet influencing the world but instead being influenced by it. In 1798, the end of the period examined, Harrison was only twenty-five years old and, like most twenty-five-year-olds, in many ways a product of his time.

Harrison the man would become a recognizable figure in American history, and not just for the laughable shortness of his thirty-two-day presidential term. His name was significant in Jacksonian politics, perhaps more for what he represented than for who he was, and he became one of the few generally successful military leaders in the War of 1812. Robert M. Owens has recently made the case for Harrison as a central figure in establishing U.S. policy toward Native Americans and their land. But all these roles are tangential to the subject of this book, Harrison's journey to maturity in a changing world.

This journey would have been illuminating even if it had been performed by someone with a less conspicuous future, uniting as it does so many theaters of the period: the crumbling world of the great Virginia planters after the Revolution, Philadelphia and the nascent federal government, the Indians of the Ohio Valley and the settlers and soldiers who sought to displace them. Major actors of the time—George Washington, Anthony Wayne, Benjamin Rush, James Wilkinson, Little Turtle—met Harrison and actively influenced his life. Complex changes in letters, science, and religion in these years—roughly speaking, the end of the Enlightenment and the beginning of the Romantic era—had major effects on the development of Harrison's intellectual interests and aspirations. In these pages, then, the reader can expect to find a great deal about Harrison's world and less about the young man himself—but the focus will remain always on the building of his character and aspirations, an examination that will, I hope, go some distance toward addressing frontier historian Reginald Horsman's admonition to his colleagues that "an attempt needs to be made to understand Harrison the man."[1]

Information about Harrison's earliest years, before he received his officer's commission at eighteen, is meager compared to that existing for the other American presidents about whom I have written, and for that reason the early chapters of this study differ from those in my biographies of James Garfield, Calvin Coolidge, and Andrew Jackson. Instead of taking a straight chronological approach, they consider the central questions about this period in his life—the nature of presidential autobiography, family relations, educational patterns, and manners, medicine, slavery, and religion in the Virginia of the 1780s and 1790s. Then, building on this examination, they try to tease out inferences and implications from the scanty documents relating to Harrison himself. After chapter 5, the writing shifts to simple narrative; the same themes are present, but they are assimilated into the narrative structure.

Just as information is scanty about Harrison's early years, so, too, are certain details of life on the frontier at the end of the eighteenth century. Of special note is the dearth of specific detail about the various Indian tribes Harrison encountered. The range and number of tribes were rarely reflected in contemporary accounts; most officials and settlers did not differentiate among them, but instead simply called them "Indians" in their reports or recollections. Therefore, although I provide the names of the specific tribes and individuals where they are available, often I could only follow my sources and use the generic term *Indian*.

No matter how authoritative this or any book may look, it is nothing more than the latest stage in an ongoing process—in this case, the process of understanding Harrison as a young man. Inevitably, time will uncover pertinent facts that I omitted because I was unaware of them and will expose errors of fact or interpretation in the material I have included. I shall be grateful to any reader who can produce additional source material bearing on Harrison's early life, or point out an error of fact or interpretation in the work as it now stands.

Despite this book's narrow focus, completing it has taken a long time, and the list of helpers is correspondingly long. In the early stages, the librarians at the State University of New York College at Purchase and the Aiken-Bamberg-Barnwell-Edgefield Regional Library in South Carolina provided invaluable aid in obtaining interlibrary loan materials, the life blood of a historian; in later years, that role was taken on by the library staff at Bucks County Community College. The rich collections of the Firestone Library at Princeton University and the David Library of the American Revolution at Washington Crossing, Pennsylvania, were central to the rewriting of the original version.

Of the many historical institutions that have provided materials and assistance for this project, the Cincinnati Historical Society deserves special mention; its staff helped not only through correspondence and in person, but also by giving space for an earlier version of chapters through 11 in the fall 1987 issue of its quarterly publication, *Queen City History*, under the title "William Henry Harrison Comes to Cincinnati" (vol. 45, no. 3). Other collections that gave me access to their manuscripts were Colonial Williamsburg; the Butler Library, Columbia University; the Connecticut State Library; the Eggleston Library at Hampden-Sydney College; the Indiana Historical Society; the Lilly Library at Indiana University; the Library of Congress; the Massachusetts Historical Society; the New-York Historical Society; the Southern Historical Collection at the University of North Carolina; the Historical Society of Pennsylvania; the Alderman Library at the University of Virginia; the Virginia Historical Society; and the Virginia State Library. Mr. Malcolm Jamieson of Berkeley Plantation also supplied valuable information.

From the many individuals who helped with different avatars of this work, five deserve special thanks. I learned basic research skills and high standards from David Donald at Johns Hopkins. Bill Harris, a fellow student of Donald's, read an early attempt and gave helpful advice. Richard

Ryerson encouraged me to resume work on Harrison after years of idleness and provided a platform for a revised version at the David Library of the American Revolution. Matt Rusnak lent me his fine ear for style and his knowledge of the eighteenth-century English-speaking world for the revision. The advice of Robert H. Ferrell was essential in finding a publisher. I thank them all deeply and absolve them of any connection with the book's flaws. Mary Young and Joyce Harrison of Kent State University Press have my thanks for shepherding the transformation of the manuscript into a book. In the process, the copyediting skills of Marian Buda substantially improved its tightness and clarity.

For the maps and the plan of Fort Greenville, I am indebted to Brian Nugent.

My last and greatest debt is expressed in the dedication.

Abbreviations

CHS	Cincinnati Historical Society
CSL	Connecticut State Library
CU	Columbia University
CW	Colonial Williamsburg
H-SC	Hampden-Sydney College
HSP	Historical Society of Pennsylvania
IHS	Indiana Historical Society
LC	Library of Congress
MHS	Massachusetts Historical Society
NYHS	New-York Historical Society
NYPL	New York Public Library
PMHB	*Pennsylvania Magazine of History and Biography*
SHC	Southern Historical Collection
UVa	University of Virginia
VMHB	*Virginia Magazine of History and Biography*
VSL	Virginia State Library
WMQ	*William and Mary Quarterly*

CHAPTER ONE

An Ardent Ambition to Become a Soldier

Various reasons exist for being concerned with the early life of a president of the United States, and each affects differently the amount and nature of source material preserved for each individual. Even before achieving the presidency, for example, a candidate for the office needs to offer the public a narrative of childhood and early adulthood that establishes a character, generates sympathy, and connects plausibly with his or her adult achievements. Although the style of presidential campaign biographies has changed over the years—a process traced in detail by Scott Casper for the nineteenth century in *Constructing American Lives*—the publication of such biographies has been a constant feature of American elections almost from the beginning. Such campaign biographies form the basis for most later studies. Despite selective omission—since nothing conceivably damaging to the candidate will be included—they are generally accurate in outline: they must be in order to establish their subject's credibility.[1]

Former presidents, with their reputation already made and less need to tell the public about the early years of their lives, have fairly often published memoirs in which those years play only a supporting part. Nevertheless, in several such cases, the material collected in the process of writing the memoir was preserved for the use of family, friends, and future biographers, and often the information not used in the memoir is more revealing than the material that actually made it into the pages. Several presidents—for example, both Adamses, James A. Garfield, and

Woodrow Wilson—saved documents from their early life, including letters and diaries, for personal reference. Such documents, steeped in the mores and the context of the times that produced them, often reveal behavior patterns and interests useful for understanding the president's career as a whole.

Some presidents have been fascinated with their own personal and political development as a theme, regardless of the possible utility of such material. Calvin Coolidge and Jimmy Carter, for example, who published autobiographies in retirement, wrote in great detail not only about their own early lives but about the society shaping those lives. Barack Obama, as a young man, turned his early life into the frame for a powerful book about racial identity in America.

Other former presidents showed less interest in their early years, and the information on them is correspondingly limited. Grover Cleveland resisted numerous invitations to write his autobiography and gave would-be biographers only perfunctory help; he was even indifferent to whether the campaign biographies accurately reported the facts of his own life. Although Chester Arthur collaborated a bit more with biographers than Cleveland, he wrote no account of his own and took care to destroy all his personal papers, while as for Zachary Taylor, modest and matter-of-fact, he neither wrote his own story nor supplied information to anyone else; his early life, consequently, is almost a complete blank. The lives of Abraham Lincoln and John F. Kennedy drew special attention and treatment. Both presidents died young, in office, by assassination, and each became a cult figure; writers and enthusiasts consequently took great pains in collecting facts and recollections about their youth and blended them into narratives quite independent of the presidents' own preferences.

On this spectrum, William Henry Harrison—the ninth president of the United States and the one serving the briefest term (only a month)—falls, not surprisingly, toward the undocumented end. Lacking the charisma of a Lincoln or Kennedy and the achievements of a Roosevelt, he was an obscure president, although a fairly famous general, and scholars are seldom interested in collecting facts about such lesser public figures. Moreover, since Harrison's national political prominence came late in his life, in his sixties, biographers found few contemporaries to interview. Finally, Harrison had moved around a good deal in the course of a military and bureaucratic life, preserving few documents. He wrote no memoir or autobiography, although he did leave two brief accounts of his early life, one in his own words and one based on information he supplied. These are where a modern biographer has to begin, and they supply a reason for writing about him, for they tell—or rather, they suggest—a more interesting story than his brief presidency offers.

The first account of Harrison's early life appeared in Philadelphia's *Port Folio* magazine in 1815, just after the close of the War of 1812, in which Harrison had won national respect through his competent generalship, actually winning a couple of battles.[2] This account was written in the third person but was clearly based on information supplied by Harrison himself. Naturally enough in the circumstances, it focused on how he happened to become a soldier in the first place. The narrative began by describing his family, one of the most prominent, wealthy, and respected in Virginia at the time of the Revolution. William's father, Benjamin Harrison, was a signer of the Declaration of Independence. "Thus honored and deserving of honor," concluded this description, "lived the father of general Harrison to the year 1791, when at the age of sixty-five he was gathered to his forefathers, leaving behind him three sons, the youngest of whom, is the gentleman of whose exploits we are now to speak, and who was born at the family seat in Virginia the ninth of February 1773."

The article went on to narrate, in smooth prose, a rather complicated sequence of events:

> William Henry, who entered upon his education after his elder brothers had finished theirs and been settled in business, was at an early age placed in a grammar-school, from which in due time he was sent to Hamden-college, where he remained till he completed his fourteenth year, when he was moved to an academy in Southampton county. There he remained until he entered his seventeenth year, at which time, being pronounced by the principal well qualified to begin the study of physic, for which he was destined by his father, he was placed for a short period under the tuition of doctor Leiper, a practicing physician of respectable standing in Richmond, and in the spring of 1791, was sent to Philadelphia to finish his medical studies.
>
> It was while he was on his journey to Philadelphia that his father died, and this event determined him to abandon altogether a profession which he had consented to enter upon, merely to gratify that gentleman. The reception he met from all the eminent professors of

> that day—Rush, Shippen, Wistar, &c., especially the first of them, on account of the services rendered by his father during the progress of the revolution, was insufficient to shake his purpose.

Having decided to quit medical study, the account continued, Harrison turned to several Virginia friends who suggested alternatives. Edmund Randolph, then attorney general, offered him a place in his office, presumably to read law. Governor Lee of Virginia made a suggestion, "more congenial with [Harrison's] taste and active disposition," to obtain a commission in the Army, and this was the course Harrison adopted.

A couple of slightly odd features are visible in this story. The restless wandering from one school to another is a little peculiar for a young Virginia gentleman of good family, but since the period of his education coincides with the years just after the War of Independence, one is tempted to attribute it merely to the unsettled conditions of the time. Again, it seems strange that, having disliked medicine as a career for some time, young Harrison had formed no alternative plan, instead spending weeks or months in a state of indecision, from which he was rescued by Governor Henry Lee.

Whatever the reasons for these shifts, the forty-two-year-old Harrison, looking back on his life, seems to have viewed it as an exciting story, as many literary-minded Americans in the early 1800s were beginning to view theirs. In this account, Harrison wanted readers to marvel, as he did, at how the repeated, inconclusive efforts of his childhood and adolescence ended at the pivotal moment when he committed himself to the Army and to the path he followed to success—hence the early, uncertain tacking from school to school, from career to career.[3]

When he retold his story in the first person, twenty-four years later, Harrison eliminated both these features. In 1839, on his way to becoming the Whig nominee for the presidency in 1840, he recounted his early life for a New York newspaper editor.[4] While this later account related essentially the same facts, Harrison laid greater stress on his early credentials and less on his frustrated youth:

> I was born at the seat of my father called Berkley on James River in the County of Charles City 25 miles below Richmond Va on the 9th of Feby 1773. For an account of my father see the lives of the signers of the Declaration of Independence.

> Having received a Classical education I commenced the study of Medicine in Richmond in the year 1790. In the Month of April 1791 I was sent to Philadelphia further to prosecute my studies & was placed under the direction of my father's intimate friend Robt Morris the Financier of the Revolution. My father died whilst I was on the passage to Philadelphia & in the following summer not liking the Medical profession & expressing that dislike to Govr Lee of Va who was on a visit to Philadelphia he recommended me to go into the Army. I immediately acquiesced. The application was made through him & in 24 hours of the first conception of the idea of changing my profession I was an Ensign in the 1st U.S. Regt. of Infantry—commission dated Augt 16th 1791.

Both versions focus on the central event of Harrison's youth: his father's death and his subsequent decision, in Philadelphia in summer 1791, to abandon medicine for a military career. That is where this chapter, too, will begin: with the seemingly distraught, purposeless young man who made the decision, the environment around him, and the factors that influenced, or may have influenced, his thought.

The young Virginian who disembarked at the Philadelphia waterfront in late April 1791, encumbered with trunkfuls of clothing, was "tall, thin, [and] puerile in his person." The description is Harrison's own, from the 1839 account; its wording is designed to point up the incongruity of his becoming a soldier a few months later. Harrison had, as he put it, been "tenderly brought up"; he looked "wretchedly qualified for the hardships to which a soldiery is liable in the wilderness."[5] No likenesses exist for this exact period of Harrison's life, but two portraits from his late twenties, a painting and a *physionotrace* (a sort of engraving in profile), depict an appearance—unblemished skin, silky brown hair, a long nose, a long, thin face—that jibes with this picture.[6] In other words, Harrison embodied a familiar kind of young Southerner: slender, graceful, and a bit delicate in build. An entry in a cousin's diary suggests that his family knew him as "Billy," and one can assume that his friends did too.[7]

Both the painting and the engraving also suggest a characteristic not apparent from Harrison's account—a mobile, expressive mouth with a humorous curl to the lips. Billy Harrison looks like a young man who might have been amusing company. Scattered sources from his early years seem to support this. He had "much resource in conversation," according to a man who met him three years later. (The men of the Harrison family, as a later chapter will show, tended to be vigorous, articulate speakers.) The testimony of another acquaintance, who knew him ten years later on the Indiana frontier, is similar but more striking: "[I]n conversation he is sprightly and gay—can repeat a theatrical performance and mimmick a blackguard as well as I ever saw a man." A long letter Harrison wrote at age twenty-one to his older brother Carter likewise suggests good humor and wit: Billy wrote in the smooth, easy style of Henry Fielding or Laurence Sterne, with graceful transitions and clever turns of phrase.[8]

That he traveled to Philadelphia by ship is evident from Harrison's reference to his father's death while he was "on the passage to Philadelphia."[9] Several contemporary accounts mention ships that plied regularly between Philadelphia and the James River around this time, carrying grain and tobacco from the plantations and luxury goods from Philadelphia, as well as occasional passengers.[10] Benjamin Harrison died on 21 April 1791; consequently his son arrived around the end of the month, and since he intended to complete a multiyear medical course, he doubtless brought a large wardrobe with him.[11]

Billy Harrison had never visited Philadelphia before, or indeed any large city (although his readings of English authors had given him impressions of London life), but even older, more experienced travelers accounted Philadelphia, then the capital of the United States, a remarkable place. Despite a population of nearly 45,000,[12] it was no longer the largest city in English-speaking North America (New York had just overtaken it), but it remained the most impressive because of what one traveler called its "Size and Regularity"; its rectangular grid of wide streets firmly asserted the primacy of human design over the natural setting, a tongue of land between two rivers, the Delaware and the Schuylkill. Remarkably level except for a few steep spots at the Delaware waterfront, the broad streets, paved in the center with cobblestones and bordered with well-maintained brick sidewalks, combined to present a soothing vision of rationality—"this splendid city," a young medical student called it in 1791. "Philadelphia seemed to me a beautiful city with wide streets," wrote a French traveler the same year; "some, lined with trees, crossed one another at right angles in regular order."[13]

Another traveler found the view of the city from the Delaware "genuinely lovely," and this was most likely the first glimpse of the city young Harrison had. As ships came closer to shore, however, arriving passengers faced an ugly, confused scene, where a part of the city had escaped from its master plan: "heaps of wooden storehouses, crowded upon each other, the chief of which are built upon platforms of artificial ground, and wharfs which project a considerable way into the river. The wharfs . . . jut out in every direction, and are well adapted for the accommodation of shipping, the largest merchant vessels being able to lie close alongside them." Narrow, crowded Water Street, which connected these wharves and warehouses, was, everyone agreed, "low and disagreeable."[14]

Once past the waterfront district, Philadelphia projected an air of moderation, regularity, and prosperity. The open brick market house on High Street, nearly half a mile long and divided systematically into sections, was notable for its decorum; a traveler in 1787 recorded that a "buzzing murmur of voices resounded through the crowds, but no clamorous noise nor crying of wares of any kind." Here farmers from the city's outskirts brought their meat, "sawed in round and appetizing shapes," their fish, milk, and produce to feed the people of the capital. The broad range of buyers and sellers at the market house reflected the multiplicity of the city itself: "The crowds of people seemed like the collection at the last day," observed one visitor, "for there was of every rank and condition in life, from the highest to the lowest, male and female, of every age and of every color." Another traveler noted the absence of profanity or billingsgate among the customers and vendors.

A few blocks distant, the State House, modern Independence Hall, had a park behind it, with small trees "judiciously arranged" and graveled walks in serpentine patterns. It was the closest thing to a ceremonial showplace in this commercial city. Elsewhere, the houses, brick or wood, were all of similar size and design; Philadelphia boasted no palaces or sumptuous churches, an absence of emphasis that led one European to label the city "cold and monotonous." Cedar posts at regular intervals kept the many carriages and coaches from running up on the sidewalks. Public pumps and street lamps likewise recurred at regular intervals. While Philadelphia did host the usual number of stray dogs for an eighteenth-century city, its streets were, on the whole, remarkably clean. Residents were soberly dressed and seemed well off. One traveler noted the absence of beggars.[15]

Philadelphia's appearance was distinctive; but like any city, it was really a set of nested boxes, each containing a different experience. An affluent young traveler like Harrison, coming to the capital to study with the leading physician in America under the guardianship of the nation's richest man, Senator Robert Morris, inhabited a different city from a sailor or laborer, coming ashore into the noise and filth of Water Street, parrying the wiles of whores and gamblers, smelling the dead animals floating in Dock Creek, and straying outside the corporate limits where the broad, straight city streets gave way to unpaved, winding lanes lined with crazy shacks.[16] A German farmer arriving on foot would experience yet a different Philadelphia, and his impressions would bear little resemblance to those of a free black visitor, tolerated but kept apart from any but the lowest levels of white society. This multiplicity was itself one of the first things likely to strike a young Virginian fresh from a state where there were no cities at all. The young Virginia medical student who called the city "splendid" went on to say, "[Y]ou would think distress was unknown in it, but the most calamatous [*sic*] scenes my eye ever beheld has [*sic*] been here." Young John Randolph, desultorily studying law with his cousin, the attorney general, made the most of the city's complexity, writing in February 1791 that he had "led a life of dissipation for the last three months." Randolph's statement implied more than mere time-wasting: by August he had run up 268 pounds in gambling debts, and it was probably in Philadelphia that he contracted the venereal disease that made him sterile for life.[17]

Other Virginians responded intellectually to the city's social complexity. Robert Carter, a neighbor of William Henry Harrison's on the James River and one year his junior, from a family as rich as the Harrisons, came to the city a little later and summed it up this way: "I was entirely ignorant of many peculiarities of my native State until I had spent some time in Phila., Pennsylvania." Philadelphia made Carter see Virginia in a new light: compared with the city, Virginia was "a part of the country devoid of science [i.e., organized knowledge] and rational emulation." Some Virginia lads, of course, accepted the city equably, or at least claimed to; John Dandridge, a kinsman of Martha Washington, noted in a letter to a friend in December 1791, "It answers my expectations in some respects, & in others it falls short. Mankind are all brethren & will be alike each other." Then he went on to analyze the looks of local women. Even Dandridge, however, was startled when he attended a presidential reception that winter and found a level of formality he had not known in Virginia: "Of all the foolish monkey shows I ever was at, a levee is the most so. I will go to no more." The national capital, it seems, exposed most young Virginians to new kinds of social relationships, provoking fresh insights.[18]

Upon his arrival, Billy Harrison's immediate destination was Robert Morris's home on High (now Market) Street, near the edge of town. He knew the senator, who had visited his family in Virginia only three years before, and could be sure of a warm welcome. Morris's three-story brick mansion, with its tree-shaded lawn, was "probably the most elegant and commodious home in the city," and Morris himself was reputed to be the richest man in the United States. However, Morris was not living there in 1791, having lent it for the duration to President George Washington and his lady. Morris occupied a more modest two-story home next door, on the corner of Sixth—modest, that is, from the street; within, it boasted china, French tapestries, and all the art objects that a successful eighteenth-century merchant could pick up through his sea captains' many voyages. Servants were plentiful and hospitality generous. Although Morris and his wife had six children, all in their teens or early twenties, they may have found room for young Billy Harrison in their home, at least for a few days. Morris himself was a large, fleshy, gray-haired man in his middle fifties, with "an energy of mind that few Men can boast of," according to a fellow delegate in the Constitutional Convention; however, although he was undeniably bright, generous, and charitable with friends, he was disliked by some Philadelphians for his arrogance and overbearing manner. It was doubtless in this house that Harrison first learned, within a week or two of his arrival, of his father's death.[19]

Only a few blocks away, on Walnut Street between Second and Third, was Billy Harrison's particular destination in Philadelphia, the home and office of Doctor Benjamin Rush. Rush's name had appeared with Robert Morris's on the Declaration of Independence, just to the right of John Hancock's, but since the war the men's lives had diverged. Rush's red brick house, though respectable, was less luxurious than Morris's. The scholarly doctor, his wife, and his children followed a restrained middle-class lifestyle. Forty-five years old, slender, high-browed and firm-lipped, Rush embodied seriousness and purpose. An eminent public figure, he lectured on medical theory and practice at the College of Philadelphia, which that year was about to merge with the University of Pennsylvania.

When he examined the sick at the Pennsylvania Hospital he was followed by a crowd of twenty or thirty students, his own and those of other doctors, intent on picking up knowledge. He used his carriage for house calls, not to impress patients but to save time for all his other activities. He wrote frequently on political and social topics and was especially active in projects to improve the condition of Philadelphia's black residents. Billy Harrison, with his father's introductory letter in hand, probably called on the doctor sometime in his first couple of weeks in the city—that is, about the same time he learned of his father's death.[20]

Even after receiving that sad news, filial piety would seem to have demanded his carrying through his father's scheme: paying Dr. Rush's apprentice fee (one hundred pounds, the highest in the city), enrolling at the College of Philadelphia for another eighty pounds, and finding lodgings close by. Although the main lecture term would not begin until the fall, one course, Dr. Barton's botany and pharmacology, began in April, and Billy Harrison could purchase his ticket for it and begin attending at once.[21] By observing Rush, Harrison would learn how to diagnose and prepare medicines. Fragments from a lecture of Rush's give some idea of the doctor's approach: "The first question you should ask your Patient whether he has pain and where the pain is seated, whether in the Bones, Head, Breast? &c. The Head is ye most dangerous part for pain to exist in—In the Bones it is not dangerous. . . . The nails are also to be inspected—red nails are favourable—I once lost a patient with malignant yellow Fever, where the nails were only tinged yellow—Never leave a sick room without naming the disease—unless you comply with this direction you will be thought ignorant."[22] After two or three years of listening and observing, Harrison would be ready to take a degree in physic.

In fact, however, Billy Harrison seems not to have carried out any part of his father's wishes. Rush kept a meticulous list of his apprentices during this period, and Harrison is not on it; thus one can be sure that no money changed hands there. Since college records were not centralized, one cannot say confidently that Harrison did not enroll, but even if he did, he could only have attended Dr. Barton's single course that spring. One thing Harrison certainly did was change his lodgings, for events a few months later make it clear that he was neither living at the Morrises' nor in regular contact with his guardian. But he took no major step toward becoming a medical student.

Harrison's reason was stated simply enough in his 1839 account: he did "not lik[e] the study of medicine," although he had been at it almost two years. His earlier account explains why he had prepared to become a physician—"merely to gratify" his father. But obedience to his father's wishes did not extend beyond the grave; once there was no fear of repercussions, it appears, Billy was eager to get out.

One influence on his decision was a letter from his oldest brother, Benjamin (usually referred to, for clarity, as Benjamin Harrison VI), the executor of his father's estate, written as the estate was being settled, some time in May or June. Ben informed Billy, according to the *Port Folio* account, "that the personal property left by his father fell short of what would be necessary to the successful prosecution of his original scheme of life."[23] Apparently the Harrison estate was rich in land and slaves but poor in ready cash. A correspondent of Thomas Jefferson's, referring to Harrison, reported, "Mr. Carrington tells me he understands [Benjamin Harrison V] fashionably died insolvent."[24] This news cannot have been entirely a surprise to young Billy Harrison; his father had been fearful of financial ruin for the previous four or five years. But as a result, Ben urged Billy to leave Philadelphia, a notoriously expensive city for strangers,[25] return to Virginia, and pursue medical study there. That idea did not appeal to Billy, quite apart from his dislike for medicine; it seems plain that he, like Robert Carter, found Philadelphia stimulating and was in no hurry to leave. Perhaps he reasoned that since he would not be spending the money allotted him for medical study he could afford the expense of living there. In any case, Billy was no quicker to comply with his brother's wishes than with those of his late father. He seemed to have wanted to distance himself from his entire family.

According to the *Port Folio* account, Rush urged young Harrison to continue with medicine. He may have done so from loyalty to the memory of Billy's father; Rush was devoted to all those who had been his companions in the great Revolutionary adventure. However, Rush had practical reasons for wanting to avoid taking Billy on himself; he had planned to devote the spring and early summer to writing and community service. Moreover, as he complained to a friend in October 1781, he already had more apprentices than he could handle. Rush may have introduced Billy to the other physicians mentioned in the account, William Shippen and Caspar Wistar, both colleagues on the college faculty. Courtly, charming

Shippen, Philadelphia's society doctor, had married a Virginia woman and boasted a wide acquaintance in Virginia. Wistar was a Pennsylvanian. Neither of them changed Billy's mind.[26]

In his two accounts of these events, Harrison left some ambiguity about when he totally abandoned medicine. According to the *Port Folio* account, he made his renunciation plain to Rush, who failed to talk him out of it. This would have occurred in May or June. The later account, however, mentions his "not liking the medical profession" only in August, in the context of his joining the army. The difference is insignificant, yet it opens up an interesting possibility. Harrison might have maintained a token connection to medicine, enough perhaps to placate his guardian or his brothers, by enrolling in Benjamin Barton's lecture course on botany and materia medica. One is tempted to suggest that he did, because one of young Dr. Barton's main interests, the study of the mysterious earthworks west of the Alleghenies left by predecessors of the Indians, was later to become a passion of Harrison's as well. Perhaps he picked it up through attending Barton's lectures, though it does not seem that he and the doctor were ever closely acquainted.[27]

In neither of his autobiographical accounts did William Harrison explain just what it was about the medical profession that he disliked. Certainly there were many features to recommend it. It was a learned profession and commanded a certain amount of automatic respect. Its practitioners could make a very comfortable income, especially those who practiced in cities, and in England, at least, they seemed to command more trust and esteem as the eighteenth century went on. However, it had obvious drawbacks as well. Eighteenth-century doctors had no real body of scientific knowledge at their command, only elaborate theory; their remedies often were no better than folk medicines and traditional cures, and consequently, they often had to accede to their patients' ideas of treatment. "We must give up to the whims of our patients," wrote a young Virginia doctor to a friend who was still studying, "or we can do nothing, which has been the case with me in several instances, where I have advised the Lancet and purge, they have insisted for the vomit and sweat, so that I find, that let them argue what they can, I insist that some quackery is essencial [*sic*]." Moreover, the more successful doctors were, the more their lives were at the beck and call of the sick. The respect people felt for them was tempered by stereotypes: they were thought to overcharge and overmedicate, and they were mocked for their backbiting and acrimony with fellow professionals. Also, the constant contact with sickroom air, blood, and bodily wastes may well have been repulsive to young men who lacked a powerful commitment.[28]

Harrison mentioned none of these factors in his reminiscences, but he did supply a piece of data that helps explain his attitude—his statement that he had read Charles Rollin's *Ancient History* three times by seventeen, the age at which he was first sent to apprentice to a physician. Rollin's book, narrated with color and energy, was an eighteenth-century take on ancient history—a blend of military strategies and engagements, moral reflections, and sketches of leaders and societies—a lively account likely to be a powerful stimulant to an adolescent imagination, especially that of a boy whose youth had been spent amid the alarms of war, whose father had been a Revolutionary leader, whose home had been occupied and its furnishings partly destroyed by the enemy. Rollin's portrayal of Pyrrhus of Epirus in action suggests the work's combination of excitement and inspiration:

> As soon as he saw a great number of Roman bucklers glittering on this side of the river, and their cavalry advancing toward him in fine order, he closed his rank, and began the attack. The lustre and beauty of his arms, which were very magnificent, distinguished him in a conspicuous manner; and his actions made it evident, that the reputation he had acquired did not exceed his merit; for while he engaged in the battle, without sparing his person, and bore all down before him, he was attentive to the functions of a general: and amidst the greatest dangers, was perfectly cool, dispatched his commands with as much tranquility as if he had been in his palace; and sprung from place to place, to reinstate what was amiss, and sustain those who suffered most.[29]

Numerous young Americans read Rollin's book in the Revolutionary years, and more than one shared the experience of James Elliot of Vermont: "From the moment when I first perused Rollin, I . . . felt an ardent ambition to become a soldier."[30] The same ambition was behind Billy Harrison's deep commitment to the book and his antagonism to medicine.

Young Billy Harrison's problem, then, was simple: from his middle teens he had dreamed of a military career, but all the roads to military preferment in Virginia led through the state government, with his father, who intended him to become a doctor, at its center. Not until Benjamin Harrison died could his son think of realizing his own dream; not until Billy's conversation with Henry Lee did he see how it could be accomplished.

CHAPTER TWO

An Education Manqué

William Henry Harrison's difficult relationship with his father, the most important person in his early life, can be best evaluated by considering it in the context of the world in which he grew up—the rich, complex world of the great Virginia and Maryland planters. The culture of what Allen Kulikoff has called Chesapeake society is so well known and its child-rearing philosophy so clearly anatomized in the work of scholars from Louis B. Wright and Edmund Morgan to Rhys Isaac, T. H. Breen, and Daniel Blake Smith that one need only assemble the scattered fragments of information about Harrison's early life and match them against the ideal model to grasp how he resembled the typical young Virginia gentleman, and how and why he differed.

Chesapeake culture centered on the ownership of large tracts of farmland, each with a manor house as its nerve center; each manor house was a consciously fashioned copy of the homes of the gentry and lesser nobility of England. Such manors embodied an ideal, as Breen puts it, of "complete personal independence," including financial and judicial control of one's own realm: the fields of tobacco that brought in money from England, the scores of African slaves laboring to produce the tobacco, the family members and employees inhabiting and working in the small clusters of buildings that, like English villages, surrounded each "great house." "Patriarchs," these gentlemen sometimes good-humoredly called themselves, in mock-biblical reference to their rural, semiwilderness surroundings, but in fact their standard of reference was that of English royalty and nobility. An English visitor in 1760 found them "haughty and jealous of their liberties."[1]

Sovereigns, as these Chesapeake gentlemen saw it, ruled under the favor of God and the king, and had a duty to represent their superiors by ruling virtuously. Thus a planter was supposed to maintain his plantation responsibly, attending closely to business and riding around his acres to supervise and assess the farming, as Roman masters in the classics he read had overseen theirs; he was supposed to take a leading part in the affairs of his neighborhood, his church, and his colony; and in his everyday actions, he was expected to exemplify gracious, educated behavior.[2] Control, David Hackett Fischer stresses in *Albion's Seed,* began with self-control; a male of the planter class was on stage all the time, whether dancing, riding, attending church, dining with his family, or disciplining his slaves; he had to learn early to "bend his will" to exhibit proper behavior.[3]

The proper raising of a great planter's son, the future ruler of a domain, was a serious matter, and one to which planters gave serious thought. A son was expected to master the extensive code of manners that governed social relationships; to be familiar with the classics in their original language and with the most approved modern authors; and to know and understand the texts and rituals of the Anglican communion, which was seen in Virginia less as a matter of personal salvation than as an important part of the social order. Often a planter father made the education of his sons a central project of his life. He taught them horsemanship, which was a major part of a man's appearance, and he took them from an early age around the plantation and neighborhood to acquaint them with its operations. They accompanied him to local social occasions—Anglican worship, court sessions, horse races, fish fries—to meet neighboring planter families and to get a clear idea of gender roles. The father sought out proper teachers to drill his sons in the languages, mathematics, and dancing, and periodically reviewed their progress. This was the ideal, and it was realized, or approximated, surprisingly often.[4]

All this was only the formal part of a son's education. Equally important was the education he received from the family, friends, and dependents in his daily orbit. From the women in his family, typically, he learned current standards of dress and manners and, often, basic literacy. From his playmates, companions, and servants among the slaves, he learned simple diversions and knowledge of the natural world as they roamed the woods and fields, playing and fishing; one planter's son recalled lying together with slave companions on a grassy bank, black and white side by side, like so many packed herrings. Later on, in his early teens, he learned from his age mates in the social group (and perhaps from observing his father and brothers) the accepted rules of gambling, swearing, drinking, and sexual behavior for males.[5]

The formal education of a Chesapeake gentleman followed a sequence that, by the middle eighteenth century, was fairly standardized. A boy learned basic reading skills from his mother, or from a tutor if there was a good one in the neighborhood. Around the age of nine or ten, he began studying Latin and Greek in earnest. For these, a tutor with some learning was required. Often the local Anglican rector filled the bill; if not, a college-educated young man from the Northern colonies or Scotland might be engaged and liberally paid. Philip Vickers Fithian, a New Jersey native and graduate of Princeton who was hired in just this way by the Carter family, noted that several plantations in his neighborhood also shared a dancing teacher, bringing together all the boys and girls for repeated training. In his early teen years, when a boy had acquired enough strength and skill to have his own horse and ride alone or with the companionship of his personal slave, it became possible to think of sending him on to college—almost always to the College of William and Mary, in Williamsburg, Virginia's capital. William and Mary had no age requirement; how early a boy attended might depend on his aptitude, whether he had relatives in Williamsburg, or other circumstances. As Kulikoff points out, a boy attended college less to acquire further education than to polish what he had learned by associating and competing with other young men of his class. Whether he went to Williamsburg or stayed home for a few more years, these were perhaps the critical years of a boy's education, as he wrestled simultaneously with the intricacies of Horace and Livy, the promptings of puberty, and the seductions of friends; Fithian's account of the Carter boys and Landon Carter's account of his grandson and namesake illustrate some of these stresses and strains. Many a planter's son, if he got through these years successfully, was ready for an adult role in society by his later teens.[6]

Around the time of William Henry Harrison's birth, two revolutions began transforming this firmly established pattern. One was the gradual ebbing of power of the great Chesapeake planters, who were being weakened by their own inattention to business and their increasing load of debt to London merchants. The other was the rise in tension between Great Britain and its American colonies that came to an abrupt head in 1774, the year after Harrison was born.

The Harrison family in 1774 was securely at the center of the vast web of cousinage that made up Virginia's leadership class—the Harrisons, among Virginia's first families in both land and wealth, were related by marriage to the Randolphs, Carters, Byrds, and Bassetts, and through them to every other family of importance in the colony. As with most great planting families, different branches resided on several plantations scattered across the colony; the two largest and best known, both headed by patriarchs named Benjamin, were at the Brandon and Berkeley plantations, both in the James River valley. This part of Virginia had a name even among the planter class for wealth and pride; a northern Virginia planter in 1785 forbade his children to mingle in James River society "lest they should imbibe more exalted notions of their own importance than I should wish any child of mine to possess." Berkeley, where Billy Harrison was born 9 February 1773, was a large, two-story red-brick house, of rather simple architecture, surrounded by the usual dependencies and filled with the usual family portraits and mementos, about a quarter mile from James River.[7]

From his small office on the first floor of Berkeley, Benjamin Harrison ruled over seven thousand acres in Charles City County and another ten thousand elsewhere in the state, worked by more than one hundred slaves on the home plantation alone. But his authority in Virginia went beyond mere ownership. He was colonel of the county militia—in fact, *colonel* was the title he was proudest of and the one by which his contemporaries generally referred to him—and he had been a member of Virginia's legislature, the House of Burgesses, since his twenty-first year. In 1774, he was chosen to represent his colony in the Continental Congress, and two years later, he would sign the Declaration of Independence. He was a skilled and respected politician.[8]

Colonel Harrison in the flesh projected power. He was a big man, well over six feet tall—taller than George Washington—and weighing more than two hundred pounds. Handsome and athletic in youth, he had grown stout and red-faced in middle age, forceful and blunt in his speech and overbearing in personal relations. His rough wit was legendary: when signing the Declaration of Independence, he had whispered to scrawny Elbridge Gerry of Massachusetts, in the line next to him, "When the time for hanging comes, I shall have the advantage over you. It will be all over with me in a minute, but you will be kicking in the air for half an hour after I am gone." As legendary as his wit was his drinking prowess; John Adams, no admirer, described him as a "Falstaff," and recalled seeing him "very high." He called himself a "votary" of Bacchus, and when the Continental Congress took refuge in Baltimore in 1777, he wrote his friend Robert Morris that the place was "the damndest hole in the world," without even "a tavern that one can ride to for exercise and amusement." After the war, he was heard to complain that the French wines he had switched to for patriotism's sake were aggravating his gout and shortening his temper, and during Harrison's term as Virginia's governor (1781–1784), Edmund Pendleton could report to a friend that "Governor Harrison . . . is, as usual, very angry."[9]

Daniel Blake Smith, in his study of Virginia gentry families during the eighteenth century, argued that the typical father-son relationship in that era was characterized more by love and mutual respect than by fear or coercion, but even if his conclusion is broadly correct, it may not have applied to Benjamin Harrison's with his son Billy. For one thing, the personal dimension was noticeably absent in their early relationship. A year after Billy's birth in 1773, Colonel Harrison was off to Philadelphia for the Continental Congress, in which he stayed heavily involved until 1777. He then served for a few years as speaker of the House of Burgesses, preoccupied with Virginia's wartime problems and rarely able to spend time with his family. Billy may well have been closer to his mother as a child, although there is no positive evidence of this. Elizabeth Bassett Harrison was a good woman and, according to one account, a pious one, but she had borne six children before Billy and seems to have been physically exhausted. She was sick much of the time during Billy's youth. Sweet she was, beyond doubt—a Philadelphia cousin of her Byrd neighbors called her "the good old lady" of Berkeley—but she may have been too tired to take an active part in raising her youngest children. In his adult recollections of his childhood, William Harrison did not mention her at all.[10]

During Billy's boyhood (the early years of the War of Independence), his father was rarely at Berkeley. Nonetheless, the plantation was a center of activity, with a shipyard and some unspecified mills in operation—an educational place for a boy if he had someone to direct his attention.

It seems unlikely that Billy did. Hired managers ran the plantation and the manufacturing operations and Billy's adult brothers were there regularly, but the former had no responsibility for Billy and the latter had careers of their own. Ben, the older brother, was by his late twenties a merchant in Richmond and paymaster of Virginia's armed forces. His letters show him to have been a sociable, expressive man, as frank as his father but less profane and blustering. Carter, the younger of Billy's grown brothers, was studying law and may have been at home fairly often. Less is known of him than of the rest of the family, but he was characterized as a man of moderate talents and "a fluent speaker," a description that applied to all the Harrison men. As for tutors, they were hard to find during the early years of the Revolution, when many of the Virginia clergy had returned to England to escape the war and younger men were joining the Patriot armies. It is unclear just who taught Billy his letters. It may have been his mother; if so, she did a good job. He had a fondness for reading from an early age, but he was still somewhat young to profit from his father's library at Berkeley when, in the winter of 1780–81, the war came to the family home.[11]

On 31 December of that year, reports came of a British fleet at the mouth of James River. Two days later it was seen moving upstream, and the great planters with ties to the Patriot cause began moving their families and slaves to the Piedmont, out of reach of the enemy ships. Billy, his sister Sally, their mother, and their personal slaves fled as best they could, probably in the family carriage and probably to the plantation of Colonel Harrison's brother Carter, in Cumberland County. Days later, a force under Benedict Arnold camped at Berkeley and, in a studied act of vengeance, ravaged the mansion, destroyed the furnishings, slaughtered the livestock, and liberated the remaining slaves. So complete was the destruction that the family was unable to move back until 1784, three years later. This was clearly traumatic to the Harrisons: fifteen years later, Billy's brother Ben spent large amounts of money he could ill afford to restore the estate to its former grandeur.[12]

Not until 1781 in Richmond, when Colonel Harrison was Virginia's governor and may have had his youngest children, Sally and Billy, living with him, did Billy get a chance to know his father as anything but a semi-legendary figure, always dashing off to rescue his country from peril, without the time to make his son's acquaintance. And, indeed, it is not clear that Billy stayed in Richmond with the family; he may have been sent away to school, or he may have stayed with his uncle Carter, who personally tutored his sons at his plantation, Clifton. No evidence of his location during this period remains. The colonel's family was then living in a large, two-story plank house owned by the Commonwealth of Virginia, with ten slaves. Ben was helping his father with the duties of his office as governor, writing important letters for him.[13] Colonel Harrison had begun to change. There are faint suggestions in some of the surviving documents, from the 1770s on, that he may have had what is now termed a drinking problem. John Adams's censorious comments during the Continental Congress have already been noted, along with the carefully recorded changes in Harrison's alcohol consumption, often associated with serious imbibing. In 1788, his son Ben wrote Robert Morris a letter that can be read as suggesting that Colonel Harrison had given up drinking for a time: "My father is with me & desires that I would present him to you & Mrs. Morris respectfully and affectionately—The Old Gent now and then calls for a Bottle of the Claret in his old way, we seldom fail to drink your healths, but never when the Claret is passing." Ben himself had a cautious attitude toward alcohol often found in the children of heavy drinkers: "I stick to my usual ration of wine, which keeps me above those sneaking complaints that are taking Peoples Breaths from them daily." Billy's habits, to be discussed in more detail later, were equally abstemious. Colonel Harrison's sudden, unexplained loss of influence in Virginia politics in the middle 1780s may have been a result simply of his own advancing age or of changing political fashions, but his tendency to drink heavily also may have been a factor.[14]

It seems likely that it was during this period that Colonel Harrison conceived his idea of making Billy a doctor. As a typical Chesapeake planter, he had already chosen his oldest son's profession, wishing to have a merchant in the family. He had chosen Carter's as well. Up to 1783, Colonel Harrison had had a physician among his close kin—his son-in-law William Rickman, husband to his oldest daughter, Elizabeth, a popular, generally respected doctor whose plantation lay near Berkeley. When Dr. Rickman died in 1783, however, Benjamin Harrison might logically have come to see in his bookish ten-year-old son a possible successor to Rickman, a man he had liked and whose career he had promoted.[15] The following year, 1784, he enrolled Billy at Hampden-Sydney Academy, in Prince Edward County, a relatively new school and one that no earlier Harrison had attended. This academy (the "Hamden-college" of the *Port Folio* sketch) was known for its director, Presbyterian minister John Blair Smith. As a zealous Episcopalian, Harrison had no particular love for the Presbyterian faith, but he probably believed, like many of his contemporaries, that a Presbyterian education was a first step to a medical career. The center of medical learning in the English-speaking world was the University of Edinburgh in Presbyterian Scotland, and many of the leading doctors in Virginia were Scots and Edinburgh graduates.[16]

The youngest Harrison son, up to that point, had had an education quite different from that of his older brothers. His command of the ancient languages, pieced together in a variety of improvised settings, was weak. He had missed out on many of the opportunities his brothers had enjoyed, central components in the education of a great planter's son, such as dancing school and rides around the neighborhood with his father. The father Billy knew, with his overpowering physique and rough humor, was an ambiguous figure—a powerful grandee of Virginia, to be sure, yet unable to prevent enemies from sacking his home and not always able to control his own actions.

When asked about his father in later life, he tended to assert that he had not known him very well: "I was . . . the child of my father's old age," he wrote to an author who was researching the lives of the signers of the Declaration of Independence, "and know less of his public services than any of his other children." However, given that he abandoned Virginia as soon as he could plausibly leave and showed no interest in returning, the converse could be true: perhaps he knew his father too well, lost rapport with him at an early age, and took every opportunity to underscore the distance between them.[17]

The first small piece of evidence for father-son conflict concerns Billy's education. In brief, Colonel Harrison withdrew Billy from the Hampden-Sydney Academy after the tone at the school took a religious turn the father disliked. However, the dates of Billy's attendance at the academy, documented here for the first time, and the circumstances of his withdrawal raise complex factual questions that necessitate a more detailed discussion.[18]

Founded in 1776 by a group of Presbyterians (and finally chartered by the legislature in 1783), Hampden-Sydney College was only the second college in Virginia, after William and Mary. Located in Prince Edward County, a hundred miles west of Richmond, it graduated its first class in 1786. It had been founded as an academy, and even after becoming a college, it took boys as young as eleven or twelve for basic classical training as well; Dabney Carr, nephew of Thomas Jefferson (then serving as ambassador to France), came there in 1785 at the age of twelve and stayed two or three years.[19]

The school was absurdly small, however. During its early years, it had only one faculty member, its president, the Reverend John Blair Smith, a short, dark-haired, dyspeptic, learned Presbyterian minister. After receiving its charter in 1783 it added two more faculty members. As for students, it had seventy or eighty in all, sons of local planters. Its grounds consisted of one three-story brick building, the "Red House," deep in the woods; five small frame buildings, including the president's house, a library, the steward's house, and a student dining room; and the usual complement of workshops, stables, and so on. Francis Asbury, the traveling Methodist preacher who had seen a great deal of the United States in his journeys, commented in 1787: "The outside has an unwieldy, uncommon appearance for a seminary of learning. What the inside is I know not." Its location was so isolated, being far from any town, main road, or river, that in 1786 James Mercer of Fredericksburg considered it "too rustic" a place to send his son.[20]

Colonel Harrison probably never set foot on the campus, but he was well acquainted with the place. He was Virginia's governor in 1783 when the academy's charter was passed, and he personally knew some of the trustees, notably Patrick Henry and James Madison. Moreover, he may have been impressed that the institution, though founded under Presbyterian auspices, had several Anglicans on its board and took pains to emphasize its religious tolerance. Most important, perhaps, was his brother's influence: Carter Henry Harrison, who lived in nearby Cumberland County and represented it in the House of Burgesses, knew the school and had sent or was planning to send his son Randolph to study there. At the end of his governorship in November 1784, Colonel Harrison, looking for a school at which Billy could begin his medical education, thought of Hampden-Sydney.[21]

At eleven, Billy was not yet old enough to manage a long journey on horseback by himself; his cousin Randolph or another of Carter Harrison's sons probably rode with him to enroll for the winter term, which began 1 November.[22] Billy must have found it a strange journey. He was riding away from the comparatively social, cultured environment of Richmond and Tidewater Virginia, where he had spent his early life, into the Southside, a newly settled area in central Virginia south of the James River whose character was summed up in the name of one of its plantations—Hors du Monde, meaning "outside the world." The Southside was a region populated mostly by the younger sons of Tidewater planters who were just beginning their tobacco plantations, a region of thick forests and red clay roads that wound confusingly through them. Benjamin Henry Latrobe, visiting the area a few years later, wrote:

> I could have fancied myself in a society of English Country Gentlemen (a character to which I attach everything that is desireable [*sic*] as to education, domestic comfort, manners, and principles) had not the shabbiness of their mansions undeceived me. Of the latter I do not mean to speak disrespectfully. It is the necessary consequence of the remoteness of the Country from towns where Workmen assemble and can at all times be had. An unlucky boy breaks two or three squares of Glass. The Glazier lives fifty miles off. An old Newspaper supplies their place in the mean time. Before the mean time is over the family get used to the Newspapers.[23]

Southside people spoke with a different accent from those in Tidewater Virginia. John Randolph, Billy Harrison's exact contemporary, recorded more or less phonetically a scrap of Southside speech, a young man addressing his slave: "Cuffy bresh my coat might clean us I'm agwine a coatin un doan tetch it with yo finguz a'ter you've done; else you'll dutty it." The Harrisons' own speech was heavily accented after the Tidewater fashion, pronouncing Carter as "Cyartuh" and garden as "gyarden" and calling their home "Barclay," but as Billy accustomed himself to his classmates at Hampden-Sydney he must have noted their Southside accent as one of their many alien features.[24]

Almost no record survives of Billy's stay at Hampden-Sydney; in fact, only two or three pieces of evidence permit placing him there at a particular time. A fragment of the program for the student exhibition of April 1786, at which the boys memorized and declaimed speeches, shows a student whose name ended in "rrison" delivering Cicero's "Pro Archia Poeta." This might have been either Billy or Randolph—but the odds favor Billy, as Randolph is said to have attended for only a single term.[25]

Less equivocal is a bill from Doctor Francis Joseph Mettauer, dated August–September 1785, to "William Harrison, College." It includes charges for treatment, medication, and apparently an operation of some sort, perhaps for an abscess. Evidently the illness came on suddenly, since Billy was treated at school rather than in Richmond or at his home; and in all likelihood it was serious, since the doctor's attentions lasted six weeks. The number of laxatives prescribed suggests a gastrointestinal problem, which would be consistent with other sources that show Harrison to have suffered from delicate digestion all his life. The whole episode also reinforces Harrison's description of himself in youth as having an appearance "apparently but illy suited to sustain . . . fatigue and hardships."[26]

Dr. Mettauer, by the way, probably was better qualified than many Virginia physicians. A Frenchman from Alsace, he was a military doctor who had come to Virginia with the French army at the close of the war, married a local girl, and settled in the remote Southside. With his Continental training, he may have undertaken a surgical procedure more readily than an American; most native-born doctors were poor at surgery and avoided it when possible.[27]

Billy saw the doctor once more, toward the end of his stay at Hampden-Sydney. Mettauer's accounts show a visit in April 1787, during which he prescribed more laxatives and a number of ointments. They also note that the earlier bill was still unpaid: Colonel Harrison had the habit, common among Virginia planters of the old school, of "never disputing a bill, and seldom paying a debt until, like their Madeira, it had acquired age"; moreover, he was in rather serious financial straits. It is not clear that the Harrisons ever paid Mettauer what they owed him. Billy left the school shortly after this last medical consultation, when he had "completed his fourteenth year"—that is, some time in 1787. Why he left is the subject of the rest of this chapter.[28]

The doctor's bill reveals that young Harrison lived upstairs in the Red House, the college's main building. He shared his sleeping quarters, barracks-fashion, with four or five other students and perhaps one of the tutors. The lack of privacy would not have distressed him or any of his roommates, who all were accustomed from boyhood to sharing their bedrooms with brothers, cousins, and male visitors. Their adolescent lifestyle could be labeled as either Spartan simplicity or rustic squalor. Slaves from the college steward's staff lit fires in the bedrooms, brought water for washing from the college spring, and periodically washed the students' bedding to get rid of the bedbugs. The Red House had no bathroom; to avoid "defil[ing] any part of the College with urine or excrements," for which they could receive a public reprimand, the boys had to make for the privy or the surrounding woods.[29]

Apart from the Latin and Greek that occupied most of the day, the college routine was the simple one of a boys' camp, including the enforced quiet of study hours until nine P.M., loud games of "fives" (a kind of handball) against the college buildings when weather permitted, and occasional raucous episodes of harassing an unpopular tutor. Since the students were generally from farms or plantations, most kept horses in the college stables and many kept dogs. On weekends, most left to spend Saturday night and Sunday on visits with each other's families in the surrounding country. Those who stayed at the school were required to observe Sunday as a day of rest and attend divine service, if any was held nearby. Most often, however, there was no service; in many parts of Virginia, where Anglican ministers had supported the British, the war had pretty much destroyed the Anglican Church, and St. Patrick's Parish in Prince Edward was abandoned. A Presbyterian church a few miles from the school met occasionally, pastored by Smith, the school's president. For the students, as a rule, religion consisted of brief morning and evening prayers led by the president—simple formalities that suited their taste, since most Virginians tended to regard religion as a series of largely perfunctory formalities. Not a student on campus possessed a Bible.[30]

In the early months of 1787, as Billy's fourteenth birthday approached, this situation suddenly changed. Over Christmas break, Cary Allen, a droll, popular student a few years Billy's senior, attended a Methodist revival meeting near his home in Cumberland County. Methodism, a movement within the Anglican clergy, had stirred up a powerful revival in southern Virginia just before the war, its members speaking to crowds on the personal aspect of religion: the consequences of sin, the need to accept Jesus into one's life, the overwhelming power of God. Methodist meetings were often highly emotional, marked by outbursts of what Virginia gentlemen contemptuously called "enthusiasm"—weeping, outcries, spontaneous prayer, and physical movements. Their revival had been cut short when many preachers returned to England during the war; but now, with the advent of peace, the movement enjoyed a resurgence, this time as an independent church. Young Allen found himself touched by the preacher's message and decided to commit his life to Christ. He returned to school in January an enthusiastic Christian, the only one on campus, and had to face the ridicule of his classmates.[31]

Allen's new devotion influenced his stepbrother and fellow student William Hill, who had been brought up in a fairly religious home, even though he played cards and had fun on the Sabbath as his classmates did. Hill began to question his own thinking and to talk with other students. Gradually he found several who felt the same way and wanted to consider the serious aspects of life. These young men often found the approach to conversion an emotion-laden experience; twenty-one-year-old James Blythe, for instance, burst into tears when Hill mentioned the Bible to him. By the spring, Allen, Hill, Blythe, and two or three other students had joined together to hold surreptitious meetings in the woods around the campus for prayer and hymn-singing.

One of these meetings ended up bringing the conflict of religious styles—between the new, heartfelt Methodism and the traditional cultural Anglicanism of upper-class Virginia—before the whole college. This meeting took place on a rainy Sunday. Hill, whose roommates were away for the weekend, suggested to the group that they gather in his room. They did, singing and praying quietly enough, they thought, to escape attention, but other students in the building heard them, realized what they were doing, and gathered at the door of Hill's room to taunt them. Before long a "noisy mob" had formed out in the hall, swearing, yelling, banging on the door, and threatening them if they did not stop. This noise attracted the tutors, Drury Lacy and William Mahon, who broke up the crowd and reported to President Smith. At prayers that evening, when Smith demanded an explanation, one of the students used the most damaging comparison he could think of: Allen and his group had been "singing and praying and carrying on like Methodists, and they were determined to break it up." Smith took a middle course: he invited the prayer group to meet with him in his house. There, convinced of their sincerity, he soon joined in with them.[32]

All this took place in spring 1787, around the time Billy was again receiving treatment from Dr. Mettauer. He was at the school when the confrontation took place, living in the same building where it occurred. Doubtless he knew all the students involved; his personality, to judge from later documents, was outgoing, friendly, and somewhat impulsive, whatever his family problems may have been. He made friends easily and remembered them for years. The affair became the talk of Prince Edward, and when Billy went home in May on vacation, he doubtless gave his father an account of the incident. When classes resumed in June,

Billy did not attend—or if he did, he came home before the term was over. In September, he was in the James River area, visiting family.[33]

No account states why Colonel Harrison did not let his son continue at Hampden-Sydney. Billy's health or the colonel's own finances may have played a part, but there is little doubt that the colonel disliked the revival. A strong defender of the Anglican Church, with its formal, emotionless service, he had fought vigorously in the legislature to keep it as Virginia's established religion. Very likely he agreed with his brother Carter Henry, who said that the worst curse God had placed on Virginia was the sending of dissenters—Presbyterians, Methodists, and the like—into it. If he had the impression that Hampden-Sydney was succumbing to Methodist enthusiasm, Colonel Harrison would have been unlikely to give it any further business or money.[34]

The colonel's choice of an alternate school for Billy to attend suggests his feelings. The account in the *Port Folio* says merely that it was an academy in Southampton County, some fifty miles from Berkeley on the other side of the James, but local tradition in Southampton unanimously identifies it as Millfield Academy, a school started in January 1788 by the Reverend Henry John Burges, who formerly had been rector of the Surry County parish attended by Billy's brother Carter Bassett Harrison. Burges, forty-four years old and an experienced teacher, was a substantial planter and a sound Anglican, who would board boys at his home for fourteen pounds a term, less than Hampden-Sydney. The academy's prospectus stressed "the Latin and Greek Languages, Geography, and the most useful branches of the Mathematicks." In no way superior to Hampden-Sydney, Burges's school was even newer, smaller, and more isolated. It was not a glorious choice for a young Harrison of Berkeley, but some other planters' sons attended it, and it was religiously sound.[35]

Even the assumption that his father withdrew Billy from Hampden-Sydney because of the revival leaves some ambiguity about the course of events. Did Colonel Harrison withdraw his son simply because Hampden-Sydney was becoming religiously offensive to him, or did he have reason to suspect that Billy had been affected by the spiritual uproar? No direct evidence exists; little source material of any kind mentions Billy's departure from the school. Detective work is needed even to establish when Billy was withdrawn and where he was sent next. One can get a hint of an answer, however, by looking at a much less ambiguous confrontation between father and son taking place only three years later.

CHAPTER THREE

Friend of Human Liberty

At the beginning of 1790, Benjamin Harrison took his sixteen-year-old son out of Millfield and launched him into an inexpensive, second-class preparation for a career in medicine.

The Reverend Burges's school, like most one-man schools in Virginia, had no set list of requirements and awarded no degrees. Boys studied the ordinary texts in classics and mathematics until their fathers or guardians judged that they had made enough progress to go on to the next step. This Colonel Harrison did in 1790.

Virginia planters who wanted their sons to practice medicine had a variety of options for preparing them for that career. Most prestigious was study in Europe, in either Edinburgh or Paris, but this was a choice available only to young men who had graduated from a college and were fluent in French or Latin. An attractive alternative was study at one of the medical institutions in Philadelphia; every year a handful of young Virginians commenced their training there. Lowest in prestige, though not necessarily in quality, was becoming an apprentice to a local practitioner.[1]

Colonel Harrison, conscious of his family's standing, undoubtedly would have preferred one of the first two options; that he chose instead to apprentice Billy to a local doctor merely confirms what he had been saying for several years, that he was in desperate financial straits. Even before the war, Benjamin Harrison had been in debt from reckless spending. In Philadelphia at the Continental Congress, he had borrowed heavily from the merchant Thomas Willing, the brother of his Virginia neighbor

Mary Willing Byrd, to cover his expenses. As governor of Virginia, he had been unable to devote enough attention to his property, ruined by British raids, to restore it to working order. By 1786, with his debt to Willing and associated lawsuits hanging over him, Harrison was facing, he told a friend, "the ruin of myself and family, let me do what I can." As the situation dragged on, Colonel Harrison offered various pieces of his property, including part of Berkeley, for sale, but found no takers. By 1789, Willing was out of patience. "It now embarrasses me much," he wrote to Alexander Donald of Richmond, "to be kept longer out of Money wh I have so long paid on this Gentlemans Account—he can't make me amends for the trouble & anxiety he has given me." During this same period, the colonel was writing to political friends begging for a job in the new federal government, which he had opposed; "the distresses brought upon me by the ravages of the British," he wrote Charles Carroll of Maryland, "and the great fall of landed property here, have reduced me so low, that some prop is necessary for the support of a numerous family." By "family," he meant, as any James River planter would, his slaves and employees as well as his blood kin.[2]

Billy, acquainted with his family's money problems, must have been aware that the training contemplated for him was second-rate by Virginia standards. Indeed, one could call it third-rate. The doctor who was to be his teacher was not even the leading physician in Richmond; that would have been William Foushee, a popular, elegant man who was active in the town government. Next in prominence were two Edinburgh graduates, James McClurg and James Currie, both in their early forties; then Andrew Leiper, an unmarried Scot around forty who had come to America as a young man and studied with Rush. It was Leiper who was to be Billy's master.[3] No evidence remains to indicate how Billy felt about this choice, but it is not unreasonable to suppose that he compared his opportunities with those given to his older brothers before the war and realized the comparative shabbiness of his treatment. Ben and Carter Harrison had both graduated from William and Mary College, and Ben had apprenticed in Philadelphia with Robert Morris before opening his own firm in Richmond, while Carter had studied law, it is not certain with whom.[4]

According to one Richmonder, Leiper was esteemed a good doctor, but his practice does not seem to have included many leading families. He was a public-spirited man and thoroughly professional, not afraid of dirt or danger. In 1798 he would serve as quarantine physician for the port of Richmond. With Billy's brother-in-law Anthony Singleton and Ben Harrison's clerk William Wiseham, he belonged to the Amicable Society, a charitable organization in town, and conceivably that connection led to his becoming Billy's preceptor. In 1787 John Marshall, whose regular physician was Foushee, called Leiper in to treat a sick slave, a choice that may indicate something about Leiper's practice. His house, at the corner of Franklin and Eighteenth streets, was in the southern part of Richmond, close to the port, where the poorer class of citizens lived. Census and tax records show that he ordinarily had between one and three apprentices living with him. Besides attending him on his visits, they assisted in mixing prescriptions, compounding blends of common and exotic ingredients—sulfur, camphor, mercury, South American bark, and Asian gums. Like many apprentices, they may have slept behind the "greasy counter" in the office next to his house.[5]

Richmond at least had the charm of familiarity; Billy had already lived there for part of the three years when his father was governor. But the little capital—one could scarcely call it a city, with only four thousand residents—was continuing to grow and change. The new Capitol building, designed by Thomas Jefferson after a Roman temple in France, was perched on the hill, nearing completion, and there were a few new residences as well. Billy's situation, however, had also changed: he was no longer living in the governor's residence on the hill, but down in "Rockett's," a section "much less beautiful and not so healthy," in the words of one traveler, separated from the hill by Shockoe Creek and mud streets notorious for their impassibility. "One of the dirtiest holes of a place I ever was in," said a traveler of this part of town in 1786.[6]

Frequently, one supposes, Billy mounted his horse and rode through the mud up to his brother's frame house. Ben was now a widower with a three-year-old son; he would have enjoyed his younger brother's company at mealtime, in addition to that of his brother-in-law Captain Singleton, likewise a merchant, and his own business household—John Satchell, John Richard, and William Wischam, a likable Englishman who "turn[ed] up his nose at any porter not made within the sound of bow bells," all of whom worked for him in his store, selling goods like china, wines, sugar, French hair powder, and other imports.[7]

No doubt the slender, well-bred, well-connected youth from Berkeley was in demand for other social gatherings as well—in company with his fellow apprentices at Leiper's, if they were also from the planter class.

Richmond had an active social scene. It offered theater at various seasons of the year—in October 1790, a company performed both *Know Your Own Mind, or The Rover Reclaimed,* and *Venice Preserved*—accompanied by much flirtation in the boxes. ("He remained long in our box," wrote a breathless young woman in 1785, "but as our friend Eliza was with me, who has the knack of attracting more certainly than the Loadstone, I took it for granted that her charms had riveted him.") Dances were held in the winter season, commencing "with minuets, of which there shall not be more than four," according to the managers' rules, followed by "fancy dances, to be succeeded by country dances." And in November, when the Assembly met and the large, commodious Eagle Tavern on the hill filled up with a great gathering of gentlemen who "sat all together around the fire, drinking, smoking, singing, and talking ribaldry," there were still more opportunities.[8]

If young Harrison tired of company, he could derive another kind of enjoyment from simply walking or riding around Richmond. His wide reading had probably instructed him in the fashionable ways to appreciate natural beauty; Richmond's location at the falls of the James River, amid broad water and steep hills, made it a place full of vistas. "The ride along the river is extremely beautiful and romantic," wrote a sensitive traveler approaching from the east in 1791; "the road winds on the brow of a hill over the river & commands a fine view of the Town, the river, the little town of Manchester, on the opposite side, and woods scattered about. The roaring of the water over the rocks & the noise of the workmen working below, with the noise of the explosion made in blowing the rocks up [they were building the James River Canal], render the scene curious & pleasing. On my return I was struck with the grandeur of the scenery; the different views of Richmond, with its immense Capitol towering above the Town on a lofty eminence, arrested my attention."[9]

All these activities are predictable, given what one knows of Billy Harrison, his family, and Richmond, but the one documented event of Harrison's stay in the Virginia capital belongs in a totally different category. "At the age of eighteen," he wrote in 1822, "I became a member of an Abolition Society established at Richmond, Virginia; the object of which was to ameliorate the condition of slaves and procure their freedom *by every legal means* [italics in original]. My venerable friend, judge Gatch, of Clermont county [Ohio], was also a member of this society, and has lately given me a corroborative statement that I was one."[10]

Gatch's statement ran:

> More than thirty years ago, I was at a meeting of the Humane Society in the city of Richmond, Va. The society was formed first by the Quakers, and others joined the same. The intention of the institution was to abolish slavery, as far as they possibly could in all things. I was at the time living in Virginia, and William H. Harrison presented himself a candidate for membership. One of the members opposed his admittance, and but one, as his father owned a great number of slaves. The Harrison family were wealthy and respectable. I was unwell, and left the meeting, but understood that Mr. Harrison was admitted a member of the aforesaid society. All were rejected that held slaves.

The records of the society have not survived to confirm this statement, but it seems credible enough. Gatch was at the time a Methodist minister and a recognized opponent of slavery; his brother-in-law James Smith was secretary of the society.[11]

It was not too surprising, in the aftermath of the Revolution, that a young man of the planter class should be openly hostile to slavery; many of these youths' fathers were likewise unhappy with the system. The Marquis de Chastellux, who visited Virginia in 1782 and interviewed many leading men, found that "in general they seem grieved at having slaves, and are constantly talking of abolishing slavery and of making other means of exploiting their lands." Robert Pleasants, the Quaker founder of the Abolition Society, could confidently write to the Virginia patriot Patrick Henry, "I well know thy sentiments on slavery, & that thou don't need any thing on that subject to convince thee of the injustice of laws which restrain the liberation of that highly injured people."[12]

For most Virginia planters, however, the real uneasiness they felt about slavery was more than outweighed by skepticism about the consequences of freeing the slaves; they feared ending up with a large number of uneducated, landless, needy neighbors whom they would have to control without deriving any benefit from their labors. Although an increasing number of planters freed their slaves in Virginia in the 1780s, often with fervent mea culpas written into their wills, such acts were spasmodic and occasional; most held back.[13] Patrick Henry refused either to join or to collaborate with the Abolition Society, and some planters, Benjamin Harrison among them, even resisted the idea of allowing their neighbors to emancipate their slaves. Apart from a few young idealists, only Quakers and Methodists in Virginia felt enough support from their fellow believers to take that step, and even for them it could be difficult. In joining the Abolition Society, Billy was deliberately taking a position opposed by and offensive to his father.[14]

Among Billy Harrison's contemporaries, sons of the great planters, a number condemned slavery even more harshly than their fathers. As young men, they could afford to do so, for they had less to lose. They were particularly attracted by Revolutionary ideals of liberty and enlightenment; young Richard Randolph, for instance, in the early 1790s denounced slaveholding in his will as a "most lawless and monstrous tyranny" and railed at "the tyrants of the earth, from the throned despot of a whole nation to the most despicable, but not less infamous, petty tormentors of single wretched slaves." Some of these young men were also attracted by the humanitarianism of the era. A few years later, Billy's contemporary Robert Carter would reject the idea of "becoming a slave-holder and witnessing many cruelties, even at this enlightened day, when the rights of man are so well ascertained."[15]

The experiences of a boy growing up on one of the great plantations would include much likely to feed these perceptions of torment and cruelty. Slaves, he learned, were a group set apart. They had little in common with one's own kin; they had not sacrificed for the Revolution as whites had; they were, in fact, aliens in Virginia, not quite Americans. Moreover, slaves were treated quite differently from white servants, tutors, overseers, and artisans who came and went from the plantation with more freedom and never experienced a beating or a whipping. Slaves typically lived at some distance from the big house, in primitive cabins that often had dirt floors; they wore simple, coarse, ragged clothing of cheap linen or homespun cotton; and they behaved with exaggerated respect, sometimes stammering with fear in whites' presence, sometimes kneeling if they had a request to make.[16]

To a white adolescent, perhaps the most striking difference in condition between slaves and whites was the one that impressed many Northerners and Europeans visiting Virginia for the first time: their nakedness. Slave children ran around entirely naked in warm weather, as no planter's child was permitted to do. On some plantations, slave boys in their teens waited on table wearing a shirt that reached only to midthigh and left their genitals exposed; a visiting Pennsylvanian remarked in his diary,

"It would surprize you to see some of these d___d black boys how well they are hung." Likewise, slave girls waited on gentlemen with their breasts uncovered. Members and guests of the master's family were not supposed to notice. "Our Girls never think of these things," several Richmond women assured Benjamin Henry Latrobe in the 1790s; "they appear to them as a different race, neither objects of desire, nor actuated by the same refined passions as themselves." Perhaps their claim was broadly true, but the difference, in terms of human dignity, was so striking that, if a young person's view of slavery changed only a little by virtue of a perception derived from reading or a personal relationship, it could seem stark and cruel, an index of the odiousness of slavery.[17]

Humanitarianism, by the Revolutionary era, had become a staple element of British and American culture; and Virginia youths in the 1780s were frequently exposed to works by Northern or British writers, most often poetic but sometimes in prose, dwelling on the basic likeness of Africans and whites and condemning slavery as "lawless and monstrous" for drawing distinctions between the races and using them as pretexts for mistreatment. While these had their effect, their verbal fervor and emotion did not inspire action. Indeed, from the 1780s onward such works began to shade into sentimentality, a style of writing that strove for emotional effect and aimed to evoke from readers a frisson, not necessarily a feeling of commitment. Winthrop Jordan and David Brion Davis have argued that these tear-jerking depictions were as much a substitute for ending slavery as they were a stimulus.[18]

Harrison, like his contemporaries, read humanitarian poems and essays. Reading was important to him. "Inferior to many in my class at College as a Latin and Greek scholar," he recollected, "I was inferior to but one in Belle [*sic*] Lettres information & particularly in history. I was acquainted with all the battles from Homer to Julius Caesar." (Harrison's mention of his "class at College," which has misled many biographers, doubtless refers to Hampden-Sydney, the largest educational institution he is recorded as having attended; but it cannot mean the collegiate division, for which he was too young. He meant the dozen or half-dozen boys at the same stage of instruction as he in the academy.) The *belles lettres* he mentioned encompassed essays, memoirs, travel writing, and, as he said, history. He read not only for information and guidance but also to learn to express himself formally. The two books he chose to carry when he went west with the army, Cicero's *Orations* and "the large edition of Blair's Lectures" (an immensely popular eighteenth-century book on rhetoric, or effective writing and speaking), indicate his seriousness. No doubt he had read more than one condemnation of the evils of slavery.[19]

It was not these readings, however, that propelled Billy Harrison, in 1791, to walk in the door of the dusty, obscure church on the south side of James River, across from Richmond, to join the Virginia Abolition Society, uniting with men who publicly rejected slavery as "an odious degradation . . . utterly repugnant to the precepts of the gospel" in an organized protest. Evidently he knew the time and place of the meeting; he also knew some of the people there, definitely Gatch and probably others. He was, in other words, part of a social network, the basis of which was probably religious. As Gatch pointed out in his account, Virginia Quakers had organized the group and then had been joined by "others," principally Methodists, the other large religious group in the state with a strong testimony against slavery. As between Quakers and Methodists, it is not hard to decide which group must have constituted the social network to which young Harrison belonged. He had had little contact with Quakers during his upbringing, whereas he had been present at Hampden-Sydney when the Methodist revival broke out there. Indeed, a Hampden-Sydney schoolmate of his, William Spencer, now a Methodist minister, had passed through Richmond only months earlier, preaching particularly to blacks, whom he found "more engaged" in religion than the whites. Although direct documentation is lacking, therefore, it seems evident that Billy Harrison established a close connection with Methodists at Hampden-Sydney, becoming either a convert or a sympathizer; that this connection had something to do with his abrupt removal from the school; and that his joining the Abolition Society three years later sprang from this association.[20]

Questions remain, however. If young Harrison was put under the care of the Reverend Mr. Burges in order to win him back to a rational, acceptable Anglicanism, one wonders why the process was so unfruitful. It is worth remembering, though, that northern Southampton and the adjacent counties were at the epicenter of the Methodist revival in Virginia. Enormous revival meetings that attracted gentry and plain folk, white and black, took place regularly. These meetings drew thousands and lasted for hours. A majority of Billy's schoolmates were from local gentry families; if he visited at their homes on weekends, as most

Virginia boys tended to do when away at school, he would have heard animated conversation about the religious revival, with both believers and nonbelievers expressing their views, an exposure that would have counteracted Burges's efforts. (An example of such table conversation, occurring in Spotsylvania County during just this period, appears in the memoirs of Archibald Alexander.) Far from returning to the Anglican fold, Billy might have become more committed to "Christian experience" and more acquainted with its followers.[21]

Virginia Methodists were not all of one mind with regard to liberating the slaves. William Spencer was unmistakably sincere when he wrote in his diary of the slaves to whom he preached, "God bless the dear Creatures, my Soul loves them, and I humbly hope and trust that my dear Lord Jesus will bless my Labours among them"—but he said nothing about freeing them. The circuit rider Jesse Lee of Sussex County was sure that immediate emancipation would be unwise, and tangled on the subject with Thomas Coke, a visiting English preacher who argued for freedom now. Philip Gatch had freed all his slaves in 1780 upon becoming a Methodist, but Coke knew a committed Virginia Methodist who was "a violent friend of slavery" and "would have been a dreadful thorn in our sides, if the Lord had not in mercy taken him away."[22]

Becoming an enthusiastic Christian did not, then, entail public opposition to slavery, although it did encourage white converts to view Africans as equals and brothers. What prompted Harrison to take the extra step of openly supporting abolition is unknown. In November 1790, his sister Elizabeth Rickman died and left him a slave in her will. That bequest could have triggered some sort of moral crisis. Or perhaps Billy became a member of Richmond's Abolition Society and made his public declaration just to nettle his father. There is simply no information.[23]

Since public opposition to slavery played no further part in Harrison's life, one is entitled to ask how sincere his youthful convictions were, recognizing the obvious fact that beliefs are apt to change over time. After he disposed of the slave left him by his sister, it is not clear from the records that he ever owned slaves again. In adulthood, living in the free Indiana Territory, he bought slaves from Kentucky, freed them, and concluded a labor contract with them for a period of years, a proceeding that suggests that the two types of unfree labor, similar as they may seem to twenty-first-century observers, were very different to him. Apparently he had no objection to enjoying the services of a bound servant; his objection, founded in religion, was simply to owning another human being. This point of view was not uncommon. The Founding Father John Dickinson freed fifty slaves during the war, convinced, as Gary Nash and Jean Soderlund put it in their history of emancipation in Pennsylvania, that "the recording Angel stood ready to make Record against him in Heaven had he neglected" to manumit them—whereupon he immediately bound them to twenty-one years of contract labor. William Harrison's attitude likewise may have been consistent in a way many modern Americans reject: he wanted to keep his own conscience clear and avoid offending God while feeling no compulsion to reform the system as a whole. He was indignant in 1822 when political opponents called him "friendly to slavery." "From my earliest youth to the present moment," he responded extravagantly, "I have been the *ardent friend of Human Liberty* [italics in original]."[24]

Billy's gesture of joining the Abolition Society took place around his eighteenth birthday, early in 1791. As he anticipated, it provoked an immediate reaction from his father—but that reaction was a surprisingly mild one. Colonel Harrison, doubtless embarrassed at having a quasi-Methodist agitator in his family, decided within weeks to get him out of the state. Almost surely at a considerable financial sacrifice, he would send his youngest son north to study in Pennsylvania, a state where slavery was being gradually phased out, with Benjamin Rush, a committed Christian, a pamphleteer against slavery, and the most celebrated doctor in America. Evidently he thought he could still save his son for a medical career. The fact suggests the degree to which he failed to grasp the depth of Billy's alienation.

CHAPTER FOUR

The Grand Gesture

In consequence of his father's plan for him, Billy Harrison found himself in Philadelphia in the summer of 1791, where the blistering hot days of early June gave way to thunderstorms that brought some relief toward the end of the month. It was a relatively healthy season without major epidemics—just the dysentery and stomach disorders that formed a normal part of summer in the capital. On 4 July, militia companies in bright uniform paraded the level brick streets. "Places of entertainment in town and country were thronged with company," reported the *Pennsylvania Gazette.* At Gray's Gardens, outside town on the Schuylkill River, a "slight disturbance" marred the celebration of independence: several people were thrown into the river, but no one drowned. Two days later, cannon boomed and bells pealed all over the city, as President Washington returned from his Southern tour.[1]

Billy Harrison, lodging somewhere near the center of the city, was doubtless aware of Washington's return. More important to him, though, was the question of his own future; still pretending to be a medical student, he was trying to work out how to avoid returning to Virginia and his family, an environment that, all evidence suggests, had become intolerable to him. A letter from his brother Ben that arrived in June or July increased the pressure on Billy. As the executor and principal heir of Colonel Harrison's estate, Ben had every reason to be annoyed at the sums his father had planned to spend on Billy's education in Philadelphia, simply to gratify his son's whim about slavery. Perhaps skeptical, as he had every reason to be, of the depth of his brother's commitment to freeing the blacks, Ben insisted that Billy give up his junket and return to Virginia for a more serious (and less expensive) course of medical study.

Quite naturally in the circumstances, Billy sought help and advice from people outside the medical profession. With Attorney General Randolph he discussed a post with the federal government, though nothing came of it. Randolph was a fellow Virginian, which made him a likely person to approach: Harrison was a lone young man in a large city, and Virginians were a conspicuous, cohesive group in the capital. Although scorned by some for their "Frothy Manners" and their constant talk of food ("Canvas-backs, ham & Chickens, Old Madeira"), riding, dueling, and the glories of the Old Dominion (like the country gentlemen of Henry Fielding's England), they were often ready to assist one another. They included so many medical students that some Philadelphians were said to believe that all medical students in the city were from Virginia.[2]

Philadelphia's resident Virginians often met at the Indian Queen, the City, or another of the city's major taverns to socialize over glasses of wine or rum, and heavy drinking was common. Billy's participation in these social evenings must have been limited, however; he was a consistently moderate drinker, whether because of his father's example or because of his own sensitive stomach. Thus he probably saw little of Jack Randolph, the attorney general's nephew and a youth his own age, who theoretically was studying law in his uncle's office but actually was dissipating his time with other young Southerners in the city, aided by his hard-drinking older brother Theodorick, who came up for a visit that summer.[3]

Had it been winter, the social season in Philadelphia, Billy probably would have received invitations to many dances and balls. Young Virginia men were much in demand with Philadelphia hostesses because of their vivacity and dancing skills. ("Virginians are of genuine Blood—They will dance or die!" commented one visitor.) Like carousing, this kind of socializing took energy. A Philadelphia woman Billy probably knew well, the sister of his family's Virginia neighbor Mary Willing Byrd, hinted as much in her letter to Bushrod Washington, the president's nephew: "Dancing until two or three oclock in the Morning, confined air, the Vapor from a number of Candles, & still greater number of Breaths, are not beneficial to any one." In summer, however, fewer dances were held. Many of young Harrison's encounters with Virginians seem to have been with family friends passing through the capital on business, whom he met at taverns to discuss the news of the day over a glass or two of wine. At these affairs he was, as always, talkative, cheerful, and sociable. At the Morrises', he struck up a friendship with a young South Carolina lawyer, Robert Goodloe Harper, who was working on one of Morris's many land deals.[4]

That summer the Philadelphia newspapers were full of reports of conflict, both looming and actual. In the Caribbean, the French island of Saint-Dominque was showing signs of a burgeoning slave rebellion—the event that most terrified slaveholding Americans; several whites had been killed, and the French government was sending more soldiers. In France itself, the ongoing revolution was arousing more and more hostility both within and outside the country; a June attempt by King Louis XVI and his family to flee Paris, reported in Philadelphia in August, was ominous. In the Western American territories the Army had been called out for an expedition against Indians attacking new settlements along the Ohio River. It was to be led by the Revolutionary general Arthur St. Clair. To a young man whose thoughts ran to military glory, it must almost have seemed that the world was erupting in war everywhere except where he happened to be, in placid, orderly Philadelphia.[5]

This was the complexion of things in late July or early August, when Billy Harrison ran into Henry Lee. The exact date of their interview is uncertain. Years later, in old age, Harrison thought it happened the day before he got his commission in the Army that is, on 15 August. In fact, however, Lee had left the city by that date, probably around 6 August to judge from his correspondence. One can only assume that the meeting occurred shortly before Lee's departure, at his lodgings or a tavern.[6]

Apart from occasional visits to New York, handsome, round-faced Henry Lee had been in Philadelphia since June, on business involving the Potomac Company (a private company backed by President Washington to facilitate settlement of the Ohio Valley), so that the Western territories were on his mind when he and Harrison met. Lee, a young man about Ben Harrison's age from one of the first families in Virginia, had won fame and a colonelcy as a cavalry leader during the Revolution; his life since then had been an anticlimax, and he recalled his military service fondly. Of course he knew Billy; everyone of prominence in Virginia had called at Berkeley and met the Harrison children. Billy explained his situation and awaited Lee's response. He was probably unaware that the president, in the spring, had offered Lee command of the Virginia and Maryland troops in the Indian expedition and that Lee had declined for personal reasons, but he surely understood that Lee was interested in the Western campaign. In Harrison's account, Lee was the first to recommend his joining the Army, and Billy "immediately acquiesced."[7]

Lee can scarcely have anticipated how receptive young Harrison would be to his idea. The younger man, by his own testimony, had read "the ponderous work of Rollin" three times already, mostly during his two-year sojourn in the isolation of Millfield Academy. Its eloquence, its rush of events, and the elevated motives its subjects had worked powerfully on Billy's imagination. They probably fed his thirst for the grand gesture and the convincing utterance—an early version of the Romantic impulse, one can call it—traits characteristic throughout his career. Perhaps Harrison was also drawn by the idea of serving his country more nobly and more gloriously than his father. Now he could step into a role that he had long admired with little hope of actually filling it. Through Lee's influence, the impossible seemed suddenly attainable.

Joining the army, of course, meant joining as an officer. Nothing else would have been suitable for a son of Colonel Benjamin Harrison. Billy might have explained himself in much the same terms used by Charles Caldwell, an obscure North Carolina medical student who considered joining the Army in Philadelphia a couple of years later for much the same reasons—being "a young man of southern constitution, an ardent temperament, an imagination neither tame nor uncreative, and a general cast of mind sufficiently awake to enterprise and romance": "[M]y pride, or something else forbade me to enrol myself as a private soldier." Even a Charles Caldwell had his pride; how much more so a Harrison of James River, whose abilities lay in giving orders, not in taking them?[8]

An upbringing on a large Virginia plantation was in some ways the best possible training for an Army career. Virginia youths grew up surrounded by servants—there were, for instance, more than one hundred slaves on Berkeley plantation—and learned early how to command and be obeyed. In his teens, many a Virginia boy of the planter class was assigned an African American slave, often of his own age, to look after his needs; Thomas Jefferson had his personal servant Jupiter as he grew up, while John Randolph recalled his brother Richard's elegantly clothed man Syphax. Sometimes a boy and his slave would fight together as a pastime, like two friends of the same class, but generally their relations were governed by formality, as in the military, with the threat of physical punishment for disobedience or nonperformance looming in the background.[9]

Quite often a planter's son sent to another state to study would bring his personal servant along; if Harrison brought his, however, it was with the design of freeing him or letting him "escape" in the capital. Whatever his feelings about African slavery, however, he was comfortable with the master-servant relationship. The master commanded, the servant obeyed; the relationship involved inequality and degradation but also protection and intimacy. Twenty-first-century accounts of Virginia slavery are apt to stress instances where the system broke down, producing frustration and abuse—Jefferson's famous comment, "The parent storms, the child looks on," or the episode in which William Byrd made a slave boy drink "a pint of piss" for wetting his bed—but the less dramatic norm of master-servant relations on the plantation, as in the Army, was simple command on the one hand, deference and compliance on the other. Billy Harrison would have had no doubts about his ability to perform as an officer.[10]

Two obstacles stood in the way of Billy Harrison getting a commission as ensign, the lowest officer's rank in the army: opposition from his family (and presumably his guardian, Senator Robert Morris) and his age. Aware of the first of these problems, Billy, who relied on Lee's influence with President Washington and with Henry Knox, the secretary of war—and knew that seeking their permission was in any case the proper technique for obtaining a commission—asked Lee not to say anything to Morris about his request until it had succeeded. Of the second problem, neither Billy nor Lee may have been aware: Knox, in a letter to General Anthony Wayne the following year, asserted that he and Washington had "invariably adhered to the principle that the Ensigns should have attained the Age of twenty one," because "the lives of men are of too much importance to be confided to a raw youth." Thus granting Harrison a commission at age eighteen was an obvious violation of this policy, and it is not at all clear how he and Lee got around this obstacle. It may be, as some nineteenth-century campaign biographies asserted, that he had a personal interview with Washington to convince the president that he was promising officer material. One can imagine him in the presence of the tall, sallow-faced, solemn-voiced Father of his Country, doing his best to appear manly and capable. Perhaps his efforts succeeded; more likely, however, he got the commission because he was Benjamin Harrison's son and many men in government remembered his father with esteem.[11]

The formal decision was not made until Lee had left for Virginia. On 16 August 1791, Harrison stopped by the War Department in Carpenter's Hall, picked up his commission, and then took the officer's oath before Justice James Wilson of the Supreme Court. At his lodgings that same day, he had received a note from Senator Morris summoning him for an interview; guessing what Morris wanted to see him about, he took the precaution of picking up the commission and taking the oath first. It was as Billy suspected: the president, unaware that the commission was supposed to be a secret, had happened to mention it to Morris, who suddenly realized that amid the press of his own political and financial affairs—looming debts and negotiations for a large land purchase in western New York state—he had lost contact with his ward. The senator was angry—but probably sober, unlike Colonel Harrison—and when Billy arrived at his opulent house, he sat him down for a lecture.

Morris, a commanding figure in his 1795 portrait by Gilbert Stuart, with a broad, fleshy face, deep eyes, full, firm lips, and shoulder-length gray hair, fixed young Harrison with an intense expression. The Army, he pointed out, was a small affair, generally held in low esteem; its two regiments numbered perhaps sixty officers and sixteen hundred men. The officers, many of whom he knew well—he had dined with General Arthur St. Clair, commander of the expedition against the Indians, only that January—were mostly middle-aged Revolutionary veterans, drinkers, braggarts, and fools who had found it impossible to fit back into civilian life; the ordinary soldiers, by common consent, were dirt—"worthless and depraved" rogues enlisted from the lowest classes of the great seaports. After all, at three dollars a month, a private's pay was too low to attract any other sort. Officers' pay was not much better. Harrison, as an ensign, would receive twenty dollars a month. As for the duty, it had all the dangers of war and none of the glory. The troops, scattered over a vast, uninhabited frontier, were fighting a series of small skirmishes with the Northwestern tribes; if Harrison was killed or maimed in such an encounter, no one beyond his family would know of the fact, or even of the engagement in which it had taken place. So much for military glory; if it was epic romance Harrison was after, Morris had to point out that the Western frontier was the least suitable place in America for the literary pursuits he enjoyed. If it was eventual promotion to general, the prospects were slight as long as the Army remained at its present size; unless there was a general war, Billy could easily remain a junior officer for years. Young Harrison, sitting opposite, was mannerly and respectful as always, but absolutely intransigent. He had made his choice, he said, and did not intend to back down.[12]

Senator Morris, it has to be said, was absolutely right in trying to keep his ward from the romantic, foolish decision he was making. All the evidence suggests that Billy Harrison was simply acting out, in headstrong fashion, his frustrations as a son. For a young man, the Army was perhaps the most dangerous environment in America. As Joseph Strong of Connecticut, who was to enter the Western army as a surgeon's mate the following year, summed it up, "There are few men here whose education & feelings render them pleasing companions. Ignorance & boldness too often insult knowledge & modesty in the lines of any army & dissipation is fashionable & ruins many men here who would be useful members of a community under the mild government of temperance." James Elliot of Massachusetts, Harrison's contemporary, judged the Army even more severely, from an enlisted man's viewpoint: "In an army every thing invites and leads to dissipation, debauchery, and indeed an almost total extinction of virtuous principles and habits. . . . More real knowledge of human nature may be acquired in six months, in an army, than in an equal number of years, spent at a university. But it is a lottery, in which the disproportion of the prizes to the blanks is immense. Where a single youth has acquired a fund of useful knowledge, and improved it to advantage, by serving as a soldier, nine or ten, perhaps a much greater number, have been eternally ruined."[13] Harrison, in fact, would beat the odds; he would be the single youth who acquired knowledge and used it to advantage. But Morris could not have known that.

In the course of the conversation, as it became obvious that Harrison would not change his mind, Morris perhaps thought of his own sons, Tom and Richard, who were now out in western New York making preparations for the Indian treaty. At any rate, his tone changed. He pointed out to Billy that the Ohio Valley was a vast and fertile country, full of good business opportunities, and that an observant young man could lay the foundation for a fortune in land. He mentioned his friendship with St. Clair, who was not only commander of the Indian expedition but also governor of the Northwest Territory. This was a man who could help Billy. If Billy's mind was fixed, Morris said, he would wish him luck and put no obstacles in his way. Harrison probably paid as little attention to this last, more generous part of his guardian's harangue as he had to the rest of it. As his military career was to show, glory, not financial success, was his dream.[14]

Billy Harrison's encounter with glory was to be postponed, however. After being sworn in, he wrote in his autobiographical letter to Erastus Brooks, he spent the next few weeks in Philadelphia, in the recruiting service. This was perhaps the least glamorous of a young officer's possible duties. It took him into the late-summer stinks of Water Street and the slums at the city's edge. The customary practice was for an officer to lead a small squad with a fifer, a drummer, and a sergeant or two. Resplendent in his new uniform—cocked hat and knee-length blue coat trimmed with scarlet, with scarlet lapels and the subaltern's distinguishing epaulette on the left shoulder—he would parade the narrow streets in front of the most popular taverns and gathering places, engaging men with the offer of a three-dollar bounty, a new suit of clothes, and the arguments common to recruiters of the time: a chance to acquire "the honourable and truly respectable character of a soldier." and the opportunity "of spending a few happy years in viewing the different parts of this beautiful continent." He would then sign up all applicants who were able-bodied, over 5' 5" in height, and white—blacks, mulattoes, and Indians were excluded from the Army of the United States. When he had a sufficient number, he would be able to march them west, or join some other company en route to the frontier. In smaller towns, a recruiting officer could impress susceptible young local women and strike up pleasant acquaintances, but in the capital, recruiting was just a specialized, tedious service. Harrison, no doubt, longed to be out of it and on his way to the tests of combat. Week after week, he waited.[15]

CHAPTER FIVE

Parallel Lives

Before following young Harrison out to the frontier, where the data on his life becomes more continuous and his motivations somewhat easier to discern, I would like to consider the lives of a few other Virginia boys, contemporaries of his from the top level of the planter class, whose lives intersected or paralleled his in the years just after the Revolution. Their early lives are fragmentary too, in some cases even less complete than Harrison's, but, set side by side, they point to themes and stresses that pervaded Virginia society in those difficult postwar years. They suggest the context in which Billy Harrison grew up, and they hint that many of his friends had problems similar to his own.

William Henry Harrison and Charles Willing Byrd were only three years apart in age and grew up on plantations only six or seven miles apart. One can assume they associated as neighboring planters' sons were apt to do—rode around the country together, hunted, visited one another's houses for extended stays, and met at dancing school and after service at Westover Church, which both their families attended. (The church stood on the Byrd plantation, Westover, and its rector had married one of the Byrd girls.) True, during much of their adolescence one or the other was away—Billy with his father in Richmond and then at school in the Piedmont, Charley (at some point during these years) at school in Philadelphia—but in the late 1780s and early 1790s they were both near home. Harrison was attending the Reverend Burges's school at Millfield at that time, and so, it appears, were Byrd's younger brothers, Dicky and Billy. Then Harrison went on to Richmond to apprentice with Dr. Leiper, while Byrd remained in Charles City.[1]

The situations of the two youths were very similar: both were younger sons of great planting families that were threatened with economic disaster. Harrison's father had devoted himself to public business and politicking at the expense of his financial well-being; Byrd's father, William Byrd III, a gambler and a Tory, had taken his own life at the beginning of the Revolution. Mary Willing Byrd, daughter of a rich Philadelphia merchant (and sister of Colonel Harrison's chief creditor), lacking many resources of her own, was desperately trying to hold her children's inheritance together and arrange advantageous marriages for them.[2]

As part of this strategy, Charley Byrd was sent to Philadelphia in his teens to stay under the care of his mother's sister Elizabeth, wife of a wealthy Quaker merchant, Samuel Powel. Part of the plan was that he was to study law, and, indeed, an early sketch of his life claims that he did so there under the brilliant lawyer Gouverneur Morris, who was a partner, though no relation, of Robert Morris. This claim, like the assertion that Billy Harrison apprenticed under Benjamin Rush, seems to be an exaggeration, although Morris may have overseen Charley's education in a general way. In any case, by the time he was seventeen or eighteen, old enough for serious law study, Charley was back in Virginia, "studying with a local attorney, perhaps one of the Tylers." He understood that he was being moved from place to place because of "the ills and mortifications, which the want of wealth gives rise to," as he expressed it in a letter to a sister. Harrison might have said the same thing.[3]

Both youths ended up in the Ohio Valley in early manhood, Harrison because of his romantic decision to seek military glory on the frontier, Byrd "dragged by poverty . . . [to] a distance of six hundred miles from my brothers and sisters"; evidently an attempt by Byrd to practice law in Charles City was not thriving, and, in fact, he may have lacked money to pay his way to Philadelphia. Charley went out to Kentucky as Robert Morris's land agent in 1794, when Harrison was still a lieutenant in the army, urged to do so by Ben Harrison as a step "to future independence and happiness."

Harrison and Byrd may have corresponded occasionally during these years. Once settled in the West, they came into close contact; Byrd succeeded Harrison in 1800 as secretary of the Northwest Territory. As Byrd grew older, he appeared to be struggling with issues similar to those Harrison had grappled with, perhaps for the first time or perhaps echoing feelings from earlier years: he became known as an opponent of slavery; he abandoned Anglicanism for evangelical Christianity, indeed for a very distinct brand of it, becoming a committed Shaker; he gave up drinking; and he began to watch what he ate very carefully, weighing his daily intake, according to one account, in a pair of silver scales. All these decisions separated him from his family and his Virginia background. His preoccupations were very similar to Harrison's, only in his case they appeared at a different stage of life, apparently for the first time. (There is not enough written evidence to say for sure, except in the matter of religious experience, where Byrd admitted that as a young man he knew nothing "of the gospel scheme of salvation.") Slavery, religion, dependence, and health formed a quartet of sensitive topics.[4]

Letters from Byrd's brothers and sisters at Westover flesh out the picture of life on a James River plantation and depict a background similar to that probably experienced by Harrison. They include many playful references to romantic relationships. Byrd's brother Billy, for example, refers to "Miss Nancy Allen, who I believe was formerly your old flame," noting that she was now being courted by his brother Dick. (There were cogent reasons for the Byrd brothers to have interested themselves in Nancy Allen; her father, William Allen, was perhaps the richest planter on James River. A few months later, Billy Byrd himself was interested in a young lady with "a comfortable fortune, which would place me in an independent situation.") Byrd's sister Ann wanted to know "who the lady is [in Philadelphia] that has made the deepest impression on your heart." Billy Byrd reported the death of "the once blooming & lovely Betsy Dandridge, whom I believe you had the pleasure of being acquainted with." The letters also gave news of neighbors, including the Harrisons of Berkeley: In 1795 the youngest Harrison daughter, Billy's sister Sally, married a local boy, John Minge. Billy's older brother Carter had just purchased the Meade plantation across the river for three thousand pounds. (Carter was now a lawyer in Surry County and self-supporting—moreover, he had been enterprising enough to marry one of the wealthy Allen girls.)

In addition, the letters gave ample family news, including greetings from some of the slaves and reports on the health of some of the children of slaves who had accompanied Charley to Kentucky. Some nieces who had lost their father were planning to spend the winter at Westover. Molly Page, another niece who was staying there, wished her uncle Charley "po[c]kets full of money and a Cellar full of beer." Billy Byrd reported that their mother "has a prospect of getting out of debt this year," as the barley and wheat crops were both excellent. Unlike some other James River planters (including Benjamin Harrison), Mary Byrd had been intelligent enough to shift from growing tobacco to growing grain.[5]

In their families, Charley Byrd and Billy Harrison were the expatriates. All the other Byrd children remained in Virginia; so did all the Harrisons. The similarity is enough to make one wonder about the similar concerns that appeared to drive them.

The Harrisons of Berkeley had a family of cousins, almost equally well off, living across the James River at a plantation called Brandon, in a large, square brick house like Berkeley's, with towering chimneys. In the 1780s, both families were headed by men named Benjamin Harrison; to avoid confusion, the head of the Brandon branch of the family usually added "of Brandon" to his name to distinguish himself from Colonel Harrison of Berkeley. Benjamin Harrison of Brandon, who had married one of William Byrd's daughters, had his elderly father, Nathaniel, living with him, and Nathaniel kept a daily record of guests at the plantation—no mean effort, since Benjamin of Brandon, like most great planters, often had guests by the dozen—individuals and whole families coming for dinner or staying for days or weeks. "I'm very happy to see you, Mr. Gildon," said a fictional planter in a novel written by a son of a planter family, "and hope you will spend some weeks with us."[6]

On 19 March 1790, while Billy was serving his apprenticeship with Dr. Leiper in Richmond, Nathaniel Harrison recorded a not atypical collection of visitors to Brandon: "Colo. J. Cocke, Miss Spooner Wm Harrison W Allen junr Mr Daingerfield C[arter] B[assett] H[arrison] E[lizabeth] & M[ary] F[itzhugh] came to dinr. Mr S, WH, WA, D went away in Evg." Billy, evidently, was visiting around James River with two similarly named young men, William Allen Jr., son of the rich landowner mentioned above, and William Allen Daingerfield; they came and left together.[7]

The three Williams were cousins and contemporaries. The grandfather of each had been a child of Colonel William Bassett of New Kent County. Daingerfield was four years older than Billy Harrison, having been born in 1769, and Allen was six years older than Billy. The closeness in family and age explains their riding around together, but another fact about Daingerfield is more arresting. A few years later, he would study medicine in Europe. It is probable that, at age twenty-one, he was already preparing to be a physician, and this likelihood raises the possibility that he, like Harrison, was apprenticed at this time to Leiper.[8]

Daingerfield's family, although quite respectable, was not as eminent as those of the other youths described here. He is included in this discussion because of his kinship to Harrison and their repeated contacts over a period of five years. Three years later, when Harrison, as an army lieutenant, was stationed at Fort Washington in the territory northwest of the Ohio River, he and Daingerfield, a newly commissioned ensign in the Second Regiment, traveled west together. Harrison's success in the West most likely prompted his cousin to enlist. They served together for more than a year in the Indian campaign; then Daingerfield left the service, possibly because of illness. The next information about him places him in Paris and Edinburgh, studying medicine, in the late 1790s. In 1799 he returned to Virginia, married, and practiced a few years in Alexandria, retiring across the river to Maryland in 1806; he died in 1821.[9]

Billy Harrison and Billy Daingerfield were intimates for a time, in the army and perhaps before.[10] Like Harrison and Byrd, Daingerfield went through a period in which he experimented with several possible careers, after the death in 1793 of the planter William Allen, who was his namesake and perhaps his protector. Ultimately, his choices proved successful. One might almost say that Daingerfield had roughly the career Colonel Harrison had envisioned for his son—medical practice, modest prosperity, and respectability in a substantial Tidewater community. However, the historical record contains little beyond the bare recital of names and places; surviving sources give no idea what Daingerfield thought on questions like religion and slavery.

One other commonality exists, and it is a striking one. Like Harrison and Byrd, Daingerfield was a young man abandoned by his father. Early in 1783, when young William was thirteen, Colonel William Daingerfield of Spotsylvania County, a planter on a scale slightly below that of the Harrisons, Byrds, and Allens who was deeply in debt, committed suicide at his plantation, Belvidera, by cutting his throat.[11]

. . .

Another family with youths who were contemporaries of Billy Harrison was the Randolph family; its sons, Richard, Theo, and Jack, were close in age to Billy; in fact Jack, the youngest (known to history as John Randolph of Roanoke), was born in the same year, 1773. Like Charley Byrd and Billy Daingerfield, the Randolph boys were victims of the shipwreck of the Virginia economy; but in one respect they were more fortunate. Byrd had no father and only the incidental guardianship of Samuel Powel and Gouverneur Morris; Daingerfield likewise lost his father early, although he may have had some help from his cousin William Allen; but the Randolph boys had a generous, well-educated stepfather, St. George Tucker, a lawyer from a Bermuda planting family who had married their mother, Frances Bland Randolph, when Richard and his brothers were small.

As a professional and a non-Virginian, St. George Tucker was in a position to perceive what eluded many intelligent Virginia planters: the state's entire agricultural economy was in slow collapse, undermined by the exhaustion of Tidewater soils, the fall of tobacco prices in 1785, and the disappearance of the comfortable, secure trade arrangements that had existed under the British Empire. He insisted that his stepsons, who stood to inherit little but debts from their father's estate, prepare themselves to be professionals, not planters. As he wrote Theo in 1786, "You are now, my dear Boy, turned of fifteen—it is now high time that you should begin to reflect on your future mode of life. At sixteen I shall demand your final determination, whether you will pursue a learned profession or a laborious occupation." George Washington demonstrated the same urgency in a letter he wrote in 1790 to a nephew about to enroll at college in Philadelphia: "You must consider it as the finishing of your education, and, therefore, as the time is limited, that every hour misspent is lost for ever, and that future years cannot compensate for lost days at this period of your life."[12]

After considering the Randolph boys' abilities, Tucker concluded that the eldest and youngest, Dick and Jack, both great readers, should go into the law, while Theo, who was less studious, should study medicine. (This apparent ranking of medicine as a less demanding profession need not imply that young Billy Harrison lacked capacity; his father had different grounds for wanting him to become a doctor. But it does suggest one more way in which Billy's status seemed inferior to that of his father and older brothers.) As for the Randolph boys, the problem with Tucker's plan was that they did not want to cooperate; attached to their childhood memories of leisurely, comfortable plantation life, they rebelled against their stepfather's advice. Richard, a talented, magnetic, generous boy, fond of fine clothes, made a stab at studying law with George Wythe in Williamsburg and loyally tutored his younger brothers; but in 1789, at the age of nineteen, he managed to impregnate sixteen-year-old Judith Randolph, the daughter of an important James River planting family whom widowed Ben Harrison had been considering as a wife, and forced the two families, his and hers, to consent to their marriage, celebrated with an old-style Virginia wedding at the bride's house, including a lavish feast, replete with ten kinds of meat and seven or eight desserts, and days of dancing and festivity. The teenage couple then moved onto a plantation of their own, for which Richard ordered carpets, a carriage, and stylish furniture on credit, quickly running through the small income he had inherited from his father's estate. At the same time, inconsistently, perhaps under the influence of his reading, Richard developed a loathing for slavery in the abstract (like a notable Randolph kinsman of the previous generation, Thomas Jefferson) and wrote a searing denunciation of it into his will, claiming to want "not a single negro for any other purpose than his immediate liberation." Within a year the couple had run out of money and were obliged to move to a smaller, isolated farm deep in the Southside region, near Hampden-Sydney. Only a year later, Richard died.[13]

Theo's rebellion against his stepfather took a more conventional form: the classic adolescent routine of drinking, gambling, and wasting resources. When, in 1788, Tucker sent Theo and Jack to New York to finish their classical preparation at Columbia College (while Billy Harrison toiled away in obscurity at Millfield), Theo, "with his dissolute companions," as Jack recalled, "absolutely prevented me from reading. Often have they forced the door of my study and tossed the books over the floor; sometimes out of the window. In two years, he had undermined his constitution and destroyed his health forever." Theo returned to Virginia in 1790 and died within two years.[14]

Jack Randolph was only a few years younger than his brothers, but perhaps that gap was enough to give a slightly different emphasis to his boyhood experiences; his childhood recollections were less of prewar opulence than of wartime dislocation. When the British, under Benedict Arnold, raided the James River valley in January 1781, seven-year-old

Jack—mounted on a horse for the first time in his life—rode with his fleeing mother to an out-of-the-way plantation in the Southside. (Billy Harrison probably had a similar experience, riding for refuge to his uncle Carter's home in Cumberland County. When he returned, after the war, to the beloved "broomstraw, old fields, and sands" of Tidewater, he found that his old family life was forever gone; Arnold's soldiers had made a bonfire of the family portraits and furniture in the front yard.) Jack Randolph (and probably Billy Harrison too, one can guess) sought not prewar plantation splendor but rather a set of values that could offer stability in a world that was flying to pieces.

After the war, Randolph's life, like Harrison's, became a series of moves from school to school. (In later life he was "always a little bitter about what he considered his irregular education.") He buried himself in books and reading, becoming pedantic, critical, and arrogant. His reading led him not toward evangelical religion, but to the cocksure atheism of Hume and Paine. In Philadelphia in 1791, restive and depressed, supposedly reading law with the attorney general and offended at his mentor's lack of attention, Jack began pursuing Theo's pattern of rebellion through gambling, wenching, and drinking, but with slightly different results. First he had to beg his stepfather for two hundred pounds to pay off gambling debts, and then, that year or the following one in Richmond, he contracted a disease that ruined his health in general and his sexual capacities in particular. It was around this time that his path crossed that of Billy Harrison, but despite their similar background and interests, the two youths were following different trajectories at that point, and when Harrison left for the West to follow a naïve dream of military fame, Randolph, soured on life, returned to Virginia, where the deaths of his brothers threw on him a family responsibility that he embraced with the passion of an abstract cause. Jack Randolph became an articulate defender of the values of old Virginia and a bitter critic of the American republic. Years later, he would do what Harrison had done in his teens: become a committed Christian.[15]

Another Virginia youth in Harrison's social circle in Virginia was Robert Carter, a neighbor and second cousin of Billy's and a year younger. The Carter family, as rich in land as the Harrisons, lived only five or six miles from Berkeley, at Shirley plantation, in an imposing dark-brick mansion with towering chimneys at the bend of James River, and Colonel Harrison often dined at Shirley. The Carter family patriarch, Charles Carter, being more attentive to his business than was Benjamin Harrison, had enough wealth to take care of all of his twenty-three children (of whom seventeen survived to adolescence).

For Robert, one of the middle children, his father's success meant an absence of the fears about debts and guidance that haunted Billy Harrison and the other youths discussed here. In fact, Robert's history was in some ways the reverse of those of Richard and Theo Randolph. Charles Carter destined Robert for a planter, and since Robert was in love with a Yorktown girl, Mary Nelson, he dropped out of William and Mary College without graduating in order to marry and take up Pampetike, a twelve-hundred-acre family plantation in King William County. After a few years, however, Robert began to wonder if he had made a mistake. Plantation management, especially the corporal punishment of slaves, sickened him. The "barbarous consequences" of the slave trade had always repelled him; now he found he loathed ruling over slaves and "witnessing many cruelties, even at this enlightened day, when the rights of man are so well ascertained." Habit and upbringing, he felt, abetted by "sordid interest," were turning him into a tyrant, something he could not tolerate. Recalling his fondness for natural science at college, he began to wonder if his real calling was that of a physician, a healer. His relationship with his father cooled; while conceding the "well intended rigor of paternal discipline," Robert began looking for ways to escape it.[16]

A serious injury to his oldest child in 1800 gave Robert his chance. He took the boy to Philadelphia for treatment and seized the opportunity to approach Benjamin Rush and other doctors about studying with them. The urban North, full of scientific thought and organized charity, was a revelation to young Carter. Virginia suddenly seemed a backward, provincial dreamworld. He gave up his plantation and stayed in Philadelphia for two years, joining a Linnaean Society and receiving a medical degree in 1803. When his wife died that year, he sent his children to stay with her family and took ship for Paris. He wanted to join the age he lived in, to immerse himself in its "scientific and rational social enjoyments." Just before embarking, he wrote his children a letter of parental advice that sounded the same themes that had shaped Billy Harrison's youth: avoid strong drink, avoid scoffing at Christianity, be humane to your slaves, and hope for an end to the slave system.

Napoleonic France was, as he had hoped, the culmination of Robert Carter's life. It enlightened him—and then it killed him. After contracting tuberculosis there, Robert returned to Virginia in 1805 to die.[17]

The shipwreck of colonial Chesapeake culture at the end of the Revolution affected the young men here described far more profoundly than it did most of their contemporaries, for obvious reasons. Their families were near the summit of power in Virginia, and they had far more to lose, not only their immediate comfort and status but also, and most significantly, their future prospects. They had been groomed for a kind of leadership that was no longer sustainable. For several of them, the problem of their future was exacerbated by the loss of a mentor through the absence, death, or disability of their fathers.

Parental death was not uncommon in colonial Virginia; the typical replacement for a deceased father as adviser and facilitator was either a stepfather or a paternal or maternal uncle. Some of these lives furnish examples: the Randolph boys acquired a kind, conscientious stepfather in St. George Tucker; after the suicide of Charles Byrd's father, his uncle by marriage, Samuel Powel of Philadelphia, took over his guidance; and William Daingerfield may have leaned on his rich cousin and namesake, William Allen, for help and advice. In Billy Harrison's case, however, no older man stepped in to compensate for his father's growing incapacity, although there are indications that his uncle Carter may have tried briefly.

All these mentors, real and substitute fathers alike, recognized the impending demise of the Chesapeake plantation lifestyle and, with remarkable unanimity, came up with the same alternative for their sons or protégés. Excepting Charles Carter alone, they sent their youths to acquire professional qualifications, committing the family wealth to the hope that the status of lawyer or doctor would provide the rising generation with an income less shaky than that of a landed gentleman. (Young Carter, the only boy encouraged to become a planter, ultimately made his own decision to abandon planting for a profession.) Benjamin Harrison, who was no fool, may well have been the earliest of these mentors to realize the need to prepare the next generation for an alternate livelihood when he steered Billy's older brothers into the professions.

Although the diagnosis was sound, however, the remedy was inadequate. The decline of the plantation system arose not merely from the burden of debt it imposed and the commercial problems of planting but also from the erosion of its underlying assumptions about authority and obedience, an erosion given concrete expression through the Revolution. Rhys Isaac has analyzed this process brilliantly as it affected an older planter, using the poignant diary of Landon Carter, whose received values of rank, order, and deference had to give way before an "emergent new mythology of person, feeling, and relationship"; but a shift that was merely an annoyance to Landon Carter was a calamity to his grandsons' generation. Adolescence, in any era, is the time of life when the "structure of values and priorities becomes problematic," as one psychologist put it. The adolescents discussed here had urgent work to do; they needed a scale of values to help them construct an adult identity. Person, feeling, and relationship were not enough; they had to work out for themselves what might be the proper basis for authority and how they could benefit society, as their reading of Roman history demanded, while retaining the recognized right to a decent income, a family, and social standing.[18]

Harrison and his contemporaries were not starting from zero: that was the problem. As planters' sons, all of them had absorbed from their earliest years a set of values that now seemed at best questionable and at worst repugnant, centered on areas of authority in society: a man's relationship to his earthly rulers (notably his family); to his God; and especially to the men and women over whom he claimed ownership. Faced with the failure of these values, each youth had to find a workable substitute in order to achieve a successful adult identity. The experience of Robert Carter illustrates the consequences of ignoring this question of values. His attempt to replicate his father's life as a tobacco planter left Carter feeling like a barbarian and a tyrant. The myths that had sustained his father in disciplining slaves had no power for Robert; instead, he found that the "well intended rigor of paternal discipline" had harmed him instead of guiding him by steering him into an identity he detested. To escape the barbarity and sordidness of his life, he eventually had to separate himself from his family and his state, as Billy Harrison was also to do.[19]

Richard Randolph's case was extreme to the point of quixotism. Against his stepfather's advice, he tried to preserve some essential values of the planter identity—dynastic alliances, lavish consumption—while professing fashionable ideas (in which he may have genuinely believed) about the wrongfulness of slavery. This attempt to maintain the lifestyle of a great planter without relying on African labor was patently a formula for failure, however; his life was bound to end as it did.

In the light of these examples, Billy Harrison's conversion, if that is what it was, to Methodism at Hampden-Sydney becomes more understandable. Viscerally aware of the fundamental conflict in the values that lay before him as he tried to forge an adult identity, he listened to the experience of his schoolmates, many of whom were just then rejecting the religion of their fathers in favor of service to an all-wise, benevolent God who had promised to structure all things for good to those who loved him. Then, whether formally or informally, he committed himself to "Christian experience" along with them. This decision was certainly a rejection of his father, on several levels: of his right to authority over his son, of his cold, formalistic Christianity, and of his commitment to the traditional order in Virginia. It was also a stab at finding a new identity; as Daniel Walker Howe has noted, "The call of the preacher for people to make 'a decision for Christ,' to be 'born again' in Christ, was the first form of conscious self-reconstruction that many Americans encountered, and it remained an important and peculiarly dramatic one."[20] Acceptance of God in the Methodist sense was not difficult or alien: it was supported by the familiar mythology of the Bible, known to Harrison as to all Virginia boys; at Hampden-Sydney, and probably also later in Southampton County, it offered the fellowship and support of fellow believers, young men of similar backgrounds, from rural planting families who often owned slaves, and it prescribed a pattern of activity: prayer, Bible reading, meeting for worship. Harrison's health problems, dimly visible in Dr. Mettauer's notes, may also have contributed to his conversion in some way not now recoverable.

Of the other Virginia boys considered here, Charles Byrd, Jack Randolph, and, to some extent, Robert Carter experienced the same need, at some time in their lives, to adjust their relationship to God. Their doing so was of course part of the grand religious revival that affected the whole English-speaking world in this era, but the Virginia version of revivalist Christianity was different in some respects.[21] In the 1780s at least, giving one's life to God was a social as well as a political declaration, not only because of the historic persecution of non-Anglicans in Virginia but also because of the question of slavery. By so dedicating himself, Billy Harrison considered the question of slavery not with the vague uneasinesses about tyranny and liberty that worried his cousins but within a wholly new context: traffic in human beings was to be avoided because it was sin; God, the ultimate authority, had said so.

Harrison's conversion may have manifested itself in other ways. He did enroll in the Antislavery Society; he may have freed a slave. Perhaps his apprenticeship with Dr. Leiper rather than with a fashionable society physician was an expression of faith, although it is not clear that Leiper himself was a believing Christian. Young Harrison read his Bible and prayed, practices that he maintained to some degree through his whole life. Robert Gunderson, a careful student of Harrison's life, attributes his lifelong religious commitment to his "devout mother" and "profoundly religious wife," but it seems more likely to have been an aftereffect of his adolescent conversion; one wonders, in fact, if it did not have some part in his choice as a mate of the profoundly religious Anna Symmes.[22] In the end, Harrison's conversion to "Christian experience" failed to provide him with the identity he needed. Conversion to an otherworldly viewpoint offers only one credible earthly role, that of evangelist, warning the unconverted about their danger and urging them to save their souls. Harrison, for whatever reason, did not want to preach and could not square his Christianity with any other identity available in Virginia.

If this reconstruction is essentially accurate (though the timing has to be speculative), it was during his two or three years at Millfield that Billy Harrison began to perceive that he could not be a preacher and to cast around for another possible adult identity, possibly without recognizing himself that he was doing so. He read a lot; it was to books that Virginians often turned for guidance—first to the Bible, the culturally sanctioned guide, but also to the classics. For Harrison, as noted earlier, a primary influence may have been Rollin's multivolume *Ancient History.* Millfield Academy evidently owned a set: Harrison's confident recollection that he had read the work through three times by the age of seventeen seems intended to mark the age when he left Millfield for medical apprenticeship in Richmond. The work was suitable for a young Christian—Rollin was a believer, a French Jansenist of strong convictions. Moreover, Rollin's histories appealed to Americans for their utility, the way in which they "set forth the concept of balance of power, the cyclical view of world history, the virtues of frugality and simplicity, and the evils of luxury and excessive ambition, doomed to be punished by the condign vengeance of divine providence." Finally, they captivated many American boys with their drama and vivid style.[23]

Ancient History captivated Harrison to such an extent that he could recall whole pages and episodes in later life with no prompting. It became his mythology, a world of eloquent warriors of stern virtue leading armed men, often through wilderness, to momentous battles. He saw himself in the roles of Rollin's heroes. As a psychologist of identity puts it, "You often live out in your imagination many of the experiences you later seek. . . . You imagine long in advance the kind of home you want and the lifestyle you wish to lead, and then work toward achieving it." As Harrison left Millfield to apprentice with Leiper and to decide definitely that medicine was not for him, he may well have found Rollin's narratives percolating through his thoughts and forming themselves into the ideal identity of the classical warrior. It was hardly surprising that in Philadelphia, when Henry Lee mentioned his ability to procure Harrison a commission in the army, that Harrison's commitment to this new identity emerged full-blown, just as he portrayed it in his memoir.[24]

William Henry Harrison was far from alone as he confronted the problem of his future. Several of the young men he knew, at the very top of Virginia society, were likewise searching desperately for some sort of credible authority in a world where all the old rules and models were crumbling. Exercising authority themselves as masters of slaves seemed problematical to many of them and unacceptable to a few. Some tried to ignore the dilemma and drink themselves into oblivion; others tacked about uneasily from career to career. The whole traditional complex of Virginia plantation life—heavy drinking, fashionable skepticism, slaveholding—disquieted many. Among the various directions in which to look for a new life, Harrison's solution, to try to live out a fantasy derived from his reading and his imagination, was no more fantastic than some others—and, as events were to show, it had at least as much chance of success.

CHAPTER SIX

Introduction to the Ohio Country

Ensign Harrison had to march his new recruits to the theater of war in the West, but it is not likely that he did so alone. Standard procedure called for him to unite his new men with an existing company under a more experienced officer who had been recruiting in the Northeast and was marching to Pittsburgh, where his troops would take flatboats down the Ohio River to Fort Washington, the central command post of the Western army. Four such companies passed through Pennsylvania in the fall of 1791; they were commanded by Captains Samuel Newman, John Buell, Jonathan Haskell, and Charles Cushing. Newman and Buell, however, passed through too early for Harrison to join them; they left Philadelphia in mid-August and arrived in September. Cushing did not get away until mid-October, and possibly not then—too late for Harrison, who arrived at Fort Washington on 21 November. Haskell's company left Philadelphia on 20 September and reached Pittsburgh on 20 October, according to army records; that Harrison marched with it seems all but certain.[1]

Secretary Knox's orders specified their route: they were to go to Lancaster and pick up provisions, cross the Susquehanna at Harris's Ferry, and march to Carlisle, where they would again draw supplies, and proceed through Chambersburg, across the mountains via Bedford, and on to Fort Pitt, where they would make the necessary arrangements for descending the Ohio River. To Harrison, of course, the towns were mere names empty of any concrete image, but those names probably rang for him with the music of Marathon and Cannae, Philippi and Arbela. Knox calculated that the company's rate of march would bring it into Pittsburgh by the second week in October; in fact, however, the troops did not arrive there until 20 October, after a month's marching—a normal rate for a company of recruits.[2]

The newly augmented company, uniformed and in full military order, marched out of Philadelphia across the Schuylkill bridge at the far end of High Street, up the hill and off on the right-hand fork toward Lancaster: a mixture of youths Harrison's own age, weathered old-timers, New England farm boys, and Philadelphia Irish, together with, very probably, some soldiers' wives plodding along the dusty road beside their men. They were eighty in all, a loud, dissolute, unruly bunch; in the judgment of the time, there was no company more corrupting than a group of "common soldiers." Sergeants, marching alongside the main body, bawled commands to the men. A rear guard of about fifteen men followed at a distance, escorting the wagon that carried their tents and supplies and watching out for deserters. Haskell and Harrison walked in front.[3]

They halted, usually, around nightfall, near a tavern—the Sign of the White Horse perhaps, or the Sheaf of Wheat or the Compass—and waited for the wagon to come up. Then the men pitched the tents and cooked their supper. Haskell and Harrison might eat in camp, or they might dine in the tavern at government expense. Inevitably, some soldiers managed to secure rum and get drunk. Almost every night, Haskell held a summary court to administer punishments for drunkenness and misconduct. They were no doubt the standard punishments of the time: ten lashes or so, say, well laid on, on a man's naked back. Would-be deserters would be punished more harshly. Not long after dark, the camp slept, but in the freshness of early morning, an hour or two before dawn, the drums began beating again; the men turned out and were sleepily mustered into ranks, struck the tents, shouldered their gear, and made ready to march.[4]

It was tiring travel for officers and men alike, although they rarely exceeded fifteen miles a day. In the languorous heat and intermittent showers of late September, they marched through the rich, rolling farm country of southeast Pennsylvania, past the stubble of recently harvested wheat fields and the stares of thrifty German farmers out gathering their produce into stone barns. They marched through Lancaster itself, "a Beautiful inland town, with some Elegant houses," as one contemporary traveler put it, slumbering among its fat, well-cultivated fields. (Perhaps they halted at the captain's orders before reaching Lancaster, as a previous company had done, to smarten their appearance by donning clean uniforms and powdering their hair with flour.) As they moved westward toward the Susquehanna, the veneer of civilization began to drop from the land. Here the settlers were mostly from the north of Ireland; their dwellings were less neat and their fields less orderly than those of the Germans. Carlisle, though, was a handsome town, on level ground. The troops encamped at the old brick barracks east of town, while Captain Haskell busied himself procuring a second wagon for the provisions they would need to cross the mountains.[5]

Beyond Carlisle to the west, one could glimpse the distinct blue outline of the Alleghenies, a sight which, in Harrison's day, never failed to thrill young travelers seeing it for the first time. One described their "blue tops towering into the sky, alternately hidden and displayed by rolling and shifting clouds." Others called the vista "magnificent" or "stupendous." Educated travelers found dimly romantic intimations in the landscape, "not only novel, but beautiful and sublime." To Harrison, perhaps, they were something like the Alps, looming before Hannibal's army.[6]

Six great mountain ridges lay between Haskell's company and the Ohio River: South Mountain and North Mountain, Sideling Hill, the Allegheny Mountain itself, Laurel Hill (tallest of the six and hardest to surmount), and Chestnut Ridge. Actually, by passing through Carlisle, the company had skirted South Mountain; but after two more days' march, through deepening forest and past Shippensburg, they were ready to confront North Mountain. Now there were no more plowed fields, only small scattered settlements hacked out of the dense growth of oak, hickory, chestnut, beech, and fir, in which the first glints of autumn gold and crimson were beginning to appear. Encumbered by their knapsacks, the men stumbled and cursed on the steep, stony road. From time to time they passed a packhorse train headed downhill, loaded with furs and ginseng, the bells on the lead horse jingling, churning up dust in the clear mountain air. The slope seemed endless, as endless as the forest on either hand. When there was a break in the trees, it revealed only more mountains and more trees—"the greatest variety of timber of any place I have ever seen," one traveler commented. The march up and over the mountain took a full day, and the road on the far side was worse than the ascent. But, as Captain Haskell could have advised them, there was worse ahead.[7]

Haskell, as Harrison doubtless had occasion to learn, was an experienced guide. A Massachusetts man, he had picked up and moved across the mountains, three or four years before, to the New England settlement of Marietta, then just taking shape in the Ohio Valley wilderness. Like many army officers in the West, he was half military man and half frontiersman, a middle-aged man with a nervous habit of spitting every other second or so when there was something on his mind. He had joined the Second Regiment when it was formed early in 1791, going in as a captain by virtue of his Revolutionary service.[8]

Two days later, lame and footsore, the company had reached the foot of Sideling Hill, where the road wound up the side of an enormous, craggy ridge. The weather had turned cooler, and the foliage all around was more and more spectacular. Near the top, one could see down the steep side of the mountain and away eastward; the panorama, as one traveler noted, was completely wild, without a hint of civilization. Then came the eight-mile-long descent, down a track barely wide enough for a single wagon, into the deep, shadowy gorge of the Juniata River, overhung by twisted rhododendron and mountain laurel; according to another traveler, the gorge had "only room . . . for the river & road the Cliffs almost projecting over us." Maybe they happened to be on this stretch at late afternoon, when the sun lit up the many-colored mountainsides above the shadowed road—"one of the most romantic and enchanting scenes," a young English visitor wrote, "I ever experienced."[9]

Actually, the country was more populous than it appeared from the top of Sideling Hill. Though by no means settled, it was not quite wilderness either. It held a few clusters of fairly thick settlement, like that around the tiny village of Bedford, and every ten or twelve miles the company passed houses along the road, usually taverns; often the property of Scotch-Irish settlers, these buildings were run-down, smoky, and, as one traveler blandly put it, "surprisingly dirty." They catered mainly to the packhorsemen and wagoners who kept up a steady stream of trade between Philadelphia and the Western settlements.[10]

Despite such settlement, however, Harrison and his men did encounter many of the inconveniences and novelties of frontier travel—the deep gullies in the road, sufficient to upset a wagon or break its axle; the steeply slanting roads on high mountainsides, where men had to hold a wagon to keep it from overturning; the thick fog of a mountain dawn that left the men blundering about as they prepared to strike camp; the cold, knee-deep rivers they had to ford. They forded the winding Juniata four times.

Other obstacles also hindered progress, notably desertion. Even in this wild part of the world, men still tried to desert, and the guarding of prisoners was another inconvenience. A company traversing the same road earlier in the year had had more than a dozen men under guard, in irons or tied together, by this point on its march; Haskell's company, probably, was little different.[11]

As Harrison marched into the Ohio Valley wilderness, he was also heading toward unfamiliar social terrain. In the army he would have to rub shoulders with men from all states, including those where the Harrison family name and prestige were unknown, and to uphold his rights as an officer and a gentleman despite his boyish appearance and lack of military experience. The first problem turned out to be no problem at all. Harrison did not share his father's antipathy to New Englanders; in fact, the best friends he made in the West would be from New England and New York. But the second problem was real. Army officers were apt to be very competitive and touchy about their status as gentlemen, and in the frontier environment, with women and other softening influences absent, the struggles could become fierce. A gentleman in the military sense was not the urbane, polite, educated figure idealized in Virginia, but more like the swashbuckling, privileged European type denounced by Benjamin Rush: "To be a gentleman subjects one to the necessity of resenting injuries, fighting duels and the like, and takes away all disgrace in swearing, getting drunk, running in debt, getting bastards, etc." The way to settle quarrels over status, as Rush observed, was the duel, a recent import from Britain that had gained some popularity in Virginia, where it was generally perceived as "a vestige of barbarity" but tolerated because it was fashionable. In the army dueling was de rigueur, as Harrison understood. "I believed," he wrote later, "that no brave man would decline a challenge or refrain from giving one, when ever he felt that his rights or feelings had been trampled upon." Honor, he felt, "might be acquired from a well-fought duel." As a product of James River society, Harrison was by definition a gentleman; he would go west prepared to maintain his status, though perhaps a little nervous about doing so in the frontier army, an environment where the rules were very different from those of old Virginia.[12]

Eleven miles beyond Bedford, the company reached the foot of the cloud-wrapped Allegheny Mountain. The eight-mile climb to its summit was longer, but no rougher, than the ones the men had already made. Eighteen miles farther on, however, Laurel Hill proved to be the worst part of their journey. It was mid-October by the time they reached it, and the weather in the West had turned cold, wet, and disagreeable. Even in good weather, travelers often ran into cold rain and biting winds at the top, so Haskell's men, laboring up the nine-mile ascent, probably had to contend with heavy rains, bone-chilling cold—perhaps even with snow and sleet—and the lack of any dry place to camp. In weather of this sort, the stone-and-clay road became a morass. The rains also flooded some of the creeks they had to ford, forcing them to either struggle through the rushing current or, more likely, camp on the bank and wait for the water to subside. At length, however, they were over Laurel Hill and Chestnut Ridge, marching through a more level, still thickly forested country in the full splendor of a Western fall. Two or three days after crossing Chestnut Ridge, the company came over a rise and sighted a large river on the right. Ahead of them, in a valley, it merged with another river of equal size coming in from the left, and at their meeting point there was a small settlement, dwarfed by the wilderness around it but still the largest Harrison had seen for weeks, consisting of fifty or sixty houses, some log, some frame. The settlement was Pittsburgh and the two rivers, the Allegheny and Monongahela, which met there to form the Ohio. White-limbed sycamores lined the bank of the Monongahela, and the newcomers soon identified the pervasive smell of smoke from the coal the inhabitants dug out of the bluffs across the river and burned in their fireplaces. It was 20 October.[13]

As the junior officer, Harrison received the duty of going ahead into the village and notifying Major Isaac Craig, the commandant, of their arrival. But though the men, freshly uniformed and powdered, no doubt made a jaunty entrance into Pittsburgh, Harrison soon found that the settlement could provide no sheltered place for the troops to encamp. Old, dilapidated Fort Pitt, at one time the chief army post in the West, had been sold to some local contractors, who were now tearing it down and carting away the materials; Craig worked out of his house in the village. The rest of the village likewise afforded no shelter, consisting primarily of a long, muddy main street with two or three log taverns. The troops ended up encamped in the open, on the bluffs across the Allegheny River from the settlement. Haskell and Harrison saw them into camp the first night, and then went to dine with the major.[14]

The initial expectation, as one can see from a letter in the papers of the territorial secretary, had been for Haskell's company to follow in the path of those before it and proceed directly downriver to Fort Washington in flatboats supplied by Major Craig. In the event, however, the company stayed at Pittsburgh well into November and perhaps even longer. There are several possible reasons why. First, Haskell discovered on arriving at Pittsburgh that St. Clair's expedition into the Indian country had already set out some weeks earlier. Since he and his men were too late to contribute to the grand effort of the year, it made sense to wait and see where else Knox or St. Clair judged they could be most effective. Second, it was becoming clear that the Indians were uneasy all over the territory, even as far east as Pittsburgh, and ready for a fight with American settlers. Only two weeks earlier, a band of Shawnee had attacked a party of seven on the east bank of the Ohio just a hundred miles downriver, killing four men and taking one captive. The people of Pittsburgh had reason to be nervous; Haskell's men were the only soldiers on hand, and Pittburgh's residents had no desire to see them leave. Craig may have suggested to Haskell that he remain where he was, at least until further word arrived from the main army in the West. Finally, there was the state of the river: October was a season of low water, in which navigation was tricky and slow. As October declined into November, then, and the autumn splendor of the forest changed to ragged brown leaves, Ensign Harrison found himself becalmed in the isolated settlement of Pittsburgh at the meeting of the three rivers.[15]

As he began familiarizing himself with his new, raw, surroundings, the eager young ensign could not have imagined that, by being in Pittburgh rather than with the main army in the West, he was avoiding one of the great disasters in American military history. At dawn on 4 November 1791, while Harrison was supervising the routine of his men, Governor St. Clair's force was surprised and slaughtered by warriors from several Indian tribes, led by the Miami chief Little Turtle; a third of the whole army perished, including a third of the officers, and St. Clair and the rest barely made it back to Fort Washington alive.

St. Clair's Defeat, as it came to be called, had a major effect on the history of the West, and also on Harrison's own future, beginning with his arrival at Fort Washington. In his autobiographical letter to Erastus Brooks, he stated that he reached his destination "just as the remnant of the Army of Genl. St. Clair which had been defeated on the 4th of the Month arrived there." This statement would seem to set a clear date for his arrival: the defeat took place in the forests about a hundred miles north of the fort, and the remnants of the expedition began arriving at Fort Washington on 8 November. Two biographers of this part of Harrison's life, Freeman Cleaves and Robert Gunderson, have adopted that date. But eight years earlier, in a speech delivered on the site of Fort Washington, Harrison mentioned the cabin of a settler that had stood only a few hundred feet east of the fort, which "afforded me a grateful shelter with my small command on the 21st of November, 1791." It is not clear why the date should have remained so clearly in his mind unless it was associated with a milestone like his first arrival in the West; nor is it obvious why he and a "small command" should have spent a night sheltered in a deserted cabin within sight of the fort, unless they arrived in the middle of a massively confused situation—as the next chapter will show they did—and were unable to gain admittance. Consequently, this account accepts the position of another biographer, James Green, that Harrison reached Fort Washington on 21 November. Although this date was not, in a precise sense, "just as the remnant . . . arrived there," it was well within the weeks of confusion and panic that followed St. Clair's Defeat.[16]

If Harrison and a small body of men arrived on the 21st, they must have left Pittsburgh no later than the 14th or 15th. By November, thanks to the late fall rains, the Ohio River was high again and the downriver passage swift. In those conditions, it was quite possible, running day and night, to make the passage from Pittsburgh to Fort Washington in six or seven days. (Because of the tension with the Indians, most riverboats made the run with only a minimum of stops; the danger from Indian attacks while encamped on the shore was too great.) The distance was 490 miles; to men who had been making fewer than fifteen miles a day across the mountains, floating seventy or eighty miles a day downstream must have seemed like flying. But a six- or seven-day journey was quite possible, and indeed, by 25 November St. Clair had news from Pittsburgh as of the 14th. It is tempting to suggest that Harrison brought it.[17]

The question then remains: if Ensign Harrison and a small group of soldiers left Pittsburgh about 14 November, what was their mission? It could have had nothing to do with St. Clair's Defeat; news of that engagement had not yet reached Pittsburgh. Most likely, they were detailed to escort a supply shipment. Although St. Clair's expedition had left Pittsburgh before Harrison arrived there, goods kept coming into the village for transshipment to headquarters—barrels of flour, whiskey, and beef, kegs of salt—and once passage of the river was practicable, there was no reason to delay shipping them, with an adequate armed guard for protection. Harrison, clearly eager to arrive at the field of action, was an obvious choice for the assignment.[18]

So in the second week of November, he and a small detail of men, perhaps a dozen, boarded a flatboat at the point and set off downriver with a crew of six or eight boatmen. The "flat," as frontier people called it, was quite unlike any craft Harrison had ever seen on the lower James. In essence it was a huge raft, twelve or fifteen feet wide and fifty or sixty long, walled in with two-inch-thick planks to a height of four or five feet, and covered, wholly or in part, by a low plank roof. The Army contractors had built it in their yard on the Monongahela, and had rounded up a crew from the habitués of the riverfront taverns. The supplies went under the roof, and Harrison and his men also bedded down in that small, cramped space, lighted only by a few small windows. The livestock, if the boat was carrying any, would have been penned in the unroofed part. Like any raft, the boat simply drifted with the current, lumbering along at a rate of seventy miles a day. The crew normally had little to do beyond listening for shoals and watching for obstructions in the river ahead. Such steering as was necessary was done with the sweep, a long oar attached to the back of the craft. Enclosed in their floating box, Harrison and his men stood guard, ate their salt meat and biscuit, and watched the bare forests of the riverbank slip by.[19]

For the first day or so of their trip, the river wound through steep, hilly country. The boatmen ticked off the names of the landmarks and rivers as they passed—McKee's Rock, a huge rock overhanging the dark river, carved and painted with the names of previous travelers; the ruins of old Fort Macintosh at the mouth of Big Beaver Creek; Yellow Creek; Cross Creek; a little settlement on the Virginia side, at Buffalo creek; another at Wheeling. Below Wheeling the river grew broader and the hills gentler, but the scattered settlements they had been seeing on the east shore disappeared. Harrison and his guard scanned the forests in vain for the smoke that signaled human presence, Indian or white. This was real wilderness. By day great flocks of wild pigeons whirred overhead, and wild turkey and deer crashed in the brush; by night wolves howled. On the third day, they came to the Long Reach, where the winding river unexpectedly ran straight for ten miles.[20]

As he drifted downriver, Harrison talked with the boatmen and reflected on what he had learned at Pittsburgh about the situation in the West—the Ohio country, as it was called—from his conversations with Craig, Haskell, and other officers in the village. In all likelihood, he had known very little about it when he joined the Army; few people in the East did. What he learned was, of course, from the viewpoint of the Army and the white settlers, which became his own. It began with the assumption that the white Americans of the Atlantic coast had the right to extend their way of life into the trans-Appalachian West.[21]

The river down which he was traveling was the most important boundary in the Western country. The lands south and east of it belonged to Virginia, although a part of them was about to enter the Union as the separate state of Kentucky. Whites in this area had been much harassed by Indians in the past, but by now some parts of it were thickly settled and much of it was reasonably secure. North of the Ohio, however, was a vast tract of thickly forested federal land known as the Northwest Territory that stretched all the way to the Great Lakes. This huge area contained only three small white American settlements, all on the riverbank: Marietta, a village of New England settlers about two hundred miles downriver from Pittsburgh; Gallipolis, a French immigrant colony farther downstream; and, much farther below, a settlement called Cincinnati, where Fort Washington was. Aside from these three settlements, the territory was inhabited by Indians (or "savages," as most Army men called them)—Shawnee, Delaware, Wyandot, and Miami close at hand, and other nations deeper in the forests. Since the end of the Revolution, the American government had been trying with little success to persuade these nations to sell or cede their claims to the land. Some tribes had made treaties but later repudiated them; others had refused to treat at all. They had been promised, the Indians maintained, that there would be no white settlement north of the Ohio; and from the founding of Marietta in 1788, which they considered a betrayal of that promise, they had been carrying on a series of attacks to drive white settlers out of the territory. The fighting had been small-scale and sporadic, but also bitter and bloody. There had been sudden attacks on isolated settlers' cabins, ambushes and traps for emigrant parties on the river, and, of course, retaliatory attacks by whites on peaceful Indian towns or parties. By 1791 the war had been going on for three years, and had spilled over into Kentucky and western Virginia.[22]

The American Army had entered the conflict slowly, partly because of its ominous international overtones. Most Army men and frontiersmen believed that the Indians were backed by agents of Great Britain, a conviction that Harrison, with an anti-British bias passed on from his early years, no doubt found it easy to accept. British army units, in violation of the treaty that had ended the Revolution, continued to occupy forts on the south shores of the Great Lakes, and it seemed more than likely that they, or their superiors in Canada, were using the Indians as pawns in an attempt to keep the United States out of the Northwest. Hostile action against the Indians could mean trouble with Britain, and the United States government, fearful of a renewed war, had moved with great caution. Moreover, President Washington genuinely wanted a peaceful solution. Nevertheless, the need to respond to Indian attacks had forced the government into more and more warlike actions. In 1789 it had built Fort Washington, and in 1790 it had sent a punitive expedition under Brigadier General Josiah Harmar into the Miami country north of the fort. That expedition had succeeded in reaching and burning a major Miami village two hundred miles to the north, but Harmer had also lost 183 men in two skirmishes with the Miami, and the expedition had done more to embolden the enemy than to subdue them. (This mixed record led to Harmar, in 1791, facing a court-martial to answer for his conduct, although he was exonerated. Harrison very probably saw him in Pittsburgh that fall, returning east after the court-martial, a worn-out, dispirited man, openly pessimistic about the prospect of a quick victory over the Indians.)[23]

As Indian attacks continued unabated in 1791, Congress decided to address the problem decisively, despite the opposition of many people in the East to an Indian war. It authorized the raising of a second infantry regiment and the enlisting of almost two thousand additional six-month soldiers for a major campaign that year, led by the territorial governor, Arthur St. Clair, an old military comrade of Washington. The idea was to build a chain of permanently garrisoned forts in the interior, to overawe the tribes and establish a white presence. The government hoped the Indians might be intimidated enough to negotiate a treaty, but sought to ensure that St. Clair's force was large enough to defeat them if they resisted. On this expedition hung the immediate future of white settlement in the Ohio country, and this was the situation—to Harrison's knowledge—as he and his men began their flatboat journey to Fort Washington.[24]

On the fourth day, Harrison and his troop reached Marietta, a little village on the Indian shore at the mouth of the Muskingum River, and probably stopped there briefly to check for news. A high log stockade surrounded the village; two associated settlements, Belpre and Belleville, had stockades of their own. In addition there were small clusters of cabins on the Virginia side, where the Great Kanawha River flowed into the Ohio, followed by a ramshackle settlement called Gallipolis, with a few dozen cabins. After that, they were back in the wilderness again, with nothing to see but the mouths of large rivers flowing in from the interior—the Hockhocking, the Guyandotte, the Big Sandy, the Scioto. In the silence of late fall, the solitude was oppressive. Harrison perhaps thought of the vanguard of Alexander's army in the Persian desert, or Caesar's legions in the forest of Gaul.[25]

They met few boats on the river. Those going upriver were keelboats, pointed craft poled by a crew of boatmen, whose progress was ponderous. It was late in the year for traveling. Winter was setting in, with cloudy skies, wet snow, and "excessive" rains that made any outside work miserable. When they did meet boats, however, they hailed them for news of the campaign, and around 19 November, near the crude little river settlement of Limestone (now Maysville), Kentucky, its streets a filthy mixture of mud and hog dung, they heard the bad news from the keelboat carrying Major Ebenezer Denny, St. Clair's official courier. The official report of the defeat had gone out on the ninth, by rider through Kentucky, which was the longer but more secure route. Denny had volunteered for the more dangerous mission up the river, where the Indians might also be up in arms, and had left on the seventeenth. He sketched out the situation for them: the remainder of the army had returned safely to the fort but feared further Indian attacks. The commander was ill and the settlers were afraid. Affairs were quite disorganized. Their supplies and their presence would be welcome. Denny continued his mission to Philadelphia, and Harrison and his men, understandably apprehensive, set out downriver on the last day of their journey.[26]

CHAPTER SEVEN

Aftermath of a Disaster

Fort Washington, headquarters of federal authority in the Northwest Territory and the largest, most solidly built post west of the Alleghenies, stood on the north bank of the Ohio high above the river—an imposing compound of twelve two-story frame houses, all connected, facing inward to form a hollow square, to which a large main gate gave admittance. Twenty-foot stockades flanked it on two sides, and large blockhouses dominated the corners. Inside were officers' quarters and barracks for the men, warehouses and blacksmith shops, and the office of the governor of the territory, not to mention stores of food and clothing. The foundations were of stone, but the buildings were faced with thick plank recycled from abandoned flatboats, in which were small windows suitable for returning fire from attackers. The Stars and Stripes flew over the shingled, red-painted roof. Below it and to the west were the log and frame houses that comprised the village of Cincinnati.[1]

During the frightening days that followed the disaster of 4 November 1791, operations at the fort were being conducted under pressures that strained them to capacity and sometimes beyond. To begin with, the fort had been built to hold a regiment—roughly eight hundred soldiers—but was currently crowded with the remains of two regular regiments, plus two regiments of temporary soldiers, the six-month men or "levies" raised specifically for the expedition. Although some were seriously wounded and all were terrified of further Indian attacks, the fort simply could not house them all, so some of the men, particularly the levies, had to camp outside its walls, as near the gate as possible. As more survivors straggled in from the forest, they were added to the units camped outside. The experience of John Shaw and his small squad of drovers typified the predicament of these men. Shaw and his drovers, six-month men back from driving beef for the use of interior forts Hamilton and Jefferson, arrived at Fort Washington around 11 November. Forced to settle outside the gates, they found themselves "encamped in a very disagreeable situation, [where they] suffered extremely from the inclemency of the weather."[2]

Inside the fort, matters were not much better. Its inhabitants included the wounded, of course, who totaled, according to the count finally drawn up on 17 November by Colonel Winthrop Sargent, the tight-lipped New Englander who served as adjutant, 29 officers and 242 men. St. Clair himself had escaped injury at the battle but was seriously ill and confined to his quarters, subsisting only on bread and tea as he fretfully issued orders to improve the defenses of the fort in case the Indians appeared. Although supplies within the fort were adequate, few seemed to reach the men camped outside; it was not clear that the quartermaster general, Samuel Hodgdon, was on top of his job. But the most acute problem was pay. There was no money in the fort. Regular soldiers were accustomed to being paid late; it was almost a part of Army life, and in the meantime they lived at government expense; but the levies, frantic to get away and return to the East, demanded to be paid immediately.

The levies were of low quality even by the low standards of American soldiers in that era—"miserable beings plucked from the dunghills of the United States," as one Cincinnatian called them, many of them from the underclass, from Eastern city "prisons[,] wheelbarrows and brothels." Many had never handled a gun before in their lives and had no notion of military discipline. They had given constant trouble since arriving in the West—perpetually complaining, some threatening to desert, and some outright mutinous. St. Clair and the regulars could hardly wait to be rid of them. Sometime around the fifteenth, he ordered them paid off with certificates (government IOUs redeemable at a later date) and sent on their way. Most of the men apparently accepted the arrangement—they were as happy to leave as St. Clair was to see them go—but traded in their certificates to the tavernkeepers of Cincinnati (at a heavy discount) for one glorious spree before returning eastward.[3]

It was just at this point that Harrison and his "small command" arrived on the scene, most likely late in the day. They soon realized that they were walking into near chaos: the levies' encampment was half deserted, and many of those remaining were down in the village, "a hamlet of logs and mud" as it seemed to Harrison, spending the "mere trifle" they had received for their certificates on whiskey and other comforts, "trust[ing]," as Harrison later wrote, "to chance & charity for support in their long & wearisome journey to the Atlantic States." He added, "I certainly saw more drunken men in the 48 hours succeeding my arrival than I had in all my previous life." He also found that there was no immediate room in the fort, and had to spend the night with his men in Peter Cox's deserted cabin.[4]

Harrison had arrived at the height of the disorder. Within a day or two, most of the levies were gone, straggling homeward through Kentucky, and the interior of the fort was being made ready for his regiment, the First, to move in for permanent occupation. The appearance of the levies left an indelible impression on him, however—their clothing "reduced to rags & their countenances exhibiting strong evidence of the privations & sufferings they had encountered" on the campaign. Naturally he asked around for details, and he found many survivors who were eager to describe their disastrous defeat. It had been a tragic compound of errors: a campaign that had gotten under way too late in the year, in the fall when the Indians were at their strongest and most confident; a commander hampered by gout and by poor relations with some of his subordinates, but bent on carrying out his mission despite the late start; supply problems including spoiled powder, leaky tents, and vital provisions inexplicably delayed through the incompetence or corruption of the contractors; lack of cooperation with the Kentucky militia who were supposed to be assisting the expedition; and most of all, problems with the men themselves, who rebelled and deserted on the line of march. On the day of the battle, the First Regiment had been absent because it had been sent back to stop deserters from raiding the supply trains.[5]

The Indian attack had come just before breakfast on 4 November, while the army was encamped on a small creek 110 miles north of Cincinnati and a few days' march from Fort Jefferson, a newly built interior post. The soldiers had been encircled before anyone knew what was happening. Survivors' recollections of the next few hours made a vivid gallery of horrors: General Richard Butler, St. Clair's second in command, lying at the foot of a tree, his body riddled with bullets; St. Clair himself, mounted, trying to encourage his men to a charge; the ground "covered with the bodies of the dead and dying, the freshly scalped heads . . . reeking with smoke" and looking, in the early morning frost, "like so many pumpkins in a corn-field in December"; dead camp followers with "their bubbies cut off" burning in the camp fires; and the little ravine that led to the creek "actually running with blood." Finally, after three hours, a charge had broken through the circle of attackers, and St. Clair's men had begun a wild, headlong flight toward Fort Jefferson, throwing away their weapons and their gear in their frantic haste to get out of the trap. Four days later, disordered and still panic-stricken, they had stumbled into Cincinnati.[6]

The Indians had done little to follow up their victory. They rarely attacked fortified positions. The interior forts, Hamilton and Jefferson, whose construction had been the only successful accomplishment of the expedition, were still garrisoned, and their commanders reported nothing but occasional gunfire in the forest. The initial panic in Cincinnati and the surrounding area, the Miami country, had subsided somewhat by the time Harrison got there. Indeed, a number of Kentuckians crossed the river to aid in the defense of the settlements the day after he arrived and, finding no fighting, turned back for home. Still, the possibility of further Indian attacks made both soldiers and civilians uneasy.[7]

Sometime during Harrison's first two or three days at the fort, while he was still trying to digest the sights he had seen and the stories he had heard, he happened to recognize a familiar face among the officers thronging in and out of headquarters. It belonged to a man who had several times been a guest of Colonel Harrison at Berkeley, and who had recently captained one of the companies of six-month men—one of the few officers to have made it through the battle unscathed. If Harrison was surprised to see him, this old acquaintance was appalled to see Harrison. Drawing the younger man aside, he urged him strongly to leave the Army at once, arguing, as Morris had, that there was little glory and much misery in a war against savages—and indeed, that the Indian campaign was so mismanaged that a junior officer had no chance to distinguish himself. Harrison would have to live and work with officers who were, most of them, heavy drinkers and compulsive gamblers. Young as he was, it would be easy for him to pick up their habits and ruin himself.

The captain said that he was about to leave for the East now that his men had been discharged; he would be both glad and relieved to have Harrison accompany him.[8]

Harrison gave considerable space in his autobiographical letter to this encounter, and it is evident why: it was part of the story he wanted to tell about himself: how he had disregarded all warnings and well-meant advice about his course, and, following his own plan, managed to come out a winner. Still, there are other details to be drawn from his account. Apparently, he bristled at the captain's suggestion—"My dander was raised," he noted, using the colloquial expression for taking offense—and his subsequent account gives some hint as to why superiors, from Colonel Harrison on, found dealing with him so difficult. Having "entered the army without the knowledge of any of my relations," he went on to explain, "I had too much pride to acknowledge . . . that I was frightened by the dangers which I had well understood." Harrison had not written Ben, or even his mother, of his decision to become a soldier, a fact that throws some light on his relations with his family, yet despite his natural fear of what might lie ahead, his pride would not let him admit that fear or reconsider his choice. And finally, "I . . . prepared my mind to encounter with cheerfulness anything which the obligations of duty required me to perform." Cheerfulness, as the Army was to learn, was the signature trait of Harrison's personality. Not only as a teenaged officer but throughout his life, he had the capacity to ignore obstacles. Mark Tapley and Nellie Forbush rolled into one, he could be optimistic to a degree that made some acquaintances doubt whether he realized the gravity of the situations he faced. In any event, Harrison declined the captain's offer and within a few days was caught up in the regular round of morning parade, drill, work parties, and picket duty inside the log stockade.[9]

An ensign had few specific duties, according to Baron Von Steuben's Regulations, the official rule book of the Army. When a company was on parade, its men arranged in two equal ranks, one behind the other with the taller men in the rear, it was divided into two sections. The captain of the company stood at the right of one section, the lieutenant at the right of the other, and the ensign precisely four paces behind the center of the whole line. The ensign was supposed to check on the smartness and discipline of the noncommissioned officers, and the cleanliness of the men and their quarters. Since he also was required "to be perfectly acquainted with the manual exercise, marchings and firings," he had to spend a lot of time supervising drill and learning "to give the words of command with a loud and distinct voice," shouting, for instance, "Handle—Cartridge! Prime! Shut—Pan! Charge with Cartridge! Draw—Rammer! Ram down—Cartridge! Return—Rammer! Shoulder—Firelock! Order—Firelock!" and so on and on through the whole routine. As an officer, he wore a sword; he also carried an espontoon, a seven-foot spear that symbolized his rank.[10]

In the aftermath of St. Clair's campaign, few officers were fit for duty, and even the greenest subalterns, like Harrison, found themselves with unusually heavy responsibilities. Before he had been at Fort Washington two weeks, Harrison was given command of a twenty-man guard ordered to escort a packhorse train carrying supplies to Fort Hamilton, the nearest of the interior posts. It was a taxing assignment, not only because of the cold, foul weather but also because one had to assume that the Indians, confident after having defeated an American army, were still in the forests, ready to swoop down on the train at any point in its twenty-four-mile, two-day journey. Early one morning, the eighteen-year-old officer, his men, and the packhorse drivers, all equally nervous and vigilant, set out on the military road up the steep ring of hills surrounding Cincinnati and marched into the somber, wintry forests of the Northwest Territory. Like any junior officer, Harrison traveled on foot.[11]

The Indians let them alone, but the weather was miserable. Harrison had his first sight of Fort Hamilton, a half-sized replica of Fort Washington in a forest of huge hickories by the Miami River, and got his men safely back to headquarters. The assignment did much to ease his own doubts about being able to measure up to the duties of a frontier officer. General St. Clair, who doubtless had been as surprised as Harrison's Virginia friend to see a youth of his age and background in the Army, thought his performance worthy of a public commendation, which he issued on Harrison's return.[12]

The commander was out of bed now, still unwell but able to take something more substantial than the bread and tea he had lived on for two weeks after the defeat, and already preparing for the most dreaded interview of his life—a meeting with his old Revolutionary comrade President Washington. Since St. Clair would have to go to Philadelphia to take responsibility personally for his defeat by the Indians, Major David Zeigler, his second in command, a big, beefy officer with a thick

German accent, would command the fort in his absence while Winthrop Sargent, as territorial secretary, would look after civil affairs. Ensign Harrison was among those who, on 8 December, saw St. Clair set out on the month-long journey to the East. It was a solemn occasion: Arthur St. Clair, everyone realized, had earned a sure but ignominious place in history. Already they were making songs about him in the West. Harrison heard some in the next two or three years, perhaps the one that began:

> "'Twas November the fourth, in the year of ninety-one,
> We had a sore engagement near to Fort Jefferson;
> Sinclaire was our commander, which may remembered be,
> For there we left nine hundred men in t' Western Ter'tory."[13]

CHAPTER EIGHT

The First Regiment

The officers of Harrison's regiment, the First, were every bit as dissolute as Harrison's Virginia acquaintance had painted them and proud of it: red-faced and loud-voiced, they were a tight-knit group of men in their thirties and forties, most of whom shared a rough haughtiness and a large appetite for whiskey. Their backgrounds varied widely. Zeigler was a stolid professional who had begun his career in the Imperial Russian Army; Captain Erkuries Beatty was a well-educated, ingratiating Jerseyman, seldom sober; Captain Ballard Smith a drunken, uproarious Virginian. A few had had some education; others could hardly write their own names. However, they had good reason for being close-knit: they had been serving together in the West since 1783. All the senior officers had served in the Revolution, and every junior had been either a noncommissioned officer or a cadet with the regiment before moving up to officer rank. More recently, for five or six winters past, most of them had shared the isolation of rude log forts on the frontier, indulged by such generals as Harmar, who himself had an "unfortunate propensity to drink."[1]

The lucky chance that had kept them out of the Indian ambush of 4 November 1791 (they had been escorting a supply train to protect it from attack by deserters) had left them, Harrison noted, "unbroken, well clothed & equipt, & in a high state of discipline" compared with the rest of the army. Once the wounded and dying were cleared out of the fort, therefore, the officers of the First Regiment were looking forward to passing the winter in the same hard-drinking routine they were used to. They faced only one minor irritant: their new recruit, Ensign Harrison, whom they regarded with unconcealed distaste.

The newcomer's appearance and habits set him distinctly apart. Smooth-faced, dark-haired, and delicate in build, he looked even younger than his eighteen years. His long horse face and earnest brown eyes did nothing to lessen the impression of boyishness. He drank moderately and was not a gambler. His eager speech and enthusiasm for reading (he had brought the large edition of Blair's *Lectures* and Cicero's *Orations* all the way from Philadelphia) suggested the literary Easterner, out of place in a half-savage country. In tastes, habits, and background, he was the greatest possible contrast to Ensign Hastings Marks, the other Virginian who had recently joined the regiment, only a couple of months before. Marks, a connection of Secretary of State Jefferson in his late twenties, had led a "very irregular life" in Albemarle County and had been eased by his family into the Western army. A heavy drinker who talked big, Marks fitted right in with the First and won commendations from the officers. Over the next three years, rancor developed between Marks and Harrison that may have begun as early as January, with "some hints being thrown out of a dispute in rank" over whose commission was the earlier in date. (Harrison's was, by two months.)[2]

To cap it off, Harrison had moved into a slot the regimental officers had been reserving for someone else—the son of their senior captain, a respected, rather overbearing Connecticut Yankee named David Strong, one of the few generally sober officers at the fort. They had sent Elijah Strong's name in to Philadelphia, and instead of him had been sent this slight, bouncy young planter's son, so ignorant of military matters that he had to have obtained the appointment through some kind of political pull—"coming in through the Cabin window," as it was known in the Navy. (Marks was equally ignorant, but in his case his senior officers overlooked that deficiency.) Led by Strong and his intimates, the whole group was outraged. They expected Harrison to fold under the pressures of Western duty and to resign, but to speed the process, they resolved to make Army life as difficult for him as possible.[3]

It is not hard to imagine how they did so. Superiors gave him more than his share of dirty and tedious assignments, such as late-night guard duty in the still, icy air of midwinter. No doubt they capitalized fully on his mistakes as a novice, and managed as often as possible, out on the hard-packed earth of the parade ground, to reprimand him in front of the men. In the officers' quarters, he was pointedly excluded from the fireside conversations about gaming, or the Western lands on which the officers of the First hoped to make a killing, or women. (Most of the officers were bachelors, although a few, like Strong, had families. Dependents were housed in the village, since there was no provision for housing them within the fort.) Harrison's overtures of friendship were rebuffed; pointedly excluded from the parties the other officers got up at select taverns in the village, he apparently spent most of his spare time reading—not only Blair and Cicero, but also a book he had run across (the property of an officer slain in St. Clair's Defeat) on military tactics and drill. It was an intelligent but lonely way of passing the time.[4]

Harrison's loneliness was exacerbated by the oppression and fear in the fort and the village following St. Clair's Defeat. Beyond the village, the bare woods seemed untenanted, but in various ways the memory of the defeat and the consciousness of the Indian threat loomed in the minds of soldiers and settlers alike. Inside the fort, the rows upon rows of wounded gradually diminished. Some men recovered, but most died. One of the latter was Captain Joseph Darke, a young Virginian whom the garrison buried in the post graveyard that December with all the panoply it could muster—a black-draped coffin, a full cortege, a dead march. While not all the dead were so honored, their successive burials must have darkened the mood in the fort. Outside the walls, fear was added to grief. In the village, people scarcely stirred from their cabins without carrying a gun; in the rest of the territory, families had abandoned their isolated clearings to spend the winter within well-fortified stockades like Garrard's Station. Even in Cincinnati, settlers believed, Indians stole through the village late at night. On Christmas Eve, a flurry of gunfire from the other side of the village sparked a brief panic in the fort; the noise was later discovered to have been made by a few villagers from the Southern or Middle states celebrating the holiday with shooting, as small farmers in Virginia had traditionally done. Other than that, however, the bleak woods of the Ohio Valley, now dusted with snow, were quiet as the year drew to a close. It seemed almost reasonable for the First Regiment to settle back into its usual winter torpor. Just after the new year, however, both the regiment's inactivity and Harrison's isolation were abruptly shattered by the arrival of a new commander for Fort Washington.[5]

It was evident from the first that Lieutenant Colonel James Wilkinson meant to take hold decisively in his new job; it was equally evident that he had a flair for the dramatic. Thirty-five years of age, though he looked older, Wilkinson was an extraordinarily winning blend of Eastern planter and Western speculator. His taste in dress was fashionable, even elegant—but he also enjoyed showing up for an expedition against the Indians in Kentucky hunter's garb, complete with moccasins, hunting knife, and tomahawk. His manners were warm, genial, almost effusive. A Marylander who had been on Washington's staff during the Revolution, he had moved west after the war to dabble in trade and land. Wilkinson had been active in the Kentucky statehood movement; like many a slaveholder, he had a couple of personal servants who went with him everywhere and for whom he was trying to find places in the Army. Though not a professional soldier, he did have military experience; he had served in the Revolution and, in the West, had led two militia raids on Indian villages north of the Ohio. When his business failed in 1791, he decided to enter the Army to secure a steady income, and he had spent the last months of the year winding up his affairs (he had received his commission too late to join St. Clair's expedition) before coming to Fort Washington to take over.[6]

From the moment Wilkinson arrived, it was clear that he was hoping to succeed to full command of the Western army; he was nakedly ambitious, and something of a schemer. No sooner had he replaced David Zeigler (who left at once for Philadelphia to testify before the congressional committee investigating St. Clair's Defeat) than he announced plans for a midwinter expedition, with help from the local militia, into the Indian country. His aims were, first, to recover the cannon lost on 4 November, and, second, to raid any Indian village within easy reach. It was a novel, aggressive plan, received with enthusiasm by the settlers, though the regular officers probably thought it unnecessary exertion.[7]

Wilkinson's small force set out on 25 January 1792, 150 mounted volunteers from Cincinnati and nearby settlements and about the same number of army regulars, Ensign Harrison among them. It was the coldest winter the West had known for seven or eight years. The Ohio was frozen over at Cincinnati so thickly that it was impossible to break a channel across, and two feet of snow covered the ground. The volunteers rode ahead to break a trail, the regulars marched behind, and sleds of provisions brought up the rear. In the bitter cold, they followed St. Clair's route by way of Forts Hamilton and Jefferson, camping at night around huge heaps of blazing logs. There were the predictable number of frostbite victims, and one volunteer at Fort Hamilton awoke to find that his head had slipped from the saddle he was using as a pillow and his queue had frozen fast to the ground. But they ran into no Indian resistance in the wintry woods; the weather itself was their worst opponent.

By the time they reached Fort Jefferson, after four days of marching, it was clear that the deep snow and the cold were seriously hampering their movements. The icy crust of the snow was cutting the horses' legs. Wilkinson prudently called off the raid and ordered the infantry back to Fort Washington while he, the territorial secretary, Winthrop Sargent, and the volunteers set out to ride the additional twenty-nine miles to the battlefield. Harrison and his men, consequently, turned and marched back next day over their own frozen tracks in the snow, probably reaching Fort Washington again by 2 February, three days before the return of Wilkinson and the militia.

From Sargent and others, Harrison later learned the ghastly details of that visit to the battlefield. Fourteen miles before reaching the site, the volunteers had begun encountering bodies in the snow—mere skeletons at first, with the flesh eaten from their bones, but later, on the field itself, naked bodies, blackened by frost but otherwise well preserved by the winter cold. The cold hadn't preserved the bodies from animals and enemies, however. Surgeon's mate Charles Brown noted that the eyes and genitals of most had been eaten, presumably by buzzards. Some bodies appeared to have had limbs torn off by the enemy while some of the women killed at the defeat had had huge stakes run through their bodies. Everywhere there were signs of the savagery of the battle; one witness saw a sapling with twenty-seven bullet holes in it.

The volunteers initially attempted to collect the bodies of their people and give them decent burial, but the ground was frozen, spades were few, and too many corpses were frozen to the ground and came apart in their hands. To add to their discouragement, provisions were short and they could not locate the artillery they had come to recover. After one night on the battleground, the party returned in haste to Fort Jefferson and to headquarters.[8]

One could not really call the expedition a success. Wilkinson had accomplished neither of his main objectives: the cannon were still lost, the Indian towns undisturbed. To be sure, the armed march through the forest had reasserted an American presence and shown that the government was not willing to concede control of the wilderness beyond

Cincinnati, but an Indian ambush outside Fort Jefferson, a few days after the expedition returned, took the edge off that accomplishment, especially since the commander's son and another man were killed. The wilds of the Northwest Territory were still a battleground, not firmly under the control of either side.[9]

Wilkinson's next probe into the interior, four weeks later, came under orders from Secretary Knox, who suggested that a new post be built between Forts Hamilton and Jefferson. To that end, the colonel, two hundred men, and sixty mounted militia left Fort Washington early on the morning of 13 March. The snow was off the ground by then, and signs of spring were visible in the trees, but it was a chill, wet spring. The muddy road made for slow going. The men forded the waist-deep Miami River at Fort Hamilton the morning of 16 March and arrived at the site of the new fort, a level, well-watered spot covered with immense oaks, beeches, and tulip poplars, two days later. There they rendezvoused with a force of two hundred men sent down from Fort Jefferson. The first day, the men went to work with their felling axes; by next morning, Wilkinson could report the site completely cleared. Then followed three or four days of intense activity, as soldiers wielding crosscut saws and axes cut and shaped hundreds of twenty-foot-thick tree trunks into palings for the stockade, others used shovels to dig trenches to set the sharpened trunks in and still others shaped boards for platforms and doors with handsaws and planes. The weather, though cold, stayed dry. By 23 March, the troops had virtually completed the fort, named for Arthur St. Clair. One hundred and twenty feet square, with "small but regular" bastions at the corners, it lacked only storehouses and a magazine. A satisfied Wilkinson marched back to Fort Washington, leaving a small garrison to finish the work.[10]

Ensign Harrison took part in this expedition, as he took part in all the hard, taxing assignments that winter. A principal duty was to command part of the guard every other night. It was a task to be taken seriously, for fresh tracks seen near Fort Hamilton on the march out indicated that the enemy was watching the army's movements closely. The men stood guard in the open air, without fires so as to avoid making themselves targets for enemy bullets, and Harrison, wrapped in his warmest clothes, periodically made his rounds among them. In the raw weather, so he recalled later, it was a rare night when no one was sent to the hospital tent with pleurisy or inflammation of the lungs. The young ensign himself came through the experience unscathed, however. It was the final test: he had endured the rigors of Western army life; he had proved himself a soldier.[11]

Army life was becoming slightly more tolerable in other ways, too. After the ambush at Fort Jefferson in February, Harrison's nemesis, Captain Strong, was sent to relieve the commander there, a change that must have eased his relations with the rest of the officers at Fort Washington. His concentrated reading of Steuben's manual began to pay off, as his smartness and precision in drilling his men drew compliments from other officers. At the same time, Harrison began to form acquaintances outside the regimental circle. One of these was the territorial secretary, Winthrop Sargent, who worked in the southwest corner of the fort. A Harvard graduate, Sargent had not only a classical education but also, once one got past his cold manner, a variety of scientific interests, notably natural history and archeology, and he must have enjoyed having someone reasonably well educated to talk to.[12]

By far the greatest change in Harrison's circumstances, however, came from his burgeoning friendship with the new commander. Like Harrison, Wilkinson was new to the regiment, and he had little sympathy with the old officers of the First, whom he described to friends as a set of "rascals . . . drunkards, and fools." At the beginning of March, he had a great row with Major Zeigler ("a most insensible blockhead," he assured Knox, "as obstinate as a German Boor") upon the latter's return from Philadelphia, which ended in Zeigler's resignation. At that point, anyone harassed by the regiment's old officers had a claim on Wilkinson's sympathy.[13] The friendship had other sources as well. The urbane, smiling commander fancied himself as bringing a touch of Eastern refinement and culture to the frontier, so naturally he responded enthusiastically to those qualities in Harrison. Moreover, the young ensign's story charmed him because it resembled his own; he too had studied medicine in Philadelphia and had abandoned a medical career for the army—in his case to join the Patriot forces in the Revolution. Another tie was Wilkinson's acquaintance with Ensign Harrison's father, Colonel Harrison; both had been on the Antifederalist side during the debate over Virginia's ratifying the Constitution.

Later in the year, Wilkinson revealed to Harrison that on taking command in January he had found orders for the latter's transfer to an interior post—probably issued by Zeigler or St. Clair to remove him from the persecution of Strong and his clique. Wilkinson had countermanded them—largely, as he said, because Harrison was so very young and vulnerable and the interior post commander was a heavy drinker whose habits Harrison might too easily acquire, but also because he enjoyed the presence at headquarters of a young man of Southern vivacity and at least a smattering of classical learning. Harrison repaid his commander's kindness with esteem and affection.[14]

Wilkinson enjoyed mentoring the young, and he made much of Ensign Harrison on gala social occasions. One such event was the Washington's Birthday ball at headquarters, to which the most select female society of Cincinnati and the vicinity were invited. In all, about twelve ladies and their escorts gathered for the rockets, the fireworks, and the dancing afterward. For Harrison, a ball lit by flickering candles in the rude mess hall of the fort, with dancing to the music of a single fiddle, must have been a contrast with the dancing assemblies in Richmond, but it still was a pleasant change from what had been happening more recently in his life. As spring approached, he could feel his environment beginning to thaw in more ways than one.[15]

CHAPTER NINE

Cincinnati

The signs of spring appeared early that year, heralding a real frontier spring, wild and beautiful. A warm spell at the end of February sent gallons of melted snow hurtling down the Ohio; by 10 March, as the troops prepared for their second expedition to the interior, the river had rampaged out of its banks at Cincinnati, flooding cabins built near the water and covering the river road. The outpost of Columbia, indeed, was cut off from the other white settlements except by canoe. The fort was untouched, however, and the troops left as scheduled.[1]

The next two weeks were chilly and wet, but by the end of March, when the soldiers returned, spring had come indeed. The hills around Cincinnati were checkered with the pink of redbud and the white of dogwood and hawthorn; green and gold parakeets, redbirds, and robins twittered in the trees; and by April, according to a boy who remembered it long after, the ground "was covered with May apple, blood root, ginseng, violets, and a great variety of herbs and flowers."[2]

Ensign Harrison could take in much of this natural beauty from the fort, just by looking up at the amphitheater of hills surrounding it, but as the spring advanced he often found occasion to visit the village. Actually, there was not a great deal to Cincinnati, which was just a collection of log buildings, at most two hundred, clustered on two levels separated by a high, steep bank. The buildings on the upper level straggled up and down dusty streets laid out in a grid like Philadelphia's. Most were dwellings: primitive, mud-chinked cabins built around clay-and-stick chimneys and painted brick red on the outside. Some were primitive but grand, like the log house of the landowning Ludlow family, who kept a servant. Their inhabitants were mainly plain Pennsylvania and Jersey farmers and their families; Harrison often saw them in the morning, going to their fields outside town with tools and oxen (and the inevitable musket) to plant or cultivate their corn. Beyond their fields, which filled with sprouting corn as the season advanced and testified impressively to the richness of the soil, stood the first thickets of the forest, bright green with fresh foliage dense enough already to conceal hostile Indians.[3]

Down on the lower level by the river were buildings of a different sort, crude warehouses for the merchants like John Bartle and Thomas Gibson who did business, genial and calculating, behind the rough plank counters of their stores. These men generally sold spirits and doubled as tavernkeepers; it was from their cabins, late at night, that hunters and boatmen came reeling out, stinking of Monongahela whiskey.[4]

Cincinnati was a rough little place. It was full of frontier drifters and discharged soldiers, heavy drinkers who guzzled bitters in the morning to wash last night's whiskey from their mouths, brawlers adept in no-holds-barred fighting of the variety called "bite, ballock, and gouge" from its three principal winning holds—nose, testicles, and eyes. Even the more permanent inhabitants settled their disputes more often by fighting than by law and were not the sort to be cowed for long by the menace of Indian war.

The residents were also hard workers. Harrison, strolling about the village in spring, could hear the sound of hammering everywhere as they continued work on their settlement. In the village center, one or two substantial men of property, like Israel Ludlow, were building pretentious, two-story houses. Winthrop Sargent, the territorial secretary, was putting up a small frame house and a large vegetable garden on some land he owned behind the fort. Down by the river, Wilkinson had soldiers working on a large stockade for the artificers who made and repaired army supplies and also on a garden where he planned to sow cabbage, turnips, and lima beans, among other vegetables. Not far from the fort, a log church was under way.[5]

Harrison had a particular interest in the church, for he had contributed to its construction. The preacher was to be James Kemper, a Presbyterian minister who had come to the West in 1791, a portly, popular man whose Eastern dress—knee breeches, queue, and buckled shoes—contrasted sharply with the linsey-woolsey or deerskin hunting shirts of most other men in town. In January 1792, several villagers, hungry for the gospel, had gotten up a contribution to build him a church. They had asked for contributions from the fort as well. Sargent, who thought the village a sinkhole of vice, had eagerly put up ten dollars, and so had Wilkinson. Harrison had chipped in a smaller amount from his meager pay. Now he could see the building going up—a simple cabin of thirty by forty feet—though he took no part in building it, as Kemper and most of the civilian subscribers did. Perhaps he did attend preaching services, though, as often as he could get away, sitting with other citizens on felled tree trunks at the corner of two dirt streets near the fort, while Kemper spoke. Despite the village's rawness, attendance at such religious services, according to a visiting minister, was surprisingly large.[6]

Ensign Harrison's contribution had been made in the late winter months of early 1792, in his most miserable days at Fort Washington, when he was being ostracized by almost all his fellow officers and doubting his ability to endure the hardships of frontier service. He was almost the only junior officer to contribute, and in the circumstances his need for divine reassurance is no surprise. However, his contribution was also the last in the series of faint Christian associations marking his early years; from spring 1792 on, signs of a new identity begin to replace, or at least overshadow, his Christian faith. More and more, it seems, he embraced the identity of soldier, priding himself on his honor, his smartness, and his bravery. This identity was the one he had sought all along and, after his difficult beginning, he became a military man with remarkable speed. He did not model himself primarily on his brother officers in the First Regiment, however; his version of soldierly identity was to be more literary and more humane toward the men.

One index of Harrison's approach to his service in the Ohio country relates to a curious discovery he made in the spring of 1792. Sargent was probably the first to show it to him. Right in the middle of the village, where the broad track called Main Street started to descend the hill from the "second bank," where Fort Washington and half the houses stood, to the lower level, it intersected a sort of oval mound of earth, perhaps eight feet high, on the brow of the hill. At the place where it cut through, passersby were continually finding strange objects—yellowed human bones, bits of hard brown pottery, stone bowls, even pieces of ore—that evidently had washed or fallen out of what was clearly some sort of Indian burial place. Clearly, too, this mound was immensely old; Sargent, who was writing a paper on it for a Boston philosophical society, had measured the oak stumps atop it and had found them some seven feet across. Perhaps some earlier generation of Indians had built it, but its dimensions—120 feet long by 60 wide—were much larger than anything the natives of the Ohio country customarily made.[7]

The Cincinnati mound was one in a large group of similar sites, Harrison learned. All equally old and puzzling, they dotted the Ohio Valley from Marietta on down. There were others located near Cincinnati; just north of the village was an obvious one, a circular, three-foot-tall embankment six hundred feet in diameter, thickly covered with trees. A little farther west was a striking example, a conical mound fifty feet high, also densely wooded.[8]

The mounds fascinated Harrison from the time he learned of them. He felt sure—and Sargent and most other investigators would have agreed—that they could not be the work of the half-naked tribes who now lived in the Ohio Valley. Obviously they belonged to some more civilized race, lost somewhere in the past, possibly whites whom the Indians had managed somehow to displace. American naturalists were beginning to speculate about exactly who they might have been. Dr. Benjamin Barton, the medical-school lecturer whose talks on botany Harrison may have attended briefly the summer before, had collected many reports on the mounds and thought their builders might have been descendants of Viking immigrants. Some New England divines conjectured that they were the Ten Lost Tribes of the Old Testament. The earthworks spoke of a past as ancient and as epic as anything in Rollin—full of kingdoms, battles, and intrigues, but at the same time thoroughly indigenous. As to their purpose, one was free to guess. Barton and others called them "fortifications," which suggested a military past at the very site of Fort Washington. The thought captured Harrison's imagination; it endowed his army experience with a colorful, significant past that only an avid reader of history like himself could fully appreciate.[9]

From the gate of the fort, Harrison and the other officers could look across to the little settlement on its mound of bones and artifacts. They did so with detachment, even with some suspicion, for relations between the soldiery and Cincinnatians in general were not good. That February, in particular, there had been a nasty little flare-up, when quick-tempered Lieutenant Thomas Pasteur of the First Regiment, believing himself cheated in trade by John Bartle, had invited the storekeeper to the fort and there, guarded by his men, had beaten him up. Bartle had sued. At the trial his lawyer, the village shyster John Blanchard, had denounced Pasteur so severely that, a few nights later, a sergeant and about thirty men from Pasteur's company had come down into the village to give him a beating too, presumably at their commander's instigation. Sergeant Nesbit's mission, however, had turned into a free-for-all in front of the cabin of Judge William McMillan: McMillan, John Riddle the blacksmith, and twenty or so other men from the village, with arms, had routed Nesbit and his band, although Mrs. McMillan was struck with a "ponderous club" as she tried to help her husband. As a result, Nesbit had been fined and broken to private, while Pasteur, against whom nothing was proved, received a reprimand from Wilkinson.[10]

Only the possibility of a major Indian attack kept a measure of peace between soldiers and civilians. It was the question in everyone's mind. The Indians seemed more than ready. One of the Marietta settlers described them that year as "a People Insolent when Victorious": confident of their ability to keep whites out of their land, they had had raiding parties out since the beginning of spring in different parts of the Northwest Territory, killing settlers' stock outside Columbia and Cincinnati and lying in wait for lone travelers in the interior. In later March, a party killed a woman and three children near Belpre, south of Marietta; in April, another group ambushed and slew Captain Montfort of the First Regiment outside Fort Jefferson. Still, it seemed very unlikely that they would try to storm any of the forts; nor would they try a direct assault on Marietta or Cincinnati as long as the Army was there to protect the settlers. In light of St. Clair's Defeat the previous November, however, offensive action by an American force was even less likely; the army was reluctant to risk a repetition of that disaster. There seemed little prospect of open battle in the Northwest, only constant raids and danger—unless the government decided to do something new.[11]

As the weather warmed up and regular communication with the East resumed, Harrison and his fellows began learning how their government had received the news of St. Clair's Defeat. The president, it was said, had been furious. Congress had entered into weeks of agitated debate. Some Easterners had argued that the nation had no business wasting lives and money on invading the Indian country—in effect, that St. Clair had gotten his just deserts—and that the army, and perhaps the settlers, should withdraw. Others had urged the necessity of standing up to the Indians because of the British influence behind them. In the end, the second party had prevailed in the main. The army, as Harrison learned toward the end of March, was to be doubled in size. Two new regiments were to be raised to fight for the Northwest Territory, and a new commander would be appointed over the whole. At the same time, though, the government intended to pursue peace negotiations with the Indians. It planned several different missions into the Indian country that spring, in hopes of finding some tribes who wanted to talk peace.[12]

One of these missions, perhaps the most important, left from Fort Washington in May. Its objective was to try to contact the hostile tribes directly, instead of going through the British-influenced Indians of the Great Lakes. Lieutenant John Hardin of the Kentucky militia and Captain Alexander Trueman of the Second Regiment were the envoys. Their task, for which both were to be liberally paid, was to travel directly into the Northwest Territory, toward Lake Erie and the Indian towns on the Maumee River, with letters from President Washington and try to talk peace with any leaders they might find. In the eyes of most people at the fort, the mission was foolhardy. The Indians, flushed with victory, were unlikely to let any white men, however peaceable, pass through their land unharmed. Trueman, Hardin, and their three attendants left the fort on 22 May. Only one of the five was to return.[13]

This extraordinary mission was only one topic of conversation in Fort Washington's officers' quarters during May. A bigger one was the coming reorganization of the Army and the chances of promotion it might create. Details about the expansion of the Army arrived piecemeal during April, both through sealed dispatches from Secretary Knox, delivered by boat from Pittsburgh, and through private letters, often more revealing, from civilians in the capital. Early in May, the fort learned that Wilkinson would not command the army in the West. Instead, the president had chosen a Revolutionary comrade, "Mad Anthony" Wayne, the hero of Stony Point, who was only a name to Harrison but was well known to many of his fellow officers. Wayne would be coming to Pittsburgh to assemble the two new regiments; when they were ready, in the fall, he would descend the Ohio with them and join Wilkinson. Then there would, most likely, be transfers and new assignments for many officers of the First Regiment.[14]

Mostly, however, the officers at Fort Washington talked of their daily concerns, the rivalries and petty scrapes of military life, and their ambitions—often vague ideas of leaving the service to take up trade in Cincinnati, or of going east to get married. Harrison listened and took some part. He was no longer a pariah; some of the senior officers, in fact, had come to have a grudging admiration for his spit and polish. They talked of the dangers of travel on the Fort Hamilton road and of housekeeping problems at Fort Washington. (Several dozen Indians, mainly women and children, were being held captive in the fort, closely confined, as a result of Wilkinson's raid the summer before. In May Wilkinson ordered a second stockade built for them by the river, "to secure the garrison from their filthy habits of living.")[15]

The officers also talked of their theatrical commander. Wilkinson, though disappointed in his hopes of command, had received a promotion to brigadier general and was at his most flamboyant that spring. Mrs. Wilkinson and their children came up from Kentucky at winter's end, and their arrival signaled the beginning of a social round unprecedented at the fort. The general had a barge built and outfitted as a pleasure boat, and he gave river parties for friends and fellow officers all spring, climaxing with a party on 26 May in a specially built wigwam by the Ohio for Mrs. Wilkinson, Sargent, Judge Symmes, leading villagers, and the officers. By that time, however, Harrison himself had become a main topic of conversation at the fort. The problem, again, was his excessive zeal—this time, military zeal.[16]

It happened this way. Toward the end of April, as the weather got warm, the general decided he could no longer keep the men cooped up in quarters. With some misgivings, in view of the past friction between soldiers and villagers, he announced that they could go into the village for pleasure, with permission from their company commanders. Within a short time he found that his apprehension had been well founded. By 11 May, two weeks after the order, he had a guardhouse full of prisoners, an inordinate number of men drunk on duty, and a steadily rising tide of complaints from settlers. That day, in preparation for the upcoming weekend, he issued a new order: any private found drunk in the village would receive fifty lashes on the spot where he was taken (instead of awaiting the sentence of a court-martial). A patrol commanded by an officer would cruise the area "at irregular hours" to enforce the order. Ensign Harrison, serious and abstemious, was one of the first to be given the duty.[17]

Sometime that weekend, probably on Saturday, 12 May, Harrison and his squad ran into two men from the fort, one of whom was very obviously drunk. With military calmness and precision, Harrison had the protesting man stripped, tied, and flogged on the spot. When the bleeding victim's soberer companion kept trying to intervene, Harrison lost patience and had him given ten lashes as well. Only later did he discover his mistake. The men were from the fort, to be sure, but they were artificers, civilian employees of the Army who worked down in the stockade, repairing gun carriages and making powder and shot. Traditionally, such men had not been held subject to military justice. On Sunday, the chief of artificers came to Wilkinson to complain of the incident; Wilkinson called young Harrison into his quarters and explained the distinction. Next day he issued an order specifically exempting artificers from the order of 11 May.

The mistake was embarrassing to Harrison, but what came next transformed the incident into a classic civil-military broil. The following week, the men who had been whipped got out, went to John Blanchard, and swore out a writ against Harrison for assault. This "seditious" gesture was too much for General Wilkinson; believing, as he explained later, that there was no reason "for me to offer further violence to the feelings of Mr. Harrison, one of the best disposed, most promising young Gentlemen in the Army," he closed the gates of the fort to the deputy sheriff who came to serve the warrant. Harrison's own behavior in the situation is not clear, but whatever it was, it was excessive, for this is the point about which Sargent wrote the War Department that "there will always be some young men in Military life." One account claims that he knocked down the deputy who brought the warrant, but this seems unlikely, given Harrison's slight build. Another version, which seems to have the Pasteur and Harrison incidents confused, suggests that he wrote the civil judges in Cincinnati a haughty letter; given his fondness for extravagant rhetoric, such an action seems possible. Whatever he did, one thing is clear: by this point, the incident had awakened all the latent grievances between the Army and the civilian administration. Harrison's actions had come to symbolize military rights, and his commander gave him full backing. The civil judges, therefore, trained their verbal fire on Wilkinson.[18]

June came with the affair at a standstill. Harrison was a virtual prisoner in the fort, subject to instant arrest (and likely to provoke a civil-military free-for-all) the moment he stepped outside. Wilkinson, trying to resolve an increasingly sticky situation, had appealed to Sargent to have the suit thrown out. At the same time, he toyed with the idea of transferring his young friend to Fort Fayette in Pennsylvania, or Fort Knox on the Wabash, or perhaps the Falls of the Ohio.

Soon, however, another idea occurred to the considerate general. Mrs. Wilkinson and the children were about to return to Philadelphia and would require an escort. Wilkinson and Sargent could write letters for Harrison to carry to Secretary Knox, explaining the incident. It would be a pleasant trip for the young man while at the same time removing him from Cincinnati just long enough for the affair to die down. He called in Harrison and broached the idea to him—would he like to accompany the Wilkinson family back to the east?

Harrison, no stranger to being asked to leave a place for his own good, needed little time to consider the proposal; as a good soldier, he followed the orders of his commander. He agreed.[19]

CHAPTER TEN

Anthony Wayne Takes Over

Toward the end of the first week in June, a small river convoy began assembling at the foot of the bluffs below the fort—two large boats, capable of carrying a hundred soldiers, who were being transferred to the new command post at Pittsburgh and on the way could provide protection for General Wilkinson's family, and two light, mobile canoes. Inside the big boats were accommodations for Mrs. Wilkinson and her sons, for Ensign Harrison, and also for the former quartermaster general, Samuel Hodgdon, who had decided to join the party. Hodgdon had been roughly handled in the report of the congressional committee that had investigated St. Clair's Defeat, and was headed for Philadelphia to try to clear himself. The river was low, as it generally was in summer, and hence suitable for upstream travel. In the fresh warmth of early June, it would (barring Indian attacks) be a pleasant journey for the passengers—none of whom, of course, had to worry about propelling the boats against the current of the Ohio.[1]

Since the trip was upriver, the boats were keelboats rather than flats: hulking, overgrown craft built of timbers and planks, sometimes seventy feet long and ten feet wide. Along their bottoms ran the keels, heavy beams four inches square, designed to absorb the shock of sunken obstructions. Along each side were the narrow walkways called running boards, where, all day long, six or nine men on each side labored in unison to drive the boat forward, planting their poles on the bottom at the command "set," walking slowly from prow to stern with the pole held firmly in a socket on their shoulders, lifting at the command "lift," and returning to the prow to repeat the operation. It was slow going; a foot traveler on the bank, had there been a clear path, could easily have overtaken them. It was also hard, sweaty work for the men who performed it, and the boat carried generous supplies of whiskey to recompense them.[2]

On 13 June, the convoy set off on the long voyage to Pittsburgh. General Wilkinson, solicitous as always of his wife's welfare, accompanied them on the first leg, as far as Limestone. The journey from there on proved uneventful. No Indians attacked; the splendid, luxuriant forests of the riverbank turned out to conceal nothing more ferocious than deer or bear, which they occasionally saw coming down to the shore in the early morning. No doubt they passed a few flatboats traveling downriver crowded with emigrants, their livestock, and their goods, for even the news of an Indian victory in the West had been unable to stem entirely the flow of westward movement. Wilkinson's boys, thirteen-year-old Jackie, eleven-year-old James, and seven-year-old Biddle, lounged on the keelboat's flat roof or fished desultorily in the still water. Ensign Harrison sat in the stern chatting with Hodgdon and Mrs. Wilkinson, perhaps sipping coffee or chocolate from a tin cup, and observing the fertility of the rich river bottoms gliding past. "The sycamore, the elm, the beach, the aspin, the hicory, the walnut, and the maple, or sugar tree, are large beyond credibility," a New England officer was to write the following spring. "The herbiage which covered the surface of the bottom, was nearly two feet high."

Mrs. Wilkinson, in both looks and manners, was agreeable company. The daughter of a rich Philadelphia family, she had been out west with her husband for eight years, and was now using the privileges of his new rank to revisit her native city; before 1792, the Wilkinsons had been unable to afford the expenses of the trip. Doubtless many of her connections in the capital were people Harrison also knew.[3]

On 22 June they passed the night at Marietta. By 2 July they were at Pittsburgh, where Harrison reported to the new commander of the Western army, General Wayne. Fleshy, middle-aged, rather overbearing and solemn in manner, with the high-colored complexion of a steady drinker, Wayne much resembled Harrison's ex-Revolutionary comrades-in-arms at Fort Washington. He was courtesy itself, however, as he provided conveyance for the Wilkinson family's trip east: a two-horse coach belonging to "Mrs. Col. O'Hara," wife of the new quartermaster general, a saddle horse for Mrs. Wilkinson, another for Harrison, and still another for the three boys to ride. He accompanied the party seven miles out of Pittsburgh when they left town on 3 July, and cautioned young Harrison to inquire for "the best and safest roads."[4]

No road across the mountains was really suitable for travel by coach, even with the good driver Wayne had provided. Ensign Harrison and the Wilkinsons picked their way carefully from tavern to tavern, down the rocky slopes of the Allegheny Mountain and up the rutted track of Sideling Hill, while Hodgdon apparently went on ahead. Within two weeks, Mrs. Wilkinson and her boys were safely in Philadelphia. Harrison took his leave of them, checked in with his friends in the capital, and stopped by the War Office to pick up dispatches for the West. His stay in Philadelphia had to be short, a week at most, for General Wayne had ordered him to be back in Pittsburgh by 1 August. Still, he had time to regale friends like the Morrises with tales of the Ohio country, to them an exotic place with curiosities like the Indian earthworks. Doubtless, in Harrison's vivid retelling, the West lost none of its fascination; but the tales established their teller not as an eccentric, headstrong youth but as a young man making his way in a promising new territory.[5]

He wasted no time getting back to his post. In contrast to his thirty-day march to Pittsburgh the previous fall, this trip, with Harrison alone and on horseback, required only eight or nine days. By 4 August he was lodged in Tannehill's tavern on the banks of the Monongahela, awaiting further orders.[6]

Pittsburgh in the summer of 1792 was a bustling place. From all over the East, companies of new recruits were on the march toward the little village. Harrison no doubt passed several of them on his return west. They seemed, on the whole, younger and more robust than those who had enlisted the previous year, although at least one company brought smallpox with it and had to be quarantined outside town, while several of the new men had virulent cases of venereal disease. The recruits had women with them, mistresses or wives whom the commanders tolerated in camp, loud and brawling as they were, because they could serve as nurses or laundresses.

As they arrived, they encamped on the shore of the Allegheny, across the river from the newly built Fort Fayette, about a mile north of the town; every week a new cluster of tents was added to the encampment. By the beginning of August perhaps four hundred soldiers had gathered there. Pittsburgh's merchants and tavernkeepers, shrewd and enterprising like those of any frontier village, welcomed their arrival. Pittsburgh already had several flourishing taverns; now, like most army towns, it was beginning to develop its own "Hell-street" or "holy ground" where, as one veteran private demurely put it, "all sorts of pastimes" were on offer.[7]

The new army was not only larger than the old one but substantially different in organization. Even its name had been changed. Drawing on the classics, Congress had decided to call the new fighting force the Legion of the United States in emulation of republican Rome, and General Wayne, who had a fondness for the showy minutiae of military organization, was planning to divide it into four sublegions, each with its distinctive sublegionary colors and uniform, into which the old First and Second Infantry would be absorbed.[8]

Harrison apparently spent the rest of August lodged at Tannehill's tavern, reporting daily to Wayne's headquarters in the village, near the site of old Fort Pitt, and doing his share by drilling the new recruits and handling many details involved in getting the Legion organized. He dined at the officers' mess and must have had frequent occasion to see and speak with General Wayne.

Wayne did not share Wilkinson's automatic fondness for junior officers, being altogether more formal and self-important in his style; but he may have had special reason to take note of young Harrison. He was a Pennsylvanian who had spent most of his life in the Philadelphia area, and he knew both Dr. Rush and Robert Morris quite well. Either of the two may well have commended young Harrison to his attention. Moreover, he had commanded in the James River theater toward the end of the Revolution, had briefly made his headquarters at Westover, and had in fact stationed some troops at the Harrisons' then-deserted estate. It seems possible that he and Harrison found a good deal to talk about, and Wayne, in the course of their conversations, can hardly have failed to be impressed by Harrison's earnestness, engaging manners, and evident devotion to military life. By September, Wayne had apparently taken a liking to the conscientious young ensign; when Wilkinson wrote that month, asking him to "send me young Harrison if you have no further occasion for him," Wayne simply ignored the request.[9]

Of all the topics discussed at the officers' mess, the likelihood of peace or war with the Indians that fall was, inevitably, the most frequently aired.

By August, as Harrison learned when he returned to the West, it was generally accepted on the frontier that the missions of Hardin and Trueman had ended in their deaths. Rumors to that effect had reached Vincennes as early as June and had been confirmed by two fugitives who appeared at Fort Jefferson in July. By 6 August, Wayne felt that the death of both officers was "a certainty." But the government at Philadelphia, conscious of its international and domestic weakness, remained committed to peace if possible. The tribes of the Northeast were to meet in council that fall, and Washington wanted to approach them there. Until the council was over, therefore, the administration was determined to refrain from renewing hostilities, even though its earlier attempts at peace had led nowhere.[10]

The Indians' intentions were less clear. No one leader spoke for all the tribes, and though an individual leader might appear at Pittsburgh to confer with Wayne (as Kiasutta, the aged Mingo warrior, did in September, with due gravity and ceremony), he could represent only his own people. As for their actions, the summer had been full of attacks on small parties of whites; they had begun increasing in number just after Harrison and the Wilkinsons had left for the east. At the end of July, when Harrison returned to the west, sporadic attacks by a marauding band of Shawnee who had killed a total of seven men on that part of the frontier were prompting general alarm in Pittsburgh and throughout the upper Ohio Valley. All this did not add up to anything like organized warfare, but it did not suggest that the Indians wanted peace.[11]

However unorganized the attacks might appear, General Wayne, like Harrison and most of the other officers, saw a clear pattern in them, a pattern not Indian but British. It was "British emissaries," the general was sure, who were inciting the Indians to attack, and he could back his contention with any number of rumors floating around the West about scarlet-coated white men seen in company with hostile natives. If they were true, Wayne reasoned, then no permanent peace would be possible in the West until the Indians were forced into submission and the British convinced they could not use the natives as their tools. Talk of slacking off in the face of such a menace made him angry. America, he argued to Knox that summer, had "more to apprehend from a temporary peace than from the Most Active Indian war." His own timetable, which assumed the failure of the negotiations, called for a drive into Indian country as soon as possible—not that fall, but in 1793. Not yet approved by Knox, the plan was common knowledge at the officers' mess. The Legion would move downriver sometime in the fall, join Wilkinson at Cincinnati, and winter there. The following spring it would be ready for an early move against the Indians, who, Wayne judged, were weakest at that season.[12]

Wayne's efforts to create an army, as captains kept marching in from the East with companies of new recruits, displayed an almost painful urgency. Desertion, both on the march and at Pittsburgh, was still a major problem, and the general, a martinet in a time when military discipline was at best brutal, dealt harshly with deserters. Some he hanged; some he wanted to brand on the forehead, if Knox would allow it, with the word "Coward." (Knox demurred.) On 1 September he had five captured deserters punished: four were shot, while the fifth, head and eyebrows shaved, acted as executioner. Drill, for the rest of the men, was long and thorough, target practice and sham fights frequent.[13]

By 1 September, there were six or seven hundred officers and men camped in tents on the bluffs outside Pittsburgh—not as many as Wayne had expected and not enough to warrant descending the river, but enough, at least, to make a detailed organization of the Legion possible. The first week of the month, Wayne issued orders dividing the recruits into sublegions, battalion, and companies, each with its own commander. Harrison, like most officers of the First Regiment, was assigned to the First Sub-Legion, with its insignia, carefully prescribed by the general himself, of white binding and white plumes on the caps. (The Second Sub-Legion had red binding and plumes, the Third, yellow, and so forth.) Harrison was to be the subaltern in a company commanded by a fellow Virginian, Captain Ballard Smith.[14]

Harrison cannot have looked forward to the assignment with much eagerness. He had known Smith at Fort Washington as a member of the old First Regiment clique—an aggressive, temperamental, heavy-drinking officer notorious for his failure to get along with his superiors. But there was nothing to be done about it, and on 10 September, the date of his assignment, Harrison presumably moved out of his quarters in the village and into one of the linen tents dotting the ground near Fort Fayette.[15]

Any misgivings Harrison had about serving under Captain Smith were soon justified. He had hardly begun his duties in the company when he became aware of bad blood developing between his captain and the camp commander, Major George M. Bedinger. A tough Kentucky frontiersman, veteran of many early Indian fights in the West, Bedinger was not an Army regular—he had just joined the Legion—and he was unimpressed by Smith, who practically personified the First Regiment's casual, swaggering approach to warfare. Smith, aware of Bedinger's disapproval, got off several loud, slighting references to the major's background and character; he also went over his head to complain to Wayne about the orders he was being given. Bedinger retaliated by arresting and publicly reprimanding Smith for jumping rank, and on 20 September, a court-martial ordered the captain to apologize publicly to Bedinger on the parade ground. But that was hardly the end of the affair.[16]

It came to a head the evening of 3 October, and Harrison had the good fortune not to be directly involved. Smith and his mistress, Polly, the common-law wife of a Sergeant Sprague, were drinking in camp. Polly got a little boisterous, picked up Smith's sword and began slashing around with it. It all seemed great fun, and both Polly and the captain were offended when a soldier showed up at the tent to disarm her, sent by Bedinger at the complaint of a soldier who had been slightly wounded by her swordplay. Smith was drunk and obstructive, and Polly, springing into his bed, seized his pistols, pointed them at the sergeant's crotch and, in what the sergeant called "blackguard and abusive" language, told him to leave or get portions of his anatomy shot off. "I'm the little queen," she crowed, "who can whip you even if you are a sergeant."

Sergeant Thorpe made off, but of course went straight to Bedinger, who promptly, and doubtless with some satisfaction, sent out a squad and had the captain placed under arrest. A court-martial two weeks later convicted Smith of drunkenness and suspended him from command for six months. Harrison, though only nineteen, succeeded to temporary command of the company, with the responsibility of seeing that the accounts, muster rolls, uniforms, and accoutrements were kept in good order.[17]

How long he held command is not recorded. It was certainly more than a month. The duty was relatively easy, according to a fellow ensign, its monotony broken now and then by "a duel for variety—then a ball—then on fatigue—then tea with the ladies." Harrison had enough experience with army procedure to turn in a decent performance, and he lacked the exaggerated haughtiness that led many officers to bully or exploit their men—as Smith, for instance, had exploited Sergeant Sprague. As a Harrison of James River, he was comfortable enough with authority to feel no pressing need to shore up his status. Then or later, he began acquiring a reputation as an officer unusually considerate of the soldiers who served under him.[18]

Smith's was not the only disciplinary problem in the Legion that fall. "Billiards lead many officers and civilians astray," wrote an ensign from Vermont, "and cards are too often introduced. . . . Our army at present contains a number of *Jack-Asses;* short will be their lives; God speed their flight." The men in general were a bad lot; too many were hardened drunkards, thieves, and marauders who continually slipped out of camp and provoked complaints from settlers for miles around for their "abuse and plundering." Much of the problem sprang from the village tavernkeepers' readiness to peddle whiskey to the soldiers; but whatever the cause, the Legion became less and less welcome at Pittsburgh as fall went on.

The soldiers' predilection for drink aggravated another problem: much of the whiskey being sold was illegal, in that its makers had not paid the federal government's newly imposed excise tax. Many had no intention of doing so. A year or two later, conflict over the tax was to explode into the Whiskey Rebellion, but already the situation was turning ugly in places, since Wayne could hardly ignore the issue entirely. Lieutenant William Faulkner of the Legion, who had been trying to enforce collection of the tax in some remote settlements, had been threatened with tar, feathers, and castration. As long as the Legion remained at Pittsburgh, there was always a possibility that a crisis might arise over the tax and that the army and settlers whom it was supposedly protecting might wind up at one another's throats.[19]

It was mainly the problem of discipline, however, that convinced Wayne of the necessity to remove the Legion from Pittsburgh. As September ended, with the river falling and still no authorization received from Philadelphia to move the Legion to Fort Washington, the general realized that if he wanted new winter quarters he had to act fast. Although he was ill with gout and attacks of vomiting and able to ride only a few hours each day, the commander himself led the search for a new camp somewhere downriver, while the men continued their drilling and rifle practice, camp chores and cavalry exercises near the town. Finally, around mid-October, Wayne found a suitable site, on the Indian shore of the Ohio, twenty-two miles below Pittsburgh, in thick forest on a fairly high bluff. On 9 November, a large party of soldiers and artificers under Quartermaster General O'Hara set out downstream to begin building the stables and ovens for the new camp, but low water in the Ohio prevented the remainder of the Legion from moving until the month's end.[20]

Harrison was still commanding Smith's company on 29 November, when, at dawn, the Legion began its move. In fact, he was now a full-fledged lieutenant, having been promoted in October. As the drums beat, he inspected his men and marched them toward the waiting flatboats, each boat marked with appropriate sublegionary colors. Other company commanders were doing the same. The cavalry, meanwhile, were making ready to cross the Allegheny and set out by land. It was an impressive, complicated operation. The Ohio was high now, as the main body of soldiers began to embark. There was a hospital flatboat for the sick, a cavalry boat for the "traveling forge, hangers & hayracks," and wagons full of tents and all the other gear of an eighteenth-century army—saws, axes, camp kettles, howitzers, kegs of sugar, flour and salt, reams of paper and boxes of sealing wax, drums, chalk, blankets, files, shoemakers' tools. With the neighing of draft horses and the oaths of the wagoners added to the drumbeats, with the sergeants' commands and boatmen's cries, it was a supremely noisy spectacle, but finally, after all the confusion, the Legion was embarked and moving downstream.[21]

CHAPTER ELEVEN

Legionville and a Trip East

Duty at the new camp was not exactly like fighting savages in the wilderness, but it was as close to it as Harrison had yet come. A few weeks before, the camp had been an unnamed spot on the high north bank of the Ohio River; now, by order of the commander, it was to become a collection of huts called Legionville, temporarily home to two thousand men; next spring, if all went well, it would again be a deserted clearing in the forest. And there were, in fact, Indians about; one or two had been seen in the woods near the site, although, cowed into inactivity by the size of Wayne's army, they gave the Legion no trouble.[1]

There was every sign of another harsh winter coming. The men had barely gotten to work, wearing the hunting shirts Wayne had issued them in lieu of the winter clothing that had not yet arrived from the east, when the snow came, falling at least six inches deep. Still the men were kept at it, felling trees, clearing brush, and shaping the fallen trunks with broadaxe and adze to fit together into huts. The soldiers' quarters were to be built first, and then the officers', with Wayne's last of all. For several weeks, then, the officers shared the men's lot, sleeping under linen tents, eating half-cooked meat and bread, and huddling around smoky fires for warmth. No doubt they all looked and felt rather grubby; in the circumstances, anything beyond minimal bathing and grooming was out of the question. By 6 December, nearly everyone was "under cover . . . warm and secure." By the middle of the month there was enough ice in the Ohio to hamper the shipment of supplies from Pittsburgh.[2]

When the men were not detailed to construction work, they resumed the routine familiar from Fort Fayette: morning parade, morning rifle practice outside camp (with a gill of whiskey for the best shots), bayonet drill, and marching over muddy snow in the afternoons. Sergeants did much of the drilling, but at parade Lieutenant Harrison would be out walking alongside his company, espontoon in hand.[3]

Harrison had been in the army for more than a year now, and it is fair to ask how much progress he had made toward assuming the role of his dreams, that of military officer. No measuring stick is readily available. The Legion of the United States, an institution less than a decade old, had no procedures for rating junior officers, and, indeed, no firm criteria for evaluating them. It did have, as William Skelton has pointed out in his masterly study of the early officer corps, a rough ideal, derived mainly from British and Continental models: an officer should be a gentleman, someone comfortable and experienced with command; he should have mastery of the practical skills that went with his position, like administration, discipline, and specifically military procedures; and ideally he should be an educated person, with a "liberal," humane point of view. To these requisites, Americans often added another, particularly significant in their own environment: a good officer needed high levels of physical strength and stamina, since his duties might well pit him against the fleet, uncivilized original inhabitants of North America in their ancestral wilderness.[4]

Lieutenant Harrison clearly met the first and third of these criteria: his Virginia gentry upbringing made him ipso facto a gentleman, while his education, though second-rate by the standards of his own class, was superior to that of most army officers. He did not need to change his behavior at all in order to fit into his new identity. As to the final criterion, however, Harrison's own account highlights the nervousness he felt about his ability to measure up. Slender and delicate in appearance, he did not look as if he belonged in a frontier military force. His accounts of his first solo assignment, the march to Fort Hamilton, and of the construction of Fort St. Clair in severe weather, show his anxiety to convince his superiors, his colleagues, and most of all himself that he was tough enough to handle the rigors of Western duty. His success in doing so was a powerful boost to his identity as a military man.[5]

Harrison' one area of weakness was in meeting the second criterion, that of professional skills. Except, possibly, for occasional attendance at militia musters, he had had no experience of drilling techniques and the handling of a firearm when he became an officer—nor did quite a few other men who received commissions. The expectation in the Legion was that such officers would learn these skills through a combination of reading standard manuals and personal guidance from more experienced officers. Because of the hostile reception he encountered in the First Regiment upon arriving in the West, however, Harrison had no one to turn to for guidance and had to rely on reading alone. Fortunately, he was a good reader, and he had the right book—Steuben's *Regulations*, or the Blue Book, as it was often called. Even more fortunately, he had entered the army at just the right time: his new commanders, first Wilkinson and then Wayne, were generals who stressed mastery of book knowledge as a basis for performance. Wayne in particular, striving to transform the Legion quickly into a disciplined fighting force, saw in the Blue Book the most effective way to get all his officers on board. To him, Harrison's ability to learn from military books made him a model for young officers, rather than the outcast he had been in the first months after his arrival.[6]

There remained the issue of discipline, and all indications are that imposing discipline on his men was the weakest part of Harrison's performance in his early years as an officer. It is easy to understand why: he was younger than most of the men he commanded and not physically imposing, even if he did manage to master the "loud and distinct voice" Steuben prescribed. His cheerful, easygoing personality may have played a part as well: soldiers who served under him then and later recalled him as a considerate commander who took an interest in their problems. Such recollections may also explain the comment, quoted earlier, of the Indiana political adversary who said that Harrison could imitate a blackguard as well as any man he ever saw: Harrison was thoroughly familiar with the lingo of disreputable lower-class men because he had no difficulty relating to them. Sympathy of this kind could interfere with command relationships. At a fairly early date, General Wayne took Harrison out of the chain of command and put him on his staff, where his handwriting, his education, and his manners could be of most use—and where discipline was not an issue.[7]

Harrison himself seems to have been thoroughly happy with his adaptation to military life. Evidence, as always, is somewhat sparse, but the brouhaha over his treatment of the artificers at Fort Washington offers some clues. The whole affair stemmed from his excessive enthusiasm for army regulations and his devotion to his commander, Wilkinson; moreover, his conduct displayed one of the hallmarks of the military personality as it was understood in the eighteenth century—a casualness about receiving or inflicting pain. He ordered the flogging administered to the artificers with no apparent qualm, just as, in a letter to his brother in 1794, he declared himself ready to personally flog an army doctor who had cheated him in a money transaction. A couple of phrases in that letter eloquently express Harrison's satisfaction with his position: "I have been long enough a soldier to have learned, that there is no disgrace in a *well meant* & *well conducted* enterprise, even if it should fail of its object," and, even more telling, "while I wear [an officer's] sword & the livery of my country I will not disgrace them by owning myself inferior to any person."[8]

As for relations with his fellow officers, his superiors had recognized his abilities with a promotion. Now, at Legionville, he was beginning to make friends among the younger officers brought in by the expansion of the army. One such congenial spirit was Solomon Van Rensselaer (friends called him "Van"), a cavalry lieutenant of Harrison's own age, the cheerful, reckless son of a rich and powerful Hudson Valley family. He and Harrison had, Harrison recalled in old age, "dispositions and tastes which induced us to seek the same employments, the same amusements and the same fellowships." Also among the junior officers of the Second Regiment were some men, "many of them graduates of the New England College's & several of talents of a superior order," as he remembered years later, who shared Harrison's fondness for reading and talking about books.[9]

One revealing indicator of Harrison's satisfaction with army life is his attitude toward dueling. Duels became a large part of his experience after the army moved to Legionville. They were a sort of military recreation. Isolated in the forest, the young officers of the Legion had little to do in their spare time except to compete among themselves for status, following the murderous rules of the code duello. There was constant prickly talk about honor; some officers, like Daniel of St. Thomas Jenifer, a new lieutenant from Maryland, managed to be involved in a shooting affray or some similar scrape almost every week. Harrison's surprise is still evident in his comment, made late in life, that there "were more duels in the Northwestern army between 1791 and 1795 than ever took place in the same length of time and among so small a body of men."[10]

There is no way to confirm or deny Harrison's statement, but it rings true. The doubling in size of the Legion had brought together a host of junior officers from all parts of the Union, many of them inexperienced and some of them unsure about their social status, but all of them determined, as Harrison was, to maintain their personal honor. For some, this was literally a matter of life or death. Because of these insecurities, aggravated by differences in regional manners, quarrels constantly arose. Personal papers and recollections of army officers in the West between 1791 and 1794 yield records of about a dozen duels, but surely there were more. They were unofficial affairs, not noted in Legion records. Wayne condoned them, even though they were forbidden by the Articles of War, because they saved him the bother of having to adjudicate quarrels between officers, and because he, like the younger officers, considered them tests of bravery and character. Their causes varied; most often they stemmed from a deliberate insult from one officer to another over some fairly trivial cause. Lieutenant Jenifer began one quarrel by declaring that a fellow officer was no gentleman; Captain William Eaton began another by leading his column the wrong way at maneuvers and then taking offense at the rebuke of Captain Edward Butler. Then, in all cases, came the hurried, agitated conferences with friends, the bearing of written challenges, and the efforts of third parties to conciliate the principals before blood was spilled. Sometimes they were successful; often, however, hot blood prevailed, and the parties met outside camp in the morning. Not all duels ended fatally. Sometimes one of the combatants was wounded; sometimes honor was satisfied at some point short of bloodshed. But the duels that were remembered were the ones that ended in death or that seemed to reflect credit on the character of one of the parties.[11]

Harrison, at the end of his long life, recalled that he turned against duelling in his early twenties—"fortunately," he added, "before I was engaged in a duel, either as principal or as second, which terminated fatally to any one." In other words, by implication, he had taken part in some nonfatal duels. In so doing, he went against the consensus of educated opinion in the country, including those of a few of his new Yankee friends. Joseph Strong of Connecticut, for example, a surgeon's mate fresh from treating a lieutenant seriously wounded in a duel, wrote a brother officer 14 May 1793, "Duelling is but a miserable recourse for the security of wounded honor. It makes wounds but does not heal them." But Harrison, it seems, despite his earlier conversion, was wrapped up for the moment in his military role and playing it to the fullest, including the casual approach of many officers to violence and manslaughter. His attitude was another example of the naïve, reckless enthusiasm that sometimes added an alarming edge to his undeniable charm.[12]

Harrison was not at Legionville all winter, and in fact, some of the particular duels mentioned above took place after he had left the camp. In midwinter he left to visit the East. The fact is remarkable in itself; General Wayne, eager to get his men trained so that he could engage the enemy at the first possible moment, was annoyed all winter by the shortage of officers, particularly subalterns. He turned down several requests for leave, and his gout and general ill health made him very testy on the subject. Harrison must have had a very good reason for his absence. In fact, he had two: his mother had died at Berkeley late in 1792, and Ben and Carter now wanted to settle the estate once and for all, so his signature was needed on various deeds. Moreover, General Wilkinson's wife planned to return west in the spring, and wanted Harrison to escort her on the return trip as he had escorted her east the year before. There was evidently a degree of intimacy by this time between Harrison and the Wilkinsons; by detaching him to serve as an escort, Wayne was doing a favor for his second-in-command. Wayne may also have felt that the young Virginian could be more easily spared from line command than an older officer because he was less forceful than an older man.[13]

To get from Pittsburgh to Richmond in midwinter, Harrison would not have needed to go to Philadelphia. He could simply have bought a horse at Pittsburgh and ridden it through the snowy defiles of western Virginia, now West Virginia, down narrow, winding roads that were safe from Indians and fairly well traveled. The journey, as one can reconstruct it from travelers' accounts, was arduous but not dangerous. He would have worn his civilian clothes and, like most male American travelers, carried only one spare shirt, changing into the clean one every four or five days and having his dirty shirt washed at one of the little log taverns where he stopped along the way. His fare was whatever he could pick up along the road, hominy and milk or fried pork for breakfast, rye mush and milk, cold corned beef and apple pie, cider, venison, or whatever his nightly hosts had, for supper. Every few days he would have shaved his beard, which was now darker and more noticeable. Except for these brief halts, however, and perhaps a day's delay if his mount picked up a stone or went lame, he started early and rode all day. His route lay down the Monongahela, across Laurel Hill, through the rugged mountains and desolate glades of western Maryland, across the fords of the icy Potomac, on to Winchester, over the Blue Ridge at Chester's Gap, until, at last, he reached central Virginia. The journey probably took him almost three weeks, longer perhaps if he ran into snow or sleet. One winter day he rode into Richmond again.[14]

Away from the military bureaucracy, Harrison's movements, not so well recorded, become more difficult to follow, but several legal documents leave no doubt about where he was and what he was doing for a couple of weeks in late February and early March: he was staying at Berkeley, near Charles City Court House where the deeds were recorded, settling the Harrison landholdings with his brothers. Ben, who had not yet dissolved his business in Richmond, stayed at Berkeley for the occasion, while Carter, who lived across James River, rode back and forth as needed. The mansion must have seemed curiously empty to Billy, lacking the animating presence of his parents. Only the house slaves, many of whom had known him since childhood, were left, and perhaps the pets his father had had during his last years—a small spaniel and a very large cat to whom Colonel Harrison had liked to teach tricks.

Lieutenant Harrison had decided to cut his ties with Virginia. On 23 February he deeded Carter his small Brown's Quarter property in Charles City County for 25 pounds Virginia money. He and Carter seem to have hit it off well; a year and a half later he would write his brother a long, bantering letter from the Northwest, and he may have borrowed a bit of cash from Carter for his further travels in the East. His relations with Ben were perhaps a different story. The eldest Harrison brother, somewhat high-strung at the best of times, was taking on the most momentous commitment of his life: he planned to use his own money to pay off all his father's debts and to reconstitute Berkeley into a showplace. He had not remarried; his whole household consisted of himself and little Ben, now six. He probably had little time for his talkative, intense younger brother. Nevertheless, they managed to agree on the estate. On 5 March Billy agreed to trade Ben his remaining land in Virginia for some land in Kentucky and five additional annual payments; on 9 March, he put his signature, "Wm Henry Harrison," in spiky, slanted letters, to a deed selling his portion of Berkeley for three thousand pounds.[15]

In addition to winding up family business, Harrison used the opportunity to revisit old friends in Virginia, perhaps Charley Byrd or Robert

Carter. He called on Doctor Leiper in Richmond and on his favorite sister, Lucy, Captain Singleton's wife. He got to know some of Ben's circle, to whom he seemed a "promising young Gentleman" who was "turning his views into the new Country." Quite possibly, he had brought his uniform with him and wore it on strategic occasions as a sort of living advertisement for the Legion. Certainly his presence made an impression on some young men in his family. Shortly after his visit, his first cousin Charles Harrison, son of his father's brother Charles, the military man of the family, joined the Legion as an ensign. Billy Daingerfield, who was perhaps still in Richmond with Dr. Leiper, was so strongly impressed by Harrison's success that he promised to obtain a commission forthwith and to join Harrison later that spring in Philadelphia.[16]

Harrison's rank as an officer and his experience of the West gave him adult status among his brother's friends. They listened with interest as he told them about the Indian campaign and the growth of white settlement. He was surprised to learn that not everyone in the East shared his high opinion of Wayne, that some well-informed men considered him "a fool, a bankrupt, & a Coxcomb" who should never have been given command. Some of Ben's friends, like Colonel Edward Carrington, owned land in the West that they wanted him to look at with a view to buying. Many had ideas of trying their own luck in Kentucky and wanted to learn as much as they could about it.

On 10 March, after concluding his final land deal with Ben, Lieutenant Harrison made ready to leave Virginia. William Wiseham gave him a note to collect for money he was owed by an officer in the West. Colonel Carrington may have thought that he was headed straight back to the Legion, for he gave him a letter to take to Winthrop Sargent. But Harrison was bound for Philadelphia first, to await Mrs. Wilkinson's readiness to leave. Doubtless he also wanted to bank his money and discuss investments with Robert Morris. He did not mind the extra miles; like most Virginia boys, Harrison enjoyed being in the saddle. Daingerfield, whose family home was near Fredericksburg, may have accompanied him on the road toward Philadelphia.[17]

Only one document provides direct evidence of Harrison's stay in the capital, but it is an illuminating one. On 21 July, Tench Coxe, a Philadelphia businessman who was an intimate of President Washington and a friend of Robert Morris, wrote to Ben Harrison in Virginia: "Your brother (of our Army) spent a day with me just before he left Philada. It was not till the week of his Departure that I knew he was your brother or I should have paid him earlier & more particular attention." Coxe's letter illustrates the patterns of eighteenth-century politeness: one cemented relationships with friends and business associates by paying "particular attention" to members of their family who were in one's city, and there is in Coxe's letter a hint of a rebuke to Ben for not letting him know that his brother was in Philadelphia. The omission may have been accidental—Ben may have been too busy with his move from Richmond to Berkeley—or it may have been quite intentional—Ben may have been still annoyed with Billy and not troubled himself to smooth his path socially. In either case, it highlights Billy's estrangement from his Virginia family. There is another implication in Coxe's letter: he had seen Harrison several times before he learned who he was, which suggests that Harrison was staying with the Morrises or at least visiting their house frequently. Affable and moneyed, he should have been a welcome guest.[18]

This fact, in turn, connects to the other main feature of Harrison's Philadelphia visit, known indirectly through his letter to Carter in November of the next year: he fell in love there. His inamorata was the daughter of rich parents in Philadelphia (as he wrote in the letter, they "must consider me their equal in every thing but fortune"); he referred to her only as Miss M. Several earlier biographers, from Freeman Cleaves to Robert Gunderson, have identified her as Robert and Mary Morris's oldest daughter, Hetty, only a year or two younger than Harrison, and the conjecture is plausible. Hetty Morris was quiet and attractive; in 1791, when Harrison first met her at the Morrises', her mother described her in a letter: "The last winter Hetty Commenced all the prerogatives of a young lady and took her place as such in society. Her extreem [*sic*] reserve in company she still possesses to such a degree as I often lament it as injurious to her appearance as well as that it may give an unfavorable opinion of her understanding. In her Person she is very Considerable improved and much hansomer [*sic*] than I expected she would be."[19]

By the midnineties Hetty was very attractive indeed, if Gilbert Stuart's portrait of her and her sister Maria is at all accurate. To Harrison, of course, she was a paragon: one could travel through the civilized world, he told Carter, without finding a lady "equal in charms and accomplishments," or even "with one half—nay—one third her charms." But Harrison did not mention whether Miss M herself returned his feelings, and the whole tenor of his letter to Carter suggests that the M family found his attentions unwelcome.[20]

In May, just after Harrison left Philadelphia, a rival appeared on the scene, though perhaps he was unaware of it at the time—a tall, raw-boned, talented Virginia businessman named James Marshall, brother of the Richmond lawyer John Marshall, nine years his senior. Marshall was returning from London on business; he won Hetty Morris's heart, sailed back to London in January 1794, and in 1795 crossed the Atlantic again to marry her. They would have a long and happy life together. Miss M's lack of interest in Harrison, therefore, had nothing to do with his Virginia background. Rather, this episode seems to be yet another case where Harrison's immature enthusiasm and disregard for protocol worked against him. Perhaps he simply refused to admit that his affections were not returned.[21]

Meanwhile, Harrison's main business in Philadelphia was to wait upon Mrs. Wilkinson, who planned to leave for the West with her small son Joseph around 1 May, leaving her older boys behind in Philadelphia to attend school. (Perhaps she was intending to use Mrs. O'Hara's coach, which she had borrowed the year before, for her return journey; the sources are silent.) Around the time fixed for departure, Harrison had a visit from Billy Daingerfield, who had recently arrived in the capital with General Thomas Posey, a tall, "powerfully built," brown-haired Revolutionary veteran and old friend of the Daingerfield family from the same part of Virginia, whom the president had just appointed to a command post in the Western army. Posey had named Daingerfield a member of his "official family," along with his son John, a newly minted cornet in the cavalry. They had stopped by the War Department to register their commissions and were now preparing to head west as well. It would have been only natural for Harrison to offer to share his knowledge of the road west, which was unfamiliar to all three of the new men. Thus, it seems, the entire party left together the first week in May. If Harrison was sad to leave his beloved behind, the prospect of a trip across the mountains with congenial companions may have done a little to ease his heartache.[22]

CHAPTER TWELVE

The March into the Woods

When the Poseys, the Wilkinson party, and their escorts rolled into Pittsburgh late in May, they found that the Legion was no longer there. It had made the long-delayed move to Fort Washington on 30 April 1793. Harrison learned that a particular officer he was looking for, Captain Samuel Tinsley, who owed William Wiseham some money, had not gone with it, but had instead been assigned to Fort Franklin in northwestern Pennsylvania. George Balfour, a little Scottish army doctor from Norfolk who was still in Pittsburgh but soon heading for Fort Franklin, promised to collect the money; so Harrison entrusted the note to him. The transaction shows how Virginians in the Legion hung together and did business together. (It also shows the hazards of third- and fourth-party business dealings; Tinsley paid Balfour the money, but Balfour never conveyed it to Harrison, whose comment next year, when he found out, was a bit of military posturing: "I shall have to be content with flogging the [little] doctor when I meet him.") While Harrison was working out this matter with Balfour, Major Craig was having a Kentucky boat especially fitted up for Mrs. Wilkinson's accommodation, and General Posey was fretting about a late shipment of stores. On 28 May, with the boat ready, General Posey and son, General Wilkinson's wife and son, Lieutenant Harrison, and one more officer boarded and set out down the river, which was fairly high. Ensign Daingerfield stayed behind to await Posey's stores.[1]

Only a day or two into their voyage, perhaps at Wheeling, where they stopped to pick up their horses, which had been ridden overland and would be conveyed in a separate flatboat with their baggage, the travelers received a pleasant surprise: General Wilkinson himself greeted them! Impatient to see his Ann, he had come upriver with a small contingent of men. It was a day of cordial reunions, reuniting Wilkinson not only with his family but also with Harrison and with Posey, who had served alongside Wilkinson in the Revolution. Now that the theatrical general was in charge, the rest of the trip took on a festive air. The day they reached Cincinnati, 7 June, he sent a barge ahead to herald their arrival to Wayne.[2]

On the way, Wilkinson brought General Posey and the other officers up to date on affairs in the Northwest Territory. Indian attacks seemed as frequent as ever, especially in the interior, with a soldier wounded at Fort Jefferson and a couple of incidents near Fort Hamilton. Wilkinson had been trying to improve the roads to the interior forts, clearly the first step to mounting a campaign.[3]

Back in Cincinnati, Harrison saw a familiar panorama with some new features. There was the ramshackle village and the fort on its bluff, but on the level ground west of the village, once covered by beech and poplar trees, he saw rows and rows, and still more rows, of white army tents. "Hobson's Choice," Wayne had wryly called the new camp, because it was the only level site anywhere near the river large enough to accommodate the Legion; the fort and the ground around it were both too small. The location was not ideal: there was swampy ground and standing water near the river, and pieces of beef carcasses and guts from the camp abattoir eddied around in a cove near the shore. But the camp itself was not bad. The tents were laid out in neat lines under tall beeches which Wayne had ordered left standing to provide shade, and the same air of busy routine as at Pittsburgh or Legionville pervaded the place. There was none of the tension, and little of the disarray, of real war. The government, as Harrison knew, had peace commissioners treating with the Indians near Lake Erie; they had left Philadelphia while he was there, late in April. The talks were mostly for show—the government expected little from them—but the "God of War," Secretary Knox, had strictly forbidden offensive operations while they were under way.[4]

Very shortly after landing, Wilkinson received Wayne's permission to relocate, with his family, to Fort Hamilton, where he had built a "handsome house" in the log-cabin style of the frontier. It was a shrewd move on the part of the general, who felt cramped by the presence of a superior. Already rumors were floating around the Western army of friction between the two commanders. One possible source of the friction was Harrison's future assignment. Wilkinson doubtless expected to have the young lieutenant at Fort Hamilton as part of his official family, but that did not happen. Instead, Harrison was given no responsibility for almost a month; then, on 9 July, he was assigned to take over a detachment previously commanded by Ensign John Michael, in Captain Suydam's company. The assignment proved a short one, possibly because he ran into difficulties commanding the men. On 28 July, a court-martial convicted Private Patrick Bigley of using "insolent language" to him. Two weeks later, after another incident of some sort, Harrison was taken out of line command entirely and named to General Wayne's staff as his second aide-de-camp, a much superior position. He was now a member of Wayne's "family," with the pay of a major of the line.[5]

Harrison's first step upon being named aide was to go into Cincinnati and spend most of his remaining money on two of the finest horses he could find, beauties worth one hundred fifty or two hundred dollars apiece. Nothing but the fastest and strongest, he thought, would do for an aide; he needed two because he would be in the saddle regularly and could not afford to be inconvenienced by an injury to one. Very gratifying to a Virginian, he would be riding most of the time. Aides rode everywhere, carrying messages from the commander. When not riding, they transcribed orders or countersigned receipts in the general's name. Harrison would sleep at the headquarters tent and take his meals with the general. He would be the first to know whatever of consequence was happening in camp.[6]

The next two months probably constituted one of the happiest times in Harrison's long life. He liked what he was doing and did it well. He rode all over camp, smartly military and pleasant, delivering messages from the commander and becoming acquainted with officers in all the other sublegions. Crossing the creek into the village, he was astonished at the number of new stores and taverns created by the Legion's presence and appalled at how high the prices of ordinary goods had soared—indeed, the rise almost nullified his recent pay raise. Business in Cincinnati was booming, and nearly every merchant had a drawer full of the three-dollar banknotes, "oblongs," used to pay off the troops. He busied himself with the vast amount of paperwork, orders, correspondence, and receipts that flowed through the general's office.[7]

He enjoyed seeing old friends like Winthrop Sargent (although Sargent left in August on a visit to the East) and renewing his acquaintance with younger and newer friends as well. These included "Van" Rensselaer, who returned to Cincinnati in August from a stint at Fort Hamilton; cousin Charles Harrison, fiery and swaggering, much more martial than he to all appearance; a number of young Virginian subalterns and some enlisted men who, he discovered, came from families near Berkeley; and two medical men from New Jersey: the witty, competent surgeon John Scott, and Joseph Phillips, a surgeon's mate who shared Harrison's taste for belles-lettres and medical chat. This circle of friends was enlarged when Daingerfield arrived from Pittsburgh in August.[8] Perhaps Harrison and his friends had suppers on occasion in Cincinnati taverns, where the young aide got as mellow as his limited tolerance for alcohol would permit. Possibly they finished up such evenings by adjourning to one of the log-cabin whorehouses in the village; Harrison, after all, was twenty, with a healthy sex drive. Considering his basic earnestness, however, it is equally likely that his get-togethers with friends consisted mainly of long, deep talks in someone's tent, over a bottle or two of wine, against a background of summer insects and frogs piping by the riverbank.[9]

Duels and honor remained a preoccupation of the officers. Early in July, Lieutenant Samuel Drake of the Second Sub-Legion received a "marked insult," of the kind designed to provoke a duel, from Captain Isaac Guion. When Drake issued no challenge, a number of his friends among the younger officers came to his tent to urge him not to jeopardize his standing among his peers by refusing to fight. Harrison was one of them. He remembered hearing with puzzlement Drake's reply, "that he cared not what opinion others might form of him, he was determined to pursue his own course," and leaving the conference with lessened respect for the lieutenant who would not put his life on the line.[10]

Harrison faced a somewhat similar situation of his own, which could have resulted in a challenge. He returned from the East to find that in his absence not only had Hastings Marks been promoted to lieutenant, which was to be expected, but also that the War Department had mistakenly listed Marks as senior to Harrison by date of promotion. The mistake, which would be difficult to rectify, could affect future promotions. Harrison kept quiet, but there was a new level of tension in his dealings with Marks.[11]

Perhaps the high point of the summer was a glorious day in August when Governor St. Clair, newly returned from the East, paid a formal visit of inspection to the Legion. General Wayne, with his retinue—Chief Aide Captain Henry DeButts; Dr. Richard Allison, surgeon to the Legion; and the other aides, including Harrison, all on horseback—escorted the governor around camp, giving special attention to the main curiosity of the area, the Indian earthworks. They rode up to the foot of the high conical mound, from which Wayne had had the topmost eight feet cut away so that a sentry box could be put there, and viewed the plain. They could see faint traces of earthworks, in an "almost endless" variety of figures, all over the ground. They ambled along leisurely beside the remains, under the hot August sun, discussing the possible origin and purpose of the figures. Harrison, enthralled, took it all in.[12]

Meanwhile, up near Lake Erie, the talks with the tribes were continuing. Nearer at hand, though, in the interior, were live Indians who remained hostile, though inactive. As long as the talks continued, Wayne was forbidden to open new roads in the interior or even to supply Fort Jefferson, and he chafed under the restriction. "The woods & roads," he wrote Knox, "are infested by savages—would to God that my hands were untied." Negotiations were bound to fail in the end, Wayne and the Legion reasoned; in the meantime, it seemed a pity to lose valuable weeks. There was time only for sham battles in which the riflemen (with blanks) impersonated attacking Indians, while Wayne urged the infantry against them with "stentorian profanity." Men did get killed, though not by Indians; one of Captain Moses Porter's artillerymen had his hand shot off in a sham battle in July and died of lockjaw. But months of brutal discipline and grueling practice had had their effect. The men Harrison had first seen in Pittsburgh the fall before were at last soldiers of some kind—still dirty, still reckless, but practiced now in what Wayne had called "the dreadful trade of death."[13]

The summer wore away. For the men there were extra rations of whiskey on holidays and periodic fracases in the village; for the officers, occasional passes to Lexington, Kentucky, where they could taste real society and decent female companionship. Then, on 11 September, the tempo changed. A small party made up of an army scout, a government interpreter, and a Seneca Indian arrived at headquarters from Lake Erie with a letter from the peace commissioners. Negotiations had failed, it said, three weeks before. The Indians had insisted on the Ohio River boundary, which the government could not concede.[14]

This news was definite enough. All the same, Wayne had to wait for express authorization from Knox before proceeding against the Indians. That authorization came five days later and was as clear an order as he could have asked for. Peaceful means had failed, the secretary repeated. War was imminent, and the government instructed Wayne and the Legion to "make those audacious savages feel our superiority in arms."[15]

For a few days Harrison and the other aides were busy writing and carrying urgent messages: orders to the various divisions to get their wagons and stores together; letters to Wilkinson and the other commanders of interior posts advising them of the imminent advance; a note to General Charles Scott in Kentucky, asking him to rendezvous at Hobson's Choice on 1 October, with all the mounted volunteers he could summon. That was still two weeks away, but it would require fully two weeks to prepare the Legion—at nearly three thousand strong the largest fighting force the West had ever seen—to move.[16]

Various special units were involved. Since St. Clair's trace was too old and narrow for the mass of troops, a corps would precede the main army to hack out a road through the wilderness beyond Fort Hamilton. Fanning out ahead of them and on both sides of the army was a band of experienced scouts led by William Wells, the man who had brought the message from Lake Erie, a red-haired, Indianized Kentuckian who had been captured as a boy and brought up among the Eel Indians. (He had married a Miami woman and was, in fact, son-in-law to Little Turtle, the Miami chief who had led the Indians at the battle of 4 November 1791. He had defected to the whites only within the past year.) Wayne, impressed by Wells's boldness and knowledge of Indian ways, had put him at the head of a remarkable group of spies, young men who were hardy, daring, and athletic even for frontiersmen.[17] Harrison, fascinated by him, watched his comings and goings with intense interest.

Indian allies also marched with the Legion. With Wells from Lake Erie had come Big Tree, a Seneca chief who had a blood feud with the Delaware and awaited a chance to kill a few Just before the appointed rendezvous, Lieutenant William Clark, the redheaded, capable Kentuckian whom Wayne had sent on a secret mission into Spanish territory, showed up with a Chickasaw chief and eight braves, allies by treaty of the American government, who would accompany the Legion. Wayne and the officers probably regarded them with the blend of aversion and amused contempt with which white men usually treated friendly Indians, but it was good politics to have them along. Harrison watched them with genuine interest, as he did Wells.[18]

As the time of departure approached, it was impossible not to be jittery. The omens for success were mixed. On the one hand, smallpox was beginning to abate among the troops; on the other, the most recent arrivals from the East had brought an equally devastating malady called the influenza, which had spread through the Legion both around Cincinnati and in the interior. By 1 October, only 380 Kentucky Volunteers had shown up, instead of the 800 or so Wayne had expected; by 5 October, Wayne estimated that the influenza had left him with only 2,600 effective soldiers in the Legion. The date of march kept being pushed back—the first, the fifth, the seventh. The trees were turning; it was already late in the year, weeks later than the time of year at which St. Clair had launched his fatal campaign in 1791, and in Cincinnati rumor held that the Indians were assembled a thousand strong on the site of St. Clair's Defeat. Arthur St. Clair himself, now in Cincinnati as governor only, not as general, was a constant presence as the Army made ready to leave, as unobtrusive as possible but nevertheless a reminder of the disaster that might lie ahead of them.[19]

The expedition finally marched on the morning of 7 October 1793, a foggy morning which, as usual in the Ohio Valley, presaged a fair, mild day. Harrison, mounted on one of his fine horses, rode with the rest of Wayne's staff up the steep trace out of Cincinnati. Following them came 50-odd companies of foot soldiers, cavalry, and artillery, more than 500 pack horses, 112 draft horses in teams of 4, 14 teams of 4 or 6 oxen, scores of creaking wagons, and scores of mounted, buckskin-clad volunteers—about 3,000 men in all, and probably a few women as well, although Wayne had successfully excluded most camp followers. All felt sure—some with bravado, some with dread—that they were on their way to a decisive encounter with the enemy.[20]

They marched ten miles that day, and the same number the next, a taxing assignment for an army the size of the Legion, whose soldiers had drilled incessantly but had not really had to march for more than a year. As one officer observed, the men had not "got properly in their geers [*sic*]"; by the end of the second day, many were faltering and footsore, worn out either by simple fatigue or by fatigue added to the aftereffects of influenza. They arrived at Fort Hamilton that second evening, where some of the garrison joined them, including General Wilkinson, himself weak from a bout with influenza; on the third day they forded the Miami and set off for Fort St. Clair. Thus far they had stuck fairly closely to St. Clair's route; now, beyond Fort Hamilton, they were cutting their own road through the thick woods and moved more slowly. The weather stayed clear and beautiful. The forests were variegated and golden.[21]

Routine on the march was simple but laborious, as Wayne insisted on the army's digging in every night. The Legion marched at dawn to the beat of the drums that, in different rhythms, governed all its movements—"ruff double" was the signal to march faster, "long march" to march slower, "retreat" to halt. It halted at two or three in the afternoon so that the quartermasters could go ahead to select a campsite. When they had chosen one and the troops came up, each company had to fell timber and build stout fortifications around its assigned position before its men could pitch their tents and cook their meals. The labor of making camp did not, of course, touch Lieutenant Harrison, who had no direct command; his duty was the more romantic one of posting from one end of the encampment to the other with orders from the commander. These were mainly routine, too, for the first few days; three days into the march, the expedition had not seen so much as a trace of the enemy.[22]

As the route of march ascended out of the rich Miami bottoms, Harrison found himself riding through higher, drier country than he had seen before, where the dominant fall colors were the dull crimson of dogwood, the warm brown of oak and buckeye, and the drab tones of withered prairie grass. On 14 October he had his first look at Fort Jefferson. Until now, the rude log fort had been the farthest outpost into Indian country; now the Legion was going deeper in, and some of the officers rode past it with a show of open disdain. Behind them, however, the line of march had been lengthening, as sick and weary men straggled behind their companies and wagons stuck fast or overturned in the marshy ground west of the Miami. At one point, the Legion was stretched out along five miles of its newly cut, deeply rutted road. Still farther back, at Fort Hamilton, most of the volunteers were still waiting to escort the contractors' supply wagons, which were only now beginning to cross the river.[23]

On the fifteenth, with the weather turning cloudy and chilly, the Legion halted only six miles beyond Fort Jefferson at the edge of a level, open oak forest. A spacious prairie stretched to the south. The head of the army had outpaced its supplies; it would have to wait there until the provision wagons could struggle up. The wait was not wholly unanticipated; Wayne had considered the spot as a site for building a new fort, but now the commander was impatient and hoped to get farther north before winter weather put an end to his campaign. Nevertheless, for the time being the Legion would have to pitch its tents, build its fortifications, and dig in on that ground.[24]

Thus situated, in the open without supplies, the head of the army was a marvelous bait to attract any large force of Indians in that part of the territory. Few in camp spoke openly of the possibility, but everyone was aware of their vulnerability. On the thirteenth, while Colonel Hamtramck was drilling his troops, some of his maneuvers had been misconstrued by other units as a flank attack. The men had sprung to their weapons, muttering "Let them come," or "We're ready for them," before the false alarm was discovered. How ready they were could be revealed only by the event; they were, at any rate, vigilant and taut.[25]

On the frosty morning of 16 October, the question whether there were Indians in the vicinity was settled definitely, when Cornet William Blue of the cavalry went out with a force of about twenty to graze the horses, and saw something moving in the grass. He thought at first that it was wild turkeys; it proved to be two Indian warriors. Blue ordered a charge, but only three or four men obeyed. Two were instantly shot down, the rest fled, and the Indians got away. Tensely the men of the army hunkered down and waited to see what would happen next. The following day an express message delivered the news that the supply wagons had been attacked on the new road near Fort St. Clair. Lieutenant Edward Lowry, a young Jerseyman who was with the escort, and a Mr. Boyd, a civilian working with the contractors, had been killed, and sixty or seventy horses had been stolen ("which would be a great obstacle to the army's moving any farther," as one officer quickly perceived). Colonel Adair and the Kentucky Volunteers had given chase, with no reported success as yet.[26]

In the circumstances, Wayne had no choice but to reinforce the escort and wait for the provisions and volunteers to arrive. Harrison, dining with the staff in the general's tent, could see the agonies of indecision through which Wayne, irritable, morose, increasingly bothered by headaches, was passing. He had hoped to move the army at least ten miles forward, to a place called Still Water on the upper waters of the Wabash, but that now seemed impossible until the supplies came up. The road was hardly passable. Wilkinson, second in command, was sick and had gone into Fort Jefferson to recuperate. And there was appalling news from the East. Philadelphia had been invaded in September by yellow fever, the mortality was staggering, and the government, including the president and secretary of war, had packed up and left town. There was no one with whom Wayne could communicate. All he could do was remain watchful and see whether his adversaries, Little Turtle or the British in Canada—or whoever was controlling Indian movements—would take the initiative.[27]

Nothing happened. Adair and his horsemen did not catch up with the band that had ambushed the supply train. Several days later, Wayne learned that White's Station, near Cincinnati, had been attacked on the nineteenth by Indians who had killed a man and two young children—perhaps the same group Adair was pursuing. Meanwhile, the supply wagons and the Kentuckians arrived, and Hamtramck was sent back with two hundred men to escort a second train. There were a few instances of firing from the woods, but no concerted action of any kind by the enemy. The weather turned colder and rawer, and wet snow fell. Wayne consulted with the senior officers of the volunteers and the Legion, but made no decision.[28]

Finally, on 2 November, he made up his mind. The Legion would go into winter quarters at the spot it was occupying. The campaign of 1793 had come to an anticlimactic end.[29]

CHAPTER THIRTEEN

Nerves

As soon as Wayne decided to "hut" the Legion (halt and erect quarters) where it was for the winter, the Kentucky Volunteers drew their provisions and galloped away, several hundred in one night, for a quick foray westward through the Northwest Territory before they returned home. The Legion remained, immobile, stalled deep in the forests of the Miami country. "After laying on this ground twenty days, without doing a single thing which could benefit the United States," as one disgruntled major put it, the entire army (except for the cavalry, who would spend the winter in Kentucky where their horses grazed) faced a hard, cheerless season separated from civilized society by a hundred miles of wilderness, both officers and men feeling, as one of them put it, like "poor devil[s] banished to another planet." They had little to fear from the Indians, who rarely made war during the winter and almost never attacked a fortified position, but their enforced sojourn was sure to be uncomfortable and dull. Within a day or so, the men were in the woods felling timber for the new post, which Wayne was calling Fort Greenville after his Revolutionary comrade Nathaniel Greene.[1]

Work on the fort went briskly. By 15 November 1793, they had raised the exterior palisade, twenty feet high and more than a mile in circumference, with two great gates facing north and south. The soldiers' huts were also up—six-man log cabins ranged along the inside of the stockade. The place was huge, dwarfing the nearby Fort Jefferson. In fact, it was the largest military post ever built in the territory, more like a town than a frontier station. A complex of log cabins occupied its center, arranged in neat rows with lanes between—here a house for Wayne, there a "laboratory" for making gunpowder, a bakehouse, a guardhouse, or quarters for the staff, all floored, chinked, and plastered on the inside between the logs.[2]

By early December, the officers' huts, Wayne's house, and the quartermaster's buildings in the center of the square were finished, plus nine blockhouses on the exterior. Some officers' wives—Mrs. Captain Ford, Mrs. Captain Butler, and Colonel Strong's daughter Rebecca, who was about to marry Dr. Allison—were on their way to visit their men. As for Lieutenant Harrison, he spent his days ensconced at his desk in the headquarters cabin writing dozens of orders, sleeping at night between clammy sheets in a freshly made log cabin, dining on venison or bear, savory pheasant or even roast raccoon when scouting parties brought them in (otherwise on bread and boiled salt beef), and trekking through freezing woods out to the camp latrine—in short, experiencing all the delights of a winter on the frontier. The men were back at the daily grind of bayonet practice and sham battles, the officers at the constant round of drinking, gambling, blustering, and complaining about the service. It was very much like Legionville the year before.[3]

But there was a difference. Around the fort, and perhaps especially in the officers' quarters, the atmosphere was oddly tense. Part of it was pent-up nerves from the abortive campaign, aggravated, for both officers and men, by the prospect of having to pass a winter in isolation, without even the taverns and brothels of Cincinnati to relieve the pressures of army life. However, the atmosphere also reflected a general unease about the commander, General Wayne, a disquiet that had been perceptible even before the Legion had marched out of Fort Washington. On 6 October 1793, the day before the campaign had begun, John Scott wrote to a friend, "In my department, having the different complaints & disorders to manage & cure, I meet with one that is pretty general & which will yield to no remedies which I can apply, Viz—*general discontent*. I believe the cause may be traced to the *head* of our Chief."[4]

Toward the end of the campaign, Wayne had not been well. Headaches had plagued him as his advance against the Indians ground to a standstill, and now, as winter set in, his gout returned. More galling than both, however, was his frustration at having failed to come to grips with the enemy that fall. Lieutenant Harrison and the other aides could see this frustration coming out in many ways: Wayne's aggressively grandiose plans for the fort; his fuming at the sudden departure of the Kentuckians; his cursing of the army suppliers, whose "evasion & equivocation" had slowed the Legion's march; his restless prowling around the post (when his gout permitted) in the earliest watches of the morning to check on the vigilance of the guard. In his letters, Wayne was more stiff and haughty than ever; in person, even with senior officers, he was irritable and rude. His moods came and went; after dealing with him for a year Robert Elliott, one of the chief contractors, described him as a man who "som times about the full of the Moon gits out of all bounds." Harrison, Captain DeButts, Dr. Allison, and the rest of the staff escaped many of the general's moods, as Wayne tended to be indulgent with his aides—"childishly familiar," some critics among the officers said. But the rest of the Legion did not escape them, for the commander had become obsessed with the need to move on against the Indians as soon as possible and grimly suspicious of anyone he perceived to be in his way.[5]

This suspicion took many forms. There was, for instance, the supply problem. Harrison had no direct responsibility for the procurement of provisions; that was the province of Quartermaster General O'Hara, whose men checked in the wagons that lumbered up from Cincinnati laden with salt, candles, vinegar, soap, flour, and other basic necessities for the army, and inspected the droves of cattle that arrived to be butchered for the use of the Legion. Wayne occasionally issued permits to other merchants from Cincinnati or Columbia for special stores—coffee, brown sugar, and even whiskey—the sale of which he could control tightly in this remote place. But his ire was directed at the official contractors, Robert Elliott and Eli Williams.

In essence, Wayne wanted to be able to move against the Indians at will, without having to wait for supplies as he had done in October. Consequently, he wanted the official contractors to send 271,000 extra rations for the men, to be stored at Fort Greenville, so that he and the Legion could set out in early spring, or even in winter if need be. Elliott and Williams protested violently. Fort Greenville was too distant, the roads too bad, and the journey too dangerous to bring up that many supplies. Wilkinson, who had made the long trip to Cincinnati in mid-November to bring up a supply train in person, corroborated the terrible state of the road. That the journey was dangerous was beyond doubt. Elliott's and Williams's drovers usually traveled under armed guard; the other merchants, who had no escort, often lost horses and provisions to Indians and seem to have reckoned it a normal business expense. The contractors thus had good reason to demur, but Wayne was outraged at their protests. His correspondence with them, much of which went over Harrison's desk, became increasingly hostile as the winter advanced.[6]

Wayne's moods were also undermining his relations with his officers. Many of them were quite as stiff and touchy as he, and very nearly as ill-tempered after the stresses of the campaign. Some had been offended by his brusqueness on the march. ("There is no calculating on any thing but insult, and oppression," Major Thomas Cushing had written a friend on 2 November. "I am sick of every thing, and almost every body around me.") When Wayne announced that the Legion would encamp for the winter, several officers, anxious to escape the prospect of "dull muddy winter quarters," immediately put in for four-month leaves to return east for the winter. To Wayne, determined to launch an early advance against the Indians, these applications bordered on treason; he turned some down and refused to act on others at all. His actions led to angry confrontations in headquarters. Some of the officers denied leave resigned from the Legion on the spot; Wayne, infuriated, refused them permission to leave the fort. A young lieutenant from Maryland, describing this situation in mid-November, concluded, "I wish it may not end seriously for somebody."[7]

By December, open hostility had developed between the general and a fairly large group of his officers. Several had resigned or been cashiered, and they, together with Wayne's opponents who were still in the Legion, had begun to write letters to newspapers and friends back in the East, detailing what was going on. Wayne, they claimed, was running the Legion like a despot; in fact, sick and frustrated as he was, he was doing just that. When Major Cushing and Captain Isaac Guion, in December, complained that Captain Edward Butler, a protégé of Wayne's, was shirking his duties as adjutant general, Wayne threatened Guion with court-martial and actually started proceedings against Cushing; he did nothing about Butler. Cushing remained in his quarters under arrest over Christmas; it was only the intervention of a senior officer, Colonel Hamtramck, that got him released after the first of the year. Even then, despite Hamtramck's expostulations, the general did nothing about Butler.[8]

To Harrison, the situation may well have recalled Rollin's accounts of the petty Greek tyrants who followed Alexander, but it made determining his own course difficult. (As one of Wayne's favorite aides, he knew all the parties involved.) No doubt he had to employ all his discretion and good temper to avoid offending someone. As the army began polarizing into Wayne's partisans and Wayne's enemies, Harrison, with uncharacteristic maturity, kept his feelings, whatever they were, to himself. But it must have been difficult, particularly toward the end of the year, when General Wilkinson, whom he respected, began to be drawn into the conflict.

Wilkinson's involvement was no surprise. Since the preceding summer, when Wayne had arrived in the Ohio country to take over, Wilkinson had been suffering all the humiliations of a former boss reduced to second-in-command. He felt that his Western experience was ignored. Wayne rarely asked his advice and disregarded it when it was offered. He also kept Wilkinson in the dark about future plans. To avoid occasions for conflict with his chief, Wilkinson moved away from headquarters, first to Fort Hamilton, then to Fort Jefferson. He also tried to keep on cordial, familiar terms in his letters to Wayne, but observant officers soon perceived that Wilkinson lent an interested ear to their complaints about the commander. While he was very discreet himself, Wilkinson had no objection to hearing others discuss "Old Toney" in language sometimes mocking and sometimes bitterly critical. By December 1793, almost everyone in the Legion was aware of two distinct groups of officers, Wilkinson men and Wayne men.[9]

All this is well documented in letters from the period, but Wilkinson's involvement poses a special problem for a biographer of Harrison, because many historians, carried away by the scoundrelly reputation Wilkinson acquired among nineteenth-century writers, have attempted to portray him as an evil schemer out to thwart Wayne's plans and prevent the success of his Indian campaign, even to the extent of stirring up sedition among the officers and causing the Legion's supply problems. The problem for a biographer of Harrison is that, throughout his army career, Harrison liked and respected Wilkinson. There are only a few ways to explain this fact: Harrison was a tool of the Kentuckian, or he was an impossibly naïve young man who failed to perceive Wilkinson's scheming, or historians have exaggerated.[10]

The evidence supports the last alternative. No credible evidence connects Wilkinson with the Legion's supply problems during the winter. As for the officers critical of Wayne, notably Cushing, Guion, Hamtramck, and Campbell Smith, they were responding to genuine grievances; nothing suggests they were mere creatures of Wilkinson. One biographer charges

Wilkinson with encouraging the contractors to drag their feet in response to Wayne's repeated demands for supplies, but as explained above, he may have had good reason for doing so. Such evidence as there is suggests that the central conflict in the Legion over the winter of 1793–94 was not Wayne versus Wilkinson, but rather Wayne versus almost everyone. Wayne's latest biographer, Paul David Nelson, agrees at one point that Wayne's problems were partly self-induced; one page later, however, he argues that Wilkinson was "the source of most of Wayne's problems in the Legion." A few months later, Wilkinson did indeed see in Wayne's difficulties a possible opportunity for himself and became his bitter, implacable enemy—but that was still to come.[11]

Just before Christmas, Wilkinson and his wife invited Wayne and his staff to dinner at Fort Jefferson on Christmas Day, promising, in Wilkinson's words, "a welcome from the Heart, a warm fire, and a big-bellied bottle of the veritable Lachryma Christi." With flowery compliments to Mrs. Wilkinson, Wayne declined, suggesting a postponement to 12 January. He had plans—which, characteristically, he had not shared with Wilkinson—to march at nine the next morning on a twenty-mile journey to the site of St. Clair's Defeat. Eight companies of infantry and one of artillery would accompany him. "I should be glad of your company," he added casually. Wilkinson declined, citing his wife's health.[12]

Lieutenant Harrison, accordingly, spent Christmas Eve not by a warm fire at Fort Jefferson but picking up skulls on the desolate forest battlefield, where the troops dug up more than six hundred in the process of breaking ground for a new fort—to be christened, hopefully, Fort Recovery. Harrison saw that the men received their extra ration of whiskey for the holiday, but cheer was unlikely to be his prominent emotion. He was probably there when Captain Butler identified the skeleton of his slain brother, General Richard Butler, by a cracked thighbone and retrieved it, and when the men dug out of a creek bed two of the cannon Wilkinson had failed to find on his earlier trek there. When the new fort was nearly finished, Wayne and most of the troops returned to Fort Greenville, leaving Fort Recovery under the command of Captain Alexander Gibson. The general issued public thanks to the officers who had accompanied him, singling out Harrison and a few others for their "voluntary aid and services" on the march.[13]

Three days after their return, Wayne and his staff kept their deferred date with the Wilkinsons, and the dinner was a splendid one. After a "grand review" in the morning, at which many of the troops appeared in new uniforms, Wayne and his entourage rode to Fort Jefferson and feasted on "roast venison, roast beef boiled, and roast mutton boiled and roast veal boiled and roast turkey and fowls; raccoons, possums, bear meat, pies made of chickens, mince, apples, tarts, &c., &c. Sweetmeats of every kind, preserves and jellies, floating island and ice cream; plum pudding and plum cake, vegetables of every kind, a plenty of the best wine, at evening we had tea and coffee in high style." The feast combined Eastern and frontier hospitality in the Wilkinsons' best manner, assisted no doubt by the black servants General Wilkinson always had in attendance.[14]

Such holiday cheer did not last, however. Around this time, Indians began to reappear near Fort Greenville, adding to the tensions within the Legion. Wayne was sure that it was his building of Fort Recovery that had stirred them into action, and he may have been right. He had been gathering intelligence on them all winter. During November and December, Wells and his scouts had ranged into the wilderness as far as the Great Lakes with instructions to spy on enemy towns and, when possible, to take captives. Harrison may have been involved in the planning for these excursions; years later, he recalled a remark by Wells and quoted it in his *Discourse on the Aborigines*. Four days after Fort Recovery had been completed, Wayne sent Captain Joseph Collins, with a small detachment, to reconnoiter the next river to the north. Just after New Year's Day, the party ran into an Indian encampment and exchanged fire. Collins lost three men, the Indians five or more.[15]

A few days later, three Indians and a white man appeared outside the north gate of Fort Greenville under a flag of truce and requested a parley with the commander. They were Delaware, it turned out, led by an English-speaking chief named George White Eyes, who was, curiously enough, a Princeton graduate; the white man was a trader named Wilson. Their immediate errand was to demand the return of three Delaware women kidnaped by Collins's soldiers, but they also brought a string of white wampum with messages from Little Turtle and from Blue Jacket of the Shawnee; both chiefs were interested in discussing peace. Wayne gave the envoys an artillery salute and a feast (at which he told them, one officer heard, that the Legion "could go any where into their Country & was determined to do it at all events, if they continued refractory"); he returned the women; and he agreed to talk peace if the Indians would return all white prisoners they were holding to Fort Recovery by 14 February, promising, in return, to make no hostile movement before that date. After four days of talks, the Indians agreed, leaving a young boy as a hostage, and disappeared back into the forest.[16]

Harrison signed the order issuing whiskey to the Indians as they left. At the talks, he must have observed them with keen attention as heirs to a vanished civilization, living pages out of Rollin whose doings were full of ancient, almost heroic interest. They wore the ordinary dress of most Eastern Indians—buckskin leggings ornamented with porcupine quills, moccasins (many white writers spelled the word "moxens") of the same material, calico or linen shirts with a blanket thrown around the shoulders—without the face and body painting, the spangles, and the silver brooches that they would have added for a formal treaty discussion. Their heads, shaven except for braided tufts of glossy black hair on the top, their expressionless faces, "yellow" or "copper coloured," as the officers described them, and the unmusical speech they used among themselves stamped them as foreign, emissaries of a fascinating and alien culture.[17]

Harrison's interest was not shared by more experienced officers, however, who cared mainly about the outcome of the talks: peace or war. Wayne doubted the Indians' sincerity and suspected they had come mainly to spy out the Legion's defenses; his opponents within the Legion, however, anxious above all to get away from Fort Greenville, hoped the talks represented a real opening that would spike the general's plans for an early campaign in the spring.[18]

One man found the talks utterly dismaying. The Seneca chief Big Tree had arrived at headquarters 1 January with Rosencrantz, the interpreter, to plead his case with Wayne. He had vowed to kill three of the enemy the previous fall, but had managed to slay only one before the end of the campaign. To fulfill his vow, he proposed to take the Chickasaw braves and a few other friendly Indians on a raid of some enemy town. Wayne vetoed the plan. Though no friend to the Northwest Indians, he wanted to regulate any action taken against them. He had no use for Indians' vendettas, and probably, like most white Americans, found savage notions of warfare repellent. He turned Big Tree down, apparently just before the Delaware emissaries arrived.

The Seneca was composed, in the main, as he listened to Wayne confer with the Delaware, but at one point he did break into a passionate tirade against them before retiring to the quarters he shared with an officer. Of all the inmates of the lonesome fort, Big Tree must have felt most lonely, isolated among a crowd of people who neither spoke his language nor appreciated his needs, and who were intent on their own struggles for power, honor, and status. A few days later he complained to his roommate of the heaviness he felt; shortly afterward, on 25 January, they found him on his bloody cot, stabbed in the heart, dead by his own hand.[19]

CHAPTER FOURTEEN

Toward a Showdown

For most of the occupants of Fort Greenville—two thousand men trying to maintain military order in the squalid isolation of what their commander called "a cold and dreary wilderness"—9 February was an ordinary day. It was a Sunday, but since the Legion had no chaplain, there was no divine service; there was only army routine. For Harrison, however, it was a special day, his twenty-first birthday. Possibly he marked his arrival at legal manhood in some way, with a small gift to the private who waited on him or a bottle of wine shared with a few friends at dinner; officers occasionally celebrated in this way to break the monotony of life on a frontier post.[1]

Although his birthday confirmed that he was, according to social custom and civil law, an adult, within the circumscribed world of the Legion he was already much more: he was one of the two or three dozen most important men at Fort Greenville, a young man in the central office with a reliable understanding of his commander's thoughts and moods. Other officers referred to him with respect, as a person of consequence: "Mr. Harrison was so obliging as to offer laying [my accounts] before Your Excellency when you should be at leasure"; "Mr. Harrison informed me that a large number of officers had applyed [for leave]." Harrison was only the second aide-de-camp; the senior aide was Captain Henry DeButts, who was even closer to General Wayne. But when DeButts was absent, as he was during January and February, Harrison was the officer with his finger most accurately on the commander's pulse.[2]

Harrison probably did not consider that his rise had been unusually rapid. In the world of Tidewater planters, it was quite common for young men to achieve honor and responsibility early. His own father, Benjamin Harrison V, had been twenty-one when he took his seat in the House of Burgesses. George Washington had been twenty when he became military adjutant for the entire southern district of Virginia. Harrison probably had the pleasant feeling that his military career was going just about as it should.

As an intimate of the commander, he sometimes received delicate assignments. Perhaps he was not aware just how delicate they were. One of the few officers on equally intimate terms with Wayne and Wilkinson, he regularly carried messages and papers between the two generals, sometimes riding the six miles between Forts Greenville and Jefferson after dark. (Doing so was not wholly safe; even during the truce, the woods were full of Indians looking for chance opportunities to attack. In January 1794, two servants of Major Buell who had gone hunting in the woods and been overtaken by nightfall were jumped; one was killed and scalped.) Wayne, who had become aware during January of Wilkinson's increasing disaffection, was rather clumsily trying to mend fences by showering the Wilkinsons with social invitations and sending James Wilkinson copies of newspapers for his amusement. "Mr. Harrison showed me a note from you," Wayne wrote 7 February, "in which you mention a wish to send a Detachment of Dragoons as an Escort to Mrs. Ernest. . . . It is with extreme pleasure I agree to that proposition."[3]

Wayne was too late. At some point in the winter, Wilkinson's dissatisfaction had crystallized into enmity, and from February on he began using all the arts he had employed successfully in Kentucky politics and the Continental Army to undermine his chief's reputation and bring about his removal. He wrote a paragraph, very unflattering to Wayne, on the Legion's recent activities, and arranged to have it published anonymously in Kentucky newspapers, from which he knew it would be copied into Eastern publications. He also began trying to undermine Secretary Knox's confidence in the general. At the same time, he maintained a façade of cordial cooperation with his commander. Doubtless he pumped Harrison whenever the aide visited Fort Jefferson for information about Wayne's plans and attitudes.[4]

Wilkinson's anonymous-letter technique was not entirely successful; there were men in the West who recognized his style. One of these was

John Armstrong, a Cincinnati merchant and former army officer who had served under Wilkinson at Fort Washington, and who wrote Wayne on 13 April to point out the article, adding, "I should be wanting in duty as well as in gratitude toward your Excellency, not to inform you in confidence that there are characters under your command, and I fear one near your person, who are placed as spies on your conduct." The reference to a spy near Wayne's person could well have been directed at Harrison; in the increasingly polarized climate of the army, it was hard for some observers to understand how Harrison could remain friendly with both generals. Armstrong's suspicions were strengthened in June when he found that Wilkinson had somehow learned about his confidential April letter.[5]

It is difficult, nonetheless, to believe that Harrison was playing a double game. He had no talent for intrigue; his behavior throughout his life was marked by a candor bordering on naïveté. Probably the strongest indication that he was not Wilkinson's agent is Wayne's reaction in November 1794 when he finally learned about Wilkinson's backstabbing. His explosive anger did not include Harrison, with whom he remained on good terms until his death in 1796. He evidently assumed that Harrison had simply been caught in the middle of a rivalry he was not experienced enough to detect.

Wayne thought highly of Harrison. The clearest proof is the attitude he took that spring toward Billy Daingerfield. At the end of the fall campaign of 1793, Ensign Daingerfield had gotten sick and stayed at Fort Washington to recuperate. On 30 January 1794, he wrote Wayne that he was feeling better but needed a short time in Kentucky to recover his strength before rejoining the Legion. This was a kind of request that usually exasperated the general; coming from any other officer, it probably would have been denied. But Daingerfield went to Kentucky and rejoined the Legion in the spring. Moreover, Wayne let him command troops marching between the forts, a very unusual assignment for an ensign, and ended by stationing him at the most advanced post, Fort Recovery, with a glowing recommendation to the commandant which could have been written, and perhaps was, by Harrison: "Permit me to recommend this Gentleman to your particular care—he is a Virginian of worth & education & descended from one of the first families of that State." Daingerfield may well have been a promising subaltern, but the stress on his education and breeding was not typical of Wayne's writing.[6]

Fort Recovery was certainly one of the key posts in the West at that time. Under Captain Alexander Gibson, it was the cockpit of Wayne's relentless efforts to probe the Indians' locations, their plans, and their relations with the British in Canada, and to discover the best routes deeper into the Indian country. Until the end of the truce period he had given the Indians, 14 February 1794, Wayne suspended these efforts—very unwillingly, for he was convinced that they had come to spy, not to negotiate—but he was eager to resume them even in the dead of winter. His immediate goal was to discover a route to the Indian towns near the Great Lakes, specifically along the river that he and other Americans in the West called the Miami of the Lakes, but which now appears on maps as the Maumee, flowing into the western end of Lake Erie near present-day Toledo, Ohio.

The country for miles north of the fort was a thick, level forest, full of springs and swampy areas. In spring, much of it was covered with water. Four of the major river systems of the Northwest Territory had their sources here. Gibson's first tasks, handed to him by Wayne, were to find a dry route across this area by which the Legion's wagons and cannon could pass, and at the same time sort out which of the creeks flowed into rivers that had an outlet in the Great Lakes, and which flowed into the Ohio.[7]

When 14 February passed without any reply from the Indians, Wayne ordered Gibson to begin reconnoitering again. He sent scouting parties out through the rain-soaked, leafless woods as far as seventy miles north, to the Maumee, and soon they began getting results. Early in March a scouting party captured a couple of Indians and brought them to the camp jail at Fort Greenville. One turned to out to be a young Kentuckian, Christopher Miller, who had been abducted by the natives as a boy twelve years earlier. Happy to be back with his own people, he told Wayne that the tribes were in disagreement on whether to attack the Legion, but that British agents from Canada were strongly urging them to do so. This news seemed all too likely; reports from Philadelphia suggested that Britain's posture toward the United States was becoming more hostile and that war might be imminent. It complicated Wayne's job by raising the possibility that the Legion might have to fight not only the natives but also a British-Canadian force of some size. Wayne, resigned to the likelihood that the tribes were "determined to have one more fight, before they will make peace," added young Miller to his corps of spies and sent for Miller's brother from Kentucky to join him.[8]

Miller's information posed another problem for Wayne. It was apparently common knowledge among the tribes of the Northwest—it must have been, for so young a man as Miller to have heard it—that a half-dozen cannon lost during St. Clair's Defeat had been concealed in the nearby woods near Fort Recovery. If a combined Indian-British force supplied with gunpowder were to advance that way and get possession of the guns, they could mount a devastating attack against the fort. Miller described to Wayne his best estimate of the hiding place of the largest gun, a six-pounder, and from late March Gibson had parties out every fair day trying to find it. He also had Fort Recovery's blockhouses enlarged so that defenders could fire straight down on a besieging force. On 11 May, the soldiers uncovered a brass three-pounder and an iron howitzer, both hidden in or under logs. The six-pounder did not turn up until June, when it was recovered thanks to information from another Indian captive.[9]

Daingerfield joined the Fort Recovery garrison in April, during this exciting time, accompanying Wells, his spies, and the Chickasaw braves, who were going on toward the Great Lakes "in quest of prisoners & scalps & information." Harrison, in contrast, remained at Fort Greenville, where the atmosphere was considerably less electric. As at Legionville, the younger officers were expressing their frustration and boredom in a steady succession of duels. Major Buell, on Washington's Birthday, reckoned that fifteen duels had been fought over the preceding year, and Captain Thomas Underwood recorded three deaths and two serious wounds from dueling that spring and early summer. Another count made it three dead and eight wounded. The most tragic duel, in which both men died, occurred in February between Ensign John Bradshaw and Lieutenant Nathaniel Huston over a minor question of respect. Harrison may have been involved somehow in the one in July between Lieutenant George Dunn and Cornet William K. Blue, in which the dying Dunn forgave his slayer. Meanwhile, Harrison's own ongoing quarrel with Hastings Marks was exacerbated that year when the War Department promoted Marks to captain ahead of Harrison. Harrison mentioned the problem to Wayne, who promised to see what could be done. Although the two men refrained from dueling, their relations when obliged to work together were described as "unpleasant." Wayne, trying to find an outlet for all this testosterone-fueled energy, ordered several construction projects to keep the men occupied, including a fives court, where officers could compete at the handball-like game Harrison's classmates had once enjoyed at Hampden-Sydney, and a citadel in the center of the camp.[10]

No one doubted that the Legion would eventually face a decisive battle with the Indians. Since the expiration of the truce, the latter had been attacking supply trains, generally near Fort Hamilton, and killing one or two men a week. From March on, Wayne was convinced that they would gather for a last stand somewhere in the Maumee Valley. But it was difficult to plan an advance without knowing the possible routes, and supply remained a serious problem. Throughout the spring, Wayne's difficulties with Elliott and Williams, the official contractors, continued; at one point he had barely a week's supply of meat on hand to feed the two-thousand-odd men at Fort Greenville. He tentatively scheduled an advance for April, then postponed it to May, then to June.[11]

Late in May, Wayne received news that added urgency to his plans. At a place called Roche du Bout, on the north bank of the Maumee not far from its outlet to Lake Erie, British forces from Canada had built and garrisoned a small fort on what was unquestionably United States territory. The gesture was evidently meant to embolden the Indians with the promise of British support, and it appeared to do just that: the Indians began moving their towns to the neighborhood of the fort, which was apparently only eighty miles north of Fort Recovery. Clearly, the United States forces needed to counter the Canadian move with one of their own if they were to remain in the contest. Wayne immediately wrote to Governor Shelby of Kentucky, asking for a force of mounted volunteers to rendezvous at Fort Greenville by 1 July. A spate of orders went out, all preparing for an early strike against the Indians.[12]

But the Indians struck first. On the afternoon of 29 June, Major William McMahon and a force of fifty men, accompanied by a detachment under Ensign Daingerfield and a force of dragoons under Captain James Taylor, escorted into the grounds of Fort Recovery a troop of 360 pack horses carrying flour intended as advance rations for the Legion when it began its march. There was no room for the escort or the pack horses inside the fort, so they encamped outside for the night, while Daingerfield and his men went inside.

Early next morning Gibson ordered the packhorsemen to take their animals down the road to graze, while McMahon and his officers had their breakfast. As they ate, they suddenly heard shots and Indian yells from down the road; the packhorsemen, about a quarter mile away, were under attack, shouting "Indians, Indians!" McMahon ran out of the fort, bareheaded in his haste, leaped on a horse, and ordered the dragoons to follow him, while Captain Asa Hartshorne started to get his unit of riflemen organized. As they arrived at the scene, however, they realized that the attackers were not just an Indian raiding party but a force of several hundred. Fire came from all sides: McMahon was hit in the head and killed; Hartshorne took a bullet in the body. His men tried to rescue him, but he shouted, "Save yourselves, boys!" The Indians laid hands on Lieutenant Hastings Marks, "a very active strong young man," who shook them off and ran back to the fort. The dragoons scattered. Gibson ordered another force out to cover Hartshorne's company, but as he realized the dimensions of the situation—he had barely three hundred men under his command and there seemed to be Indians everywhere—he ordered all the men back in the fort. The dragoons abandoned their horses and ran inside as well, leaving the Indians to run off the horses and cattle left outside the walls.

For the rest of that day, Fort Recovery was under siege. "The Savages," Gibson reported to Wayne, "fired from every Direction, and advanced as far as they could find Stumps & Trees to cover them. Some got within 60 or 70 Yards—A heavy fire was kept up by the Enemy, and also by the Garrison, untill the officers obliged the men to fire deliberately lest they should expend their amunition in vain." Any man who showed himself became a target. At one point, surprisingly, the Indians made a frontal attack on the walls, trying to climb the sides of the fort; Gibson's defenders picked off several. Gibson now had his cannon loaded and fired into the forest, with little apparent damage but considerable psychological effect. As night fell, the firing slowed and the Americans could see the Indians moving through the forest with torches, collecting their dead and wounded. By midnight, silence had fallen. Two enlisted men volunteered to carry word of the engagement to Fort Greenville through the dark woods. Next morning, Gibson's cautious scouts could find no Indians—only a few corpses, and the carcasses of some horses that had been slain for food. Their enemies had vanished as suddenly as they had come.[13]

On receiving the news that morning, Harrison may have felt a twinge of envy: Daingerfield had been in the thick of the action while he had been at his ease in headquarters. (Actually, Daingerfield had not distinguished himself—at least, his name does not appear in any of the reports.)

But the chief reaction at Fort Greenville was surprise. The Indians had appeared from nowhere in the summer woods, fought fiercely for a day in great numbers, and disappeared. Actually, there had been warnings of the attack, unrecognized by anyone. Only a couple of hours before it started, a Chickasaw brave known as Jimmy Underwood had stumbled into Fort Recovery tired, agitated, and babbling unintelligibly about something, which turned out afterward to have been the attacking force. The day before, the Chickasaw as a body had picked up the trail of a number of warriors moving south. And back at the beginning of June, a Pottawatomie, captured by Gibson near the Maumee, had warned of an assault planned "about the latter end of the moon" by two or three thousand Indians.[14]

The real surprise lay in the Indians' departure from their usual tactics: they almost never attacked a fortified post. Their decision to do so, apparently made at the last minute, seems to have rested on two factors. First, Fort Recovery was located on the very site where St. Clair had been so disastrously beaten, and was thus sacred ground, favorable for another Indian victory. Second, they were aware of the hidden cannon near the fort and of their potential for destroying it with the help of British artillerymen accompanying the army—so Harrison was told some weeks later. When the supernatural aid did not appear and they failed to locate the big guns, however, the Northwest Indians lost hope. They had had well over a thousand warriors at Fort Recovery; estimates range from twelve hundred to eighteen hundred. Never again would they be able to muster a force even close to that size against Wayne. After the engagement at Fort Recovery, the Legion's struggle for control of the Ohio country was more than half won, although the Americans were as yet unaware of the fact.[15]

To Harrison and his fellow soldiers, however, Fort Recovery was just the prelude to a drama in which the entire Legion would take center stage, confronting an Indian-Canadian force of uncertain size and intentions. All through July he checked in provisions and transmitted orders as the Legion awaited reinforcement by the mounted Kentuckians, who would bring their total numbers well above three thousand. General Wilkinson, seething with hostility inside but agreeable and dutiful in behavior, joined the main force. On 16 July the first Kentucky Volunteers arrived, followed by their general, Charles Scott. On the 28th, almost the entire Legion moved out for the Maumee.[16]

CHAPTER FIFTEEN

Consummation

Midsummer warmth and the steady beat of military drums enveloped the Legion as it began its march, an hour after sunrise. Around Fort Greenville it was the height of summer; the officers' gardens were flourishing, and on the edge of the clearings blackberries and plums were ripe. But the Legion's route lay northward, into the level, boggy, brush-choked forest. Two thousand infantrymen, organized by sublegions, led the way, with Wayne and his aides near the head; the 720 Kentucky Volunteers rode behind. Another 800 Kentuckians were said to be coming up behind to overtake the army and unite with it. Heavily loaded baggage wagons labored in the severe heat. Wayne ordered frequent halts, but the men could not really refresh themselves—all the creeks and pools in this swampy country contained muddy, undrinkable water. On the second day, before they reached Fort Recovery, several horses died.[1]

It was Harrison's first summer campaign. Sweating freely, he rode with orders up and down the length of the long, unwieldy caravan. At one point on the second day, the baggage train stretched out for four miles behind the troops. Wilkinson, commanding the right wing, fretted as always about Indian attacks. He pointed out to Harrison the length of the line and requested him to mention it to Wayne. Perhaps Harrison did, but it was a waste of effort; Wayne was in one of his driven moods, fixated on moving ahead as fast as possible to engage with the enemy. A compact formation was unimportant. The Army passed Fort Recovery, which saluted them with fifteen cannon shots, and encamped a mile farther on. Two more companies, one under Daingerfield's command, joined the main army. But impatient as Wayne was, he still proceeded with caution. The men halted at 3 P.M. and dug strong breastworks for the night.[2]

No road existed beyond Fort Recovery. Early next morning, Wayne detailed a hundred "pioneers," men with axes, to go ahead of the Legion and clear a track through the forest. In the shade the mosquitoes were "very troublesome, and larger than I ever saw," noted Lieutenant Henry Bowyer. Thick brambles and winding creeks slowed their progress, and finally, in midafternoon, they came to a patch of ground too swampy for the wagons to cross. The army had to stop and build a bridge over the morass, whose bottom was "perfect mud," as one officer put it. For the next day soldiers not engaged on the bridge scouted the muddy pools for drinkable water or stayed in camp discussing the questions on everyone's mind: where was Wayne leading them, and where were their enemies?[3]

From the scouting expeditions of Wells, Miller, and others, the general had accurate compass bearings to several possible destinations in the Maumee Valley. The rapids, where the British had erected their fort, lay somewhat east of north. Almost directly north was a large collection of Indian towns—Miami, Shawnee, and Delaware—at a place called Grand Glaize, where the Auglaize River flowed into the Maumee. This seemed to be Wayne's objective. The distance to it was a matter of debate—perhaps a week's march, perhaps ten days' march, depending on the kind of ground the soldiers had to traverse and the obstacles they might encounter. As they approached it, they were likely to run into the Indians' main force.

But in the meantime, where were the Indians and what were they doing? These questions particularly worried the Kentuckians, constituting a semi-detached unit at the rear of the main body who rode and encamped by themselves. The second night of march, believing they heard shots in the woods near them, they fired a few of their own in return, but no attack developed. The next day, when Wilkinson brought up the question, Wayne told him that he had evidence that a small body of Indians was shadowing the army's left flank. Wilkinson and many of the men, suspecting the presence of a much larger force a few miles deeper into the woods, urged Wayne to send out scouting parties for miles around the line of march. Wayne promised to do so, but Wilkinson remained nervous.[4]

With the bridge finished, the army marched again on 1 August and that afternoon reached the St. Mary's, a large river forty-five yards across. Lieutenant Bowyer and several men bathed in the cool waters; other soldiers sewed their blankets together and caught fish, which abounded in the river—"Pike, Pickeron, Pearch, Salmon, Trout," noted one diarist. The bottom was mud, however, and the water was still far from drinking quality. Here, to the exasperation of Wilkinson and some other officers, Wayne first decided to encamp on the far side of the river and then, two hours later after the crossing, changed his mind, ordering the pack horses reloaded and the soldiers to recross the river and camp on the near side. For reasons that are not always possible to reconstruct, the commander was changing plans constantly, from day to day, even from hour to hour. This trait, it is said, earned Wayne the nickname of "The Blacksnake" among the Indians, who could never predict what he would do next; it also generated a lot of criticism from subordinates.[5]

At the St. Mary's, Wayne decided to erect a small fort, on which the men spent the next two days. Early in the afternoon of the second day, a beech tree being felled for the fort landed on Wayne's marquee (tent) and that of Captain DeButts, next to Wayne's; Harrison must have been quartered nearby, but not close enough to be in danger. The accident splintered DeButts's cot while Wayne, resting on his cot, "was only preserved by an old stump," as he explained in a letter the next month, "which prevented the body of the tree from crushing me to attoms." Even so, a limb struck his left leg and he was dragged out unconscious. A few months later he expressed his suspicion that the incident, which, in Lieutenant William Clark's words, "perturb[ed] the minds of Hundreds . . . & open[ed a] large . . . field for Speculation," had been an assassination attempt, instigated presumably by Wilkinson or some other opponent within the Legion. The notion cannot be lightly dismissed. If accidental (one account blamed it on a fire "carelessly left burning" against the trunk), it was certainly a piece of extraordinary carelessness, and the records do not show that anyone was disciplined for it. A "considerable" crowd gathered at the scene, and rumors flew that the commander had been killed, but next morning, although "much bruised" and "in great bodily pain," Wayne ordered the army, reinforced by the Kentuckians, who had arrived during the night, to resume the march.[6]

At the time, few officers, including Wayne himself, spoke of the incident with great seriousness. In the Western army, military style dictated that death was to be treated lightly. Twenty-three-year-old Lieutenant Clark, for instance, who disliked some of Wayne's protégés, disparaged the incident as a "tumble"—"the downfall of Some [on Wayne's death] would have been equale to the tumble of our Chief." Cavalrymen were particularly noted for their posture of sangfroid; Harrison's friend "Van" Rensselaer, on the march with the Legion, received a letter a few days later from a brother officer at Fort Recovery: "I wish you . . . to inform me whether you have yet had an opportunity of slashing with temporary advantages; if not, I hope you soon may, and that you may even be honorably killed!! To hear of your death wou'd be a good story for me to carry home." More gallows humor came from Lieutenant James Underhill, who was left with a few dozen men, most of them ill, to garrison the fort at the St. Mary's River when the Legion moved on. Realizing that his small party's chance of survival was slim if even a modest Indian force showed up, he told Dr. Carmichael he wished "the Indians would immediately come and tomahawk himself and his own detachment, to prevent him from cutting his own throat."[7]

Three more days' march brought the Legion within a few miles of Grand Glaize, but the arduous trek, moving through "intolerable thick woods & the earth covered with Snagley underwoods & almost impassible defiles" and attempting to drink water described by various officers as "durty," "foul and disagreeable," and "stagnant," while constantly anticipating a "warm attack," brought the desire to learn the enemy's whereabouts to a new pitch of urgency. Here Harrison again appears momentarily in the record. Around midafternoon on 6 August he rode over to the right wing to tell Wilkinson that Wells and his spies, moving ahead to scout out the Indian towns, had found no guards posted. Guessing that the Indians might be unaware of the Legion's approach, Wells had suggested, and Wayne had approved, a mounted raid to catch them by surprise. Wilkinson agreed, but asked Harrison to urge the general to make the raiding force a big one; he objected to a "partial stroke." In the event, only a small force was sent to the nearest town, and they found it partially burned and deserted.[8]

Early on the morning of 8 August, the Legion marched unopposed and exultant through the heart of Grand Glaize. Captain John Cooke of the Fourth Sub-Legion noted that the center of the towns commanded "a beautiful prospect," and added, "It appears from the smoking houses and the quantity of things found, that the enemy must have recently evacuated this place and in a great hurry and confusion, we found vast quantities of vegetables which were of service to our army." Lieutenant Bowyer was more expansive. "This place far excels in beauty any in the western country, and believed equalled by none in the Eastern States. Here are vegetables of every kind in abundance, and we have marched four or five miles in cornfields down the Oglaize, and there is not less than one thousand acres of corn around the town." Everybody noticed the smoking cabins, and some troops, rummaging through the debris, found white men's goods—kettles, barrels, and tools, discarded by resident traders in their haste to get away. Evidently the Indians had evacuated when they learned of the Legion's approach, retreating to shelter near the British fort, fifty miles downriver.[9]

It was raining hard when the army entered Grand Glaize. "This was the first only Rainy day sence [*sic*] our departure from Greenville, & a Small shower fell a few evenings sence or we should have seen none," observed Lieutenant Clark, adding, "never was an army so indebted to fortune, She has certainly been perfuse in her favours—a few days rain, would have so impeded our march as to render the Country almost impassable with Waggons, &c &c." The bumptious young Kentuckian was inclined to be critical, but as Harrison and others close to the general knew, he had a point. Wayne, incapacitated by his gout and his accident, was running on willpower alone, ignoring strategy and intelligence, taking many chances, and making some mistakes. He required help mounting and dismounting his horse, he needed frequent rests, and at times he seemed to make no sense at all. And yet the Indians were falling back. A sense of impending victory was beginning to pervade the Army.[10]

At Grand Glaize Wayne ordered still another fort built, right on the north bank of the river, and named it Fort Defiance. A worried Captain Cooke deemed the site too close to the water and predicted that the Maumee would wash the fort away in three years. The third day of construction Wayne sent Harrison to summon the other senior officers for a strategy conference in his tent, where he had lain, ill and exhausted, for three days. He sketched the situation for them. The Indians, only six hundred in number, were at the foot of the rapids near the British fort. Evidently they hoped for British support, but that seemed unlikely, given the inaction of the British force so far. Or perhaps they were awaiting reinforcements. Wayne advanced two contradictory strategies, first suggesting a truce offer to the Indians and then suggesting an early military advance. Wilkinson, Scott, and Major Hamtramck could hardly make out what they were being asked to agree to. What did seem obvious was that the army could not advance until Wayne felt better. And yet something had to be done soon: only twenty days' rations were left, with no word of more supplies coming up behind. Wilkinson suggested putting the men on half rations; Wayne dismissed the idea with an oath.[11]

In the next few days, however, he adopted all three suggestions, both his own and Wilkinson's. On 13 August he sent Christopher Miller to the Indians with a flag and a proposal for a truce. On 15 August, with the fort completed, he ordered an advance and put the troops on half rations. On 16 August, Miller returned with a proposal from the Indians requesting a ten-day truce and no further advance. Most of the officers regarded it as a time-buying maneuver and an indication of weakness, but Wayne intended to answer it until Wilkinson talked him out of it. The army continued its advance toward the rapids.[12]

Their route lay along the north bank, where there was already a sort of path connecting several settlements. Lack of water was no longer a problem. The right wing of the army enjoyed a beautiful, unobstructed view across the river. On the left, up a long, gradual slope, the troops had to hack their way through thick forest, where they occasionally got entirely lost. In the center, where Wayne rode, his aides had worked out a plan in case of a surprise attack by the Indians: DeButts and Captain Thomas Lewis, the third aide, would stay with the ailing commander and try to maneuver him to a position of safety; Harrison would carry all the necessary messages and orders between one wing and the other.[13]

On the 18th, they were encamped seven miles from the British fort, at the head of the rapids, a series of falls in the river, and still they had seen almost no enemy activity. Sending Major Price of the Kentucky Volunteers ahead to reconnoiter, Wayne established a deposit for all excess baggage before moving forward to engage. There were "great Expectations of an attack" the morning of the 19th, but nothing materialized, only small parties visible at a distance and a couple of minor skirmishes with the spies. "The troops are in such high spirits that we will make an easy victory of them," Lieutenant Bowyer wrote. But those combatants who, like Harrison, had never been under fire before were experiencing a more complex set of emotions. Among the commanding officers, there was talk of a night advance, but finally the order was issued to march at five in the morning.[14]

The day dawned rainy. Advance was postponed two hours, but by the time they moved at 7 A.M., it was clear and getting hot. Ahead of the Legion lay a broad prairie cut by the steep-sided valleys of little creeks

William Henry Harrison. Portrait by Charles Balthazar Julien Févret de St-Mémin, 1800. Engraving on paper. National Portrait Gallery, Smithsonian Institution; gift of Mr. and Mrs. Paul Mellon.

Berkeley Mansion. Photograph courtesy of Berkeley Plantation.

Eighteenth-century campus of Hampden-Sydney College. Drawing by N. Douglas Payne, based on model by Richard McClintock in the Atkinson Museum of Hampden-Sydney College. Used with the permission of Hampden-Sydney College.

View of Richmond from South Side of James River, Showing Capitol from Bushrod Washington's Island. Work on paper by Benjamin Henry Latrobe, 1796. Courtesy of The Maryland Historical Society.

"Library and Surgeons Hall, in Fifth Street Philadelphia." William Russell Birch, 1800. The Library Company of Philadelphia.

Portrait of Benjamin Rush by Charles Willson Peale, 1783. Courtesy of Winterthur Museum.

Portrait of Robert Morris by Thomas Sully, after Gilbert Stuart, Accession #1957.43. Collection of the New-York Historical Society.

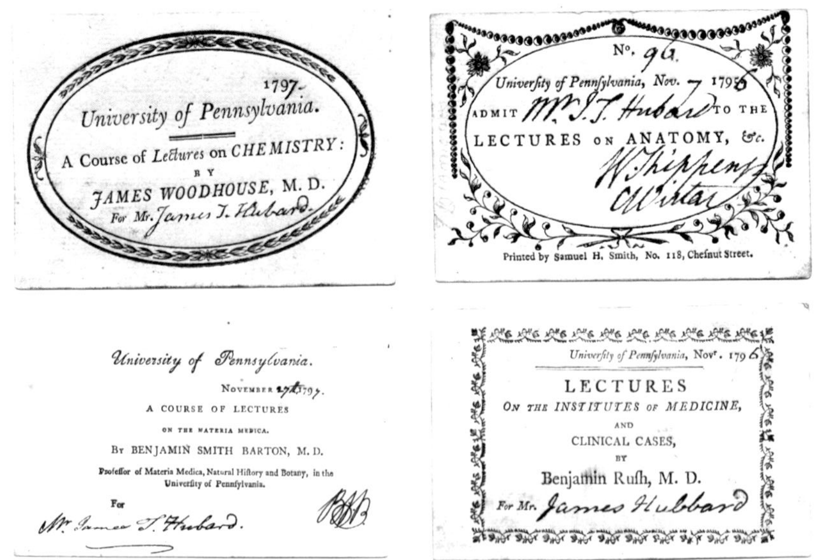

1797.
University of Pennsylvania.
A Course of *Lectures* on CHEMISTRY:
BY
JAMES WOODHOUSE, M. D.
For Mr. James T. Hubard.

No. 96.
University of Pennsylvania, Nov. 7 1795
ADMIT Mr. J. T. Hubard TO THE
LECTURES ON ANATOMY, &c.
W. Shippen
C Wistar
Printed by Samuel H. Smith, No. 118, Chesnut Street.

University of Pennsylvania.
November 1797.
A COURSE OF LECTURES
ON THE MATERIA MEDICA.
BY BENJAMIN SMITH BARTON, M. D.
Professor of Materia Medica, Natural History and Botany, in the University of Pennsylvania.
For
Mr. James T. Hubard.
BSB

University of Pennsylvania, Novr. 1796
LECTURES
ON THE *INSTITUTES* OF *MEDICINE,*
AND
CLINICAL CASES,
BY
Benjamin Rush, M. D.
For Mr. James Hubbard

Southern Historical Collection, Wilson Library, The University of North Carolina at Chapel Hill. Harrison would have purchased a ticket like these for admission to Dr. Barton's botany lectures in the summer of 1791.

"River scene showing flatboats and two keelboats" from *The Keelboat Age on Western Waters* by Leland D. Baldwin, © 1980 (1941). Reprinted by permission of the University of Pittsburgh Press.

Map of Cincinnati, 1792. Cincinnati Museum Center–Cincinnati Historical Society Library.

Fort Washington, lithograph. Cincinnati Museum Center–Cincinnati Historical Society Library. This scene is an idealized re-creation by a nineteenth-century artist, but the depiction of the fort's architecture is accurate.

Portrait of Anthony Wayne by James Sharples Sr., 1796. Independence National Historical Park, Philadelphia, PA.

Portrait of James Wilkinson by Charles Willson Peale, c. 1797. Independence National Historical Park, Philadelphia, PA.

Portrait of General Solomon Van Rensselaer. Courtesy of the Albany Institute of History & Art, Albany, NY.

Portrait of Winthrop Sargent by John Trumbull, 1790. Pencil on paper. National Portrait Gallery, Smithsonian Institution.

Portrait of John Cleves Symmes by Charles Willson Peale, 1793. Miami University Art Museum, Oxford, Ohio.

Pecan, a Native American chief of the Miami Tribe, ca. 1776–1778, by Henry Hamilton. Graphite on paper. MS Eng. 509.2 Mat 1 (4), Houghton Library, Harvard University. Though this chief was not at Fort Greenville in 1795, his portrait shows the dress and manners of the native leaders on a ceremonial occasion of that kind.

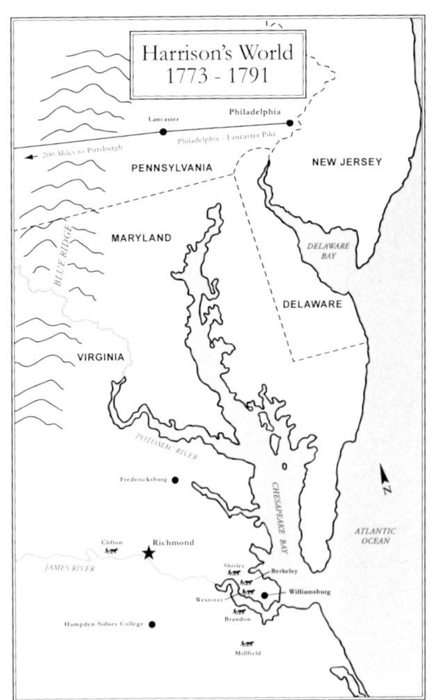

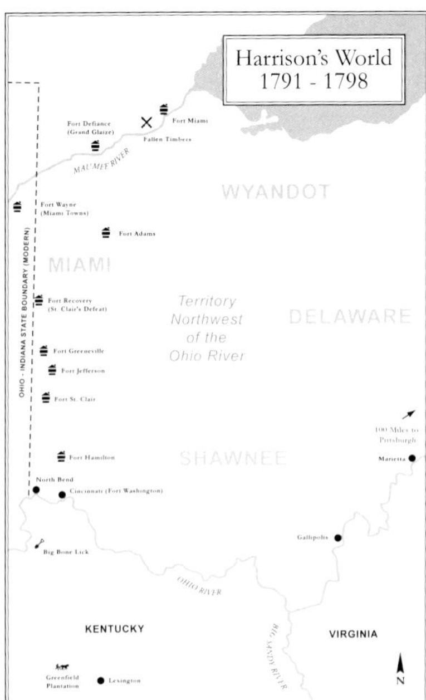

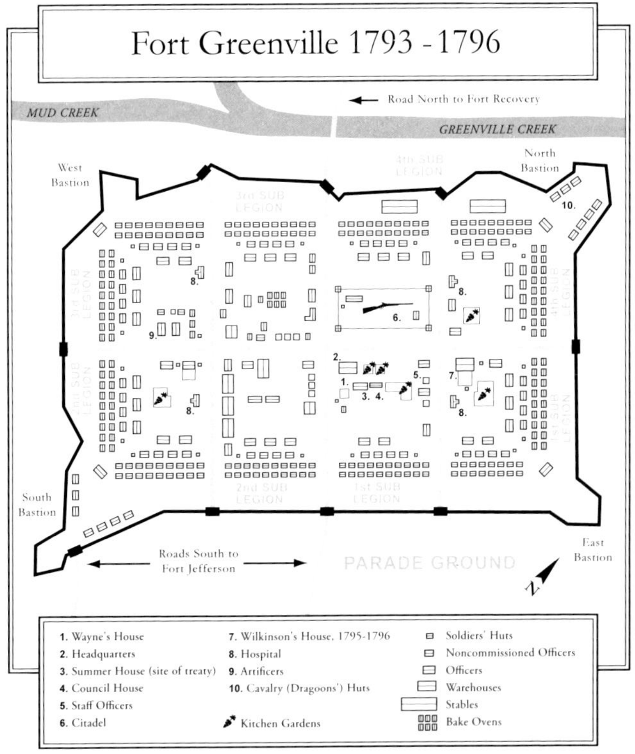

Map: Brian Nugent

running into the river. The British post was ahead, just out of sight. After they had advanced three miles without difficulty, Wilkinson, curious for a glimpse of it, requested Wayne's permission to go out onto the bluffs for a look downriver. Wayne told DeButts and Robert Elliott of the contractors to go with him. Whether they saw the fort is not recorded, for their attention was distracted. Wilkinson looked down on the tall grass of the prairie and saw a group of horsemen riding hell for leather toward the American lines. At the same time his ears caught the pop of gunfire. He ordered DeButts to inform the commander.

What had happened was this. An advance guard of volunteers, again under Major Price, had come under fire about a quarter mile ahead of the main body, turned, and were fleeing back toward the lines with dozens of Indians in pursuit. Captain Cooke, seeing them about to charge into his company's lines, ordered his men to fire at them and bring them to their senses. Wilkinson, arriving on the scene at the same time, tried to shame them into turning around, but they simply turned and charged off toward the right wing.[15]

Harrison was with the left wing when the attack started, and shouted encouragement to the soldiers to resist the Indians' onslaught. Then Wayne sent him to the far right to order the dragoons there to charge. Harrison instinctively took the most direct route, crossing diagonally in front of the First and Third Sub-Legions, which were just beginning to return the Indians' fire, and ended up taking fire from both sides. "My gallant steed bore me on so rapidly as to prevent a direct aim from the Indians," he wrote years later, with a touch of the same naïve exhilaration that some people found so odd in him, "and I was fortunate enough to escape the balls of my friends." The Indians were now about eighty yards away. The charge Wayne had ordered, led by Lieutenant Robert Mis Campbell, a friend of Harrison's, drove into their midst. Mis Campbell was shot and fell from his horse, but as the infantry began to get organized and advance, the Indians fell back.

Then there was a huge fusillade of fire from the left, and Harrison was sent over there. What had happened on the right now repeated itself there, with more intensity. The left wing, advancing, had run into more Indians, together with Canadian militia, hidden among fallen tree trunks at the edge of the forest. Wayne ordered a cavalry charge and Harrison gave the word to his friend "Van" Rensselaer, who started through the woods and took a musket ball in the chest. Hamtramck ordered his two sublegions to form up with fixed bayonets, and the enemy began retreating on that side. The whole set of encounters had taken hardly fifteen minutes. Now the Indians gave way in front of the Legion, hiding in ravines, firing, then leaping out, running to the next ravine, and firing again. Nevertheless, the Legion steadily moved forward and after about an hour, the Americans were within a mile of the British fort and had reached the natural barricade of fallen, twisted trees, uprooted by a windstorm, behind which the Indians had hidden to begin their attack. It was this barricade that gave the encounter the name it has had in the history books: the Battle of Fallen Timbers. At this point, the Indians simply disappeared into the forest. The British, immobile in their fort, which was plainly visible to the Americans, Union Jack and all, refused to get involved.[16]

The outcome of a battle, Harrison learned, was never as immediately apparent at the time as it was in a history book. This one had been, as Wilkinson correctly observed, more a skirmish than a battle; much of Wayne's force had been involved briefly or not at all. For the rest of 20 August, it was doubtful what the Indians intended to do—whether they were awaiting reinforcements, or would attack again—or who had won. Officers, "all full of expectation & anxiety," as Lieutenant Clark reported, counted casualties—about thirty dead and a hundred wounded. The next two days illuminated the situation, however. Right under the guns of the British fort the Legion laid waste the Indian villages on both sides of the river. The British did not stir, but they sent Wayne a stiff note asking his intentions. Wayne, who did not want a battle with them, simply replied that they had no right to be where they were. The British commander in turn retorted that that was a political question he was not competent to discuss.

Nevertheless, the exchange clarified the real meaning of the encounter: Britain had no intention of delivering on its promises of military support to the Indians of the Northwest Territory, and the Indians, realizing that fact, had abandoned the field in defeat. The skirmish was suddenly a major victory. On 23 August Wayne composed his official report, celebrating the triumph of American arms and giving Harrison and the other aides full credit for "communicating my orders in every direction, and by their conduct and bravery . . . exciting the troops to press for victory." Harrison at last had the glory he had dreamed of.[17]

At the same time, he was learning the human cost of even a small battle like this one. Two officers he knew and liked, Mis Campbell and

Lieutenant Henry Towles of the Fourth Sub-Legion, had been killed early in the action; their bodies were found and interred the first day. "Van" Rensselaer was found later, propped against a tree on the left side of the field, with a gunshot wound received in his right breast, blood flowing from his mouth, and a smile on his face. When soldiers moved to pick up his body, assuming the wound to be mortal, he opened his eyes and growled at them, with all the bravado of a cavalryman, "Damn you, dress me." Harrison had him brought to Wayne's marquee for treatment and saw that he received constant medical care. By the time the Legion was ready to return to Fort Defiance three days later, "Van" Rensselaer was well enough to ride. Others were less fortunate. Eli Edmondson, Towles's sergeant, was wounded along with him in the first Indian charge, but somehow escaped noticed in the aftermath of the attack. He was a neighbor of the Harrisons from Charles City County, in fact a connection of the family of small planters into which Harrison's sister Elizabeth had married. When he was finally found, two days after the battle, he had only just died, apparently "with Utmost Agony," Harrison wrote his brother Carter. There was another Edmondson brother in the Legion, and Harrison resolved to take more pains to look after him.[18]

Harrison was learning that warfare was more ambiguous and riddled with accidents than it appeared in the histories he had been reading. It was also messier—seamed with macabre humor because of the unexpected tricks bullets could play in combat. He heard the story, for instance, of John O'Brian of the Kentucky Volunteers, who was shot while retreating from the first attack—"[He] was shot in the low part of his back," Captain Underwood reported; "the ball passed through the bottom of his Belly & Lodged in a certain part in front, in his P____." O'Brian lived, but uncomfortably. Harrison began to perceive that his dream of military prowess had features as grotesque and unpleasing as the medical life he had abandoned. It had lured him as a youth from Virginia to the Ohio country; now he was reaching manhood and starting to see it more critically. Whether he knew it or not, the first phase of his life was over.[19]

CHAPTER SIXTEEN

The End of the Dream

In August 1794 William Henry Harrison experienced the thrill of battle in a good cause and won his commander's approval; he was happy in his chosen career and could reasonably expect it to continue. Yet within two years, in disillusion, he would consider leaving the Legion of the United States, and in 1798 he would return to civilian life. This chapter explains how his plans were frustrated and why he set aside his aspirations.

On 12 November 1794 "the *Skeleton* of the Legion," as Wayne described it, saluted by artillery fire, returned to Fort Greenville in triumph. As on all its wilderness expeditions, the Legion had had supply problems. Wayne's men had endured some lean days since the battle of 20 August; moreover, they had left scores of men and officers in the new forts they had built—Adams, Defiance, and Wayne. Nevertheless, even slimmed down and reduced in number, they were "in high health & spirits." They had routed the Northwest Indians and stopped the frontier war.[1]

Harrison was the first man from the expedition to return; Wayne had ordered him to ride ahead to Fort Greenville with the official notification. After that night's celebratory feast, he learned that a letter from his brother Carter, now in Philadelphia as a representative from Virginia, awaited him in the newly established Cincinnati post office. When he got it a couple of weeks later, it turned out to be a reproof for the discomfort that his attentions to Hetty (probably including letters from the West) had caused the Morris family. Harrison replied in high good humor: while conceding that his pay and his fortune would not have allowed him to support Miss Morris in the style she deserved—an insufficiency he would become increasingly conscious of over the next few years—he asserted that his status as an officer of the United States made him worthy of any young woman's hand, and referred his brother to Wayne's official report for details of the battle. He closed with greetings for Ben, perhaps another index of his good feelings, and then turned his attention back to the general's business.[2]

There was certainly business enough to occupy him. The campaign had been a triumph, but from Fort Greenville the future of the war still seemed unclear. Although Wayne had sent the tribes overtures for peace through several channels, he had to assume that the British were still actively urging them to regroup and continue their resistance. He therefore had to ensure adequate supplies to maintain his army in its isolated, squalid wilderness bastion and to respond to enemy movements. On the day the Legion returned, Harrison heard Wayne tell Wilkinson, "I don't know how soon I may want you, perhaps in two weeks, for we don't know what these fellows to the North intend," before sending his disgruntled second-in-command on to Fort Washington to visit his wife and family.[3]

Wayne was mistaken: the war was, in fact, over. The inaction of the British at the Battle of Fallen Timbers had stamped them in the Indians' mind as cowards and promise breakers, weaklings who would let the Americans come into their territory and, as one chief was quoted as saying, "piss in their spring." The tribes of the Northwest unanimously repudiated British protection, and now they wanted to conciliate the United States. Beginning in December, groups of Indians began appearing at the fort to discuss peace, drawn partly by calculation, partly by hunger, and partly from a desire to see Wayne, the "wonderful man," the supernatural hero who had overcome them. Some brought white prisoners whom they freed as a token of sincerity. Wayne and his staff responded with food and cheap symbolic gifts, making every effort to obtain a written commitment to peace, "preliminary articles" as they called it, which Wayne and his aides also signed. One by one, all the tribes sent emissaries: first the Miami; then the Wyandot, the senior tribe; finally and crucially, the Delaware and the Shawnee. Skeptical at first, Wayne gradually came to believe that this submission was genuine, and set a date of 15 June for a grand council of all the tribes.[4]

It was William Wells, the spy, who had carried the word through the Ohio country that General Wayne, "The Blacksnake," was ready to talk formally of peace. More than half Indian in his manners and habits, Wells ranged the country freely. He was often in Wayne's office, where he and Harrison, only three years apart in age, spent hours in conversation and became "warm friends," partly because of their cultural difference. Harrison learned much from Wells about the traditions and practices of the Northwestern tribes; at the same time, he "helped to educate Wells in the manners and customs of white people."[5]

More or less concurrently, Wayne learned the full truth about General Wilkinson's disloyalty. In November, Robert Newman, a soldier who had deserted just before the battle and was now back in custody at Fort Washington, gave Chaplain David Jones a statement that seemed to incriminate Wilkinson in the sending of secret information to the British. When he heard the story, a furious Wayne immediately sent Jones and his chief aide, Henry DeButts, to the War Department with the evidence of his subordinate's treason. Then in January letters from Philadelphia informed him that Wilkinson was charging him with misconduct during the campaign and wanted a hearing before the War Department. His wrath was volcanic. If not for the peace process then under way, he declared, he would not stay one more second in the army with that "worst of all bad men." He severed communication with Wilkinson and left him at Fort Washington on permanent leave, without a command, hoping he would resign on his own if the War Department found no evidence to force him out of the service. It was a ticklish situation for Harrison, who was still on friendly terms with the disgraced general.[6]

Harrison's more immediate concern, though, was relaxation from the dangers of the campaign. Now that the grand peace conference had been set for June, with boatloads of cheap goods being sent from the East for distribution to the tribes, there was time for a break, to get out of "the woods" and rejoin civilized society with its unique benefit, the company of refined young women. The general was tolerant of his younger officers' needs in this respect; young Lieutenant William Clark, who returned late from leave at the falls of the Ohio (modern Louisville) because of heavy courting, found Wayne "a reasonable as well as a Galant man, [who] had some *Idea* of my *Persute,* he treated my inatention as all other good fathers would on the Same acasion." Harrison planned to make for Lexington, Kentucky. He may have learned that his old friend and neighbor Charles Byrd had recently come there as agent for Robert Morris; in any case, the settlement was full of Virginians and had a reputation for genteel society. At the beginning of April, he and his bosom friend John Scott, a high-spirited, popular army doctor who was a little older than Harrison and likewise a bachelor, set off down the muddy track to Kentucky. Scott brought his servant, very likely a black man; they stopped for a couple of days at Fort Washington to find him a more suitable horse.[7]

As the two young men rode out of the drenched woods of the territory into Kentucky, where peach trees were blooming, matrimony was a prime topic on their minds and probably in their conversation. The need for sex was of course a component of it, but not really a central one: simple, casual sex was readily available for officers at frontier posts, and Harrison, by his own later recollection, was a champion at it. Indian women were unbelievably available by white standards, a fact commented on by many white male observers, and there were always a number of white women of varying degrees of respectability around an army. Harrison's friend Winthrop Sargent, whom they had probably just seen at Cincinnati, kept a mistress living in his house. What Harrison and Scott had in mind was the next step to full manhood: securing a loving partner who would validate their claim to success with property and offspring. She need not bring property of her own, though her doing so would be welcome; the prospect of marriage demanded that a young man collect his resources and develop a plan for adult life. Scott had his profession and his savings from some years in the frontier army; Harrison had military accomplishment and the favor of the commanding general, together with whatever cash Ben might pay him for his Berkeley land.[8]

It was with thoughts like these running through their heads that Harrison and Scott rode into Lexington. "The Philadelphia of Kentucky," Lexington was the largest city west of the mountains, three times the size of Cincinnati, with 1,800 inhabitants, an academy, a bakery, a bookseller, a coffeehouse, and about forty brick buildings, some of them "very handsome," signs of the next step toward civilization. They found the city's social tone as lively and elegant as expected. Probably they spent only a night or two lodged in one of the numerous taverns; both young men were well connected and had friends or kin living in the area. In fact, not much is known about their movements, except for one crucial episode: they rode several miles into the countryside to the residence of state senator Peyton Short, a frame farmhouse whose grounds were so improved with outbuildings that it was beginning to resemble a Virginia plantation; Short even called it Greenfield. There they met the genial Short, a Virginian, his wife, and her sister Anna or Nancy Symmes, arrived only three months earlier from New York. Both ladies were charming—Mrs. Short was tall and attractive, Nancy delicate and pretty. Harrison was immediately attracted to Nancy; despite her precarious health, she loved horseback riding and seemed to have the same zest for life as Harrison himself. Moreover, she was a sincere Christian. Thoughts of Hetty Morris evaporated, and by the time he had to return to headquarters he had plans for marriage on his mind.[9]

Marrying Nancy meant getting her father's consent, and Harrison, like almost every other officer in the Legion, recognized her father's name. Judge John Cleves Symmes was one of the best-known men in the Northwest Territory. He owned half a million acres there (the "Symmes Purchase") and was constantly litigating title disputes over his lands. Restless, energetic, and combative, he was one of the three territorial justices who administered law, and he had no special fondness for the military; in fact, unfortunately, he had been one of the judges who issued the writ against Harrison in the artificers' case back in 1792. Much to the displeasure of his new wife, Susan Livingston (a daughter of the New Jersey Livingstons), Judge Symmes lived in a cabin a few miles downriver from Cincinnati (Susan wrote her sister, "I have suffered much for the want of a good house in this country). The cabin was in North Bend, a little village of Symmes's own creation—a "wretched" place according to Sargent, who had visited it the previous year—that he had hoped would become the metropolis of the area. To see the judge, Harrison would have had to make a detour to North Bend.[10]

Most likely, then, Harrison stopped by North Bend in May to present his suit to the crusty judge and his refined wife. The answer he got was a qualified no. "We are all too much strangers to each other," was the way Symmes put it to a friend, even while conceding that Harrison made a strong first impression, with his "understanding, prudence, education, & resource in conversation." That they were all relative strangers was certainly true: the judge hardly knew his own daughter, who had been in the East with her grandparents all the years he was building his settlement in the Western country; Nancy and Harrison had known each other barely a month; and Symmes and Harrison knew each other mainly as adversaries. Nevertheless, Harrison gained some ground in the end; when he departed, Symmes was already calculating how "Captain Harrison" as a son-in-law might figure in "my own arrangements." Actually, Harrison was still a lieutenant, but as will be seen, he probably had verbal assurances from Wayne that the next vacant captaincy was his.[11]

In fact, on his return to headquarters Harrison discovered that fate had finally caught up with Hastings Marks. Exactly what Marks did is unrecorded, but it was so bad (he himself called its consequences "fatal") that he was court-martialed, appeared at the proceedings drunk, and was forced to send in his resignation, which Wayne accepted with satisfaction, and to leave camp forthwith. This cleared the way for Harrison when the next round of promotions was sent in. He could reflect that he had not stretched the truth too far when he described himself as a captain to the Symmes family.[12]

Fort Greenville, Harrison found on his return, was a changed place, not just because of the beauty of the wilderness spring, but also in preparation for the Indian treaty meeting. As the largest full-scale meeting held between the United States government and several Native American tribal leaders, both in its time and today, the planned conference was, as Andrew Cayton has pointed out, first and foremost a piece of military-diplomatic theater. Wayne wanted to exhibit United States power and discipline to the best advantage, and was preparing a great show. He had the troops on parade all the time, smart in their movements and uniforms. He had had a new council house built in the midst of the fort's garden, to be the scene of the speeches. He even permitted officers' wives to visit from Fort Washington. Lieutenant Clark, just back from Kentucky, caught the mood in his inimitable style: "All is gaiety, good humer & Devertion. The eye is constantly entertained with the Splendour of Dress and equipage, and the year [ear] with the Sounds of Drums, fifes, Bugles, Trumpets, and other Instrumeanteals." The Indians had begun appearing, and were camped in the surrounding woods, where their presence provided additional entertainment, particularly when they managed to purchase whiskey from the army sutlers and get screaming drunk.[13]

During the next few weeks Harrison was very busy, issuing orders for food and gifts to the Indians, for whiskey, equipment, and hair powder for the men. He dealt frequently with the few traders whom Wayne had allowed to stay at headquarters (most were sent away for having made whiskey too available to the guests) and formed a lasting friendship with a young Cincinnati merchant, a Pennsylvanian named James Findlay. The camp was full not only of soldiers and Indians but also of officers' ladies, interpreters, visiting Easterners, and the occasional African American servant on an errand from Cincinnati or Kentucky. There was much gawking at the Indians. "Their manners are very singular," commented one Virginia minister, "viz., their dress, paint, beads, Ear jewels, Nose d[itt]o . . . bandages, silver hoops for their wrists and arms, girdles, feathers, headdresses, ornaments of feathers, and management of hair"—that is, the chiefs' practice of plucking out the scalp hair except for a single top knot. More bands of Indians kept emerging from the forest, sometimes waving flags, and were greeted by Wayne in person with a speech and a ceremonial gift of wampum. They included important leaders: Buckongahelas of the Delaware and Little Turtle of the Miami, who had led the victory over St. Clair.[14]

Not until mid-July, however, did the crucial delegates arrive: the Wyandot, senior tribe of the region, under their chief Tarhe, The Crane, and the warlike Shawnee led by Blue Jacket. Formal talks then began; Harrison and the other two aides were constantly at their table taking notes. As was his custom, Harrison watched the chiefs with interest. Although the Miami had worn European clothing for years, he saw that Little Turtle, as a concession to midsummer heat and the gravity of the occasion, wore "no clothing but his breech cloth and moccasins; he also had on a bear-claw necklace, metal armlets on his upper arms, large metal ear hoops, a large medallion suspended by a second chain, and a headpiece of thirteen eagle feathers fastened in his hair by means of three snake rattles." Some of the chiefs spoke English; outside the council house, as opportunity offered, Harrison talked with them, inquiring about themselves and their people. His recollections years later suggest that he was consciously trying to gather information for a history of the Northwestern Indians as they had lived before the whites arrived—to become, as it were, the Rollin of the Indians, narrating their migrations and wars, perhaps incorporating the mounds that had so interested him at Cincinnati. By writing such a work, he could become a soldier-scholar on the model of Winthrop Sargent—or, for that matter, Julius Caesar. Such an accomplishment would win praise for him and perhaps impress Nancy and her father.[15]

The treaty was signed 3 August. Harrison, aged twenty-two, was the youngest of the dozen white men who put their names on it. In it the united tribes gave up most of the present state of Ohio and ended their armed resistance to white settlers. The treaty brought peace to the West. It also represented a tragic miscalculation by the Indians—that by ceremonial submission to the United States, as younger brother to older brother, or son to father, they could persuade them to leave part of the trans-Appalachian forest untransformed for Indian occupancy. It was a desperate, futile hope. The chiefs and their followers dispersed into the forest. Wayne sent his report of the proceedings to Philadelphia, with a recommendation that Harrison, "a Young Gentleman of family Education & merit," be promoted to the next captain's slot.[16]

With the paperwork on the treaty concluded, it seems evident that Harrison confided his personal hopes to his commander, explaining that he intended to marry Nancy, but could not until the return of her father, who would be holding court in the Illinois country until November. Determined to support her "in the style she deserve[d] to live in," he proposed a bold plan. Wayne would shortly be leaving for the East to receive the honors due to him for his victory, while the Wilkinsons would be moving to Fort Greenville so that Wilkinson could take command (on a very short leash from Wayne) of the Legion. Harrison proposed that, rather than going eastward with Wayne, he be allowed to marry Nancy and move into the "good quarters" at Fort Washington now occupied by the Wilkinsons. Harrison, in other words, asked to take a break from his job and have a honeymoon at government expense. That Wayne agreed to help set up this audacious arrangement demonstrates his deep fondness for Harrison, and perhaps also the glow of success both men felt after the completion of the treaty.[17]

From early September to the last week of November 1795, Harrison disappears from the documentary record. He was not working as an aide for Wayne. He had borrowed $300 from an army friend, Dr. Charles Brown, on 31 August. His biographer Freeman Cleaves coyly suggests that he had gotten an assignment leading packhorse trains to North Bend, the better to court his Nancy. But Nancy was not there; she was still at Greenfield with her sister. Where was Harrison?[18]

There is a possible answer, which has found its way into a few Kentucky histories. In 1828, on a visit to New York, Harrison casually remarked to a couple of gentlemen that "in 1795" he had organized an expedition to Big Bone Lick, Kentucky, a well-known fossil site some twenty miles downstream from Cincinnati. There he had overseen the collection of many bones of gigantic animals (the word *fossil* was not yet in general use), which he packed into thirteen hogsheads and shipped to the East, but he had never learned what became of them. The story found its way into the *Proceedings* of the Lyceum of Natural History of New York. Harrison himself may never have seen it. Undocumented in any other source, this tale suffers from all the disadvantages of a second-hand account. However, it does fit nicely with Harrison's situation in the fall of 1795. He needed an excuse to be in Kentucky (Big Bone Lick was only one long day's ride from Greenfield; he could spend Sunday with Nancy, who was raised a strict Presbyterian, in conversation and worship); he was thinking of himself as a man of letters and scientific interest; and he had just borrowed three hundred dollars. The unknown fate of the bones is not a major objection. They could have sunk in an accident on the river, as some Kentucky writers have assumed they did, and almost no one would have known, even in the West. Busy with arrangements north of the river and romance south of it, Harrison would have found it difficult to follow their journey.[19]

In early November, Judge Symmes returned to Greenfield from his Western trip. He visited for a few days with the Shorts, then gathered up his wife and Nancy and returned to North Bend by the customary water route—that is, by flatboat down the Kentucky and keelboat up the Ohio. When they came ashore at North Bend, or shortly after, there was "Captain Harrison" with a renewal of his suit for Nancy's hand and the promise of comfortable quarters in Fort Washington. The judge's answer, again, was no. This time, probably, he was more candid about his real objection: the young officer had "no profession but that of arms"; as Symmes put it in another letter, "he can neither bleed, plead, or preach." Symmes did not consider soldiering a viable or even a particularly honorable profession in the United States of 1795, and many Americans would have agreed with him. (He treated Harrison's future in the military lightly: "If he can dodge well a few years, it is probable he may become conspicuous.") But Nancy's mind was made up, and Harrison was charming and persistent. In the end, when father and daughter failed to convince each other, the judge, "inflexible," stormed out of the house. Harrison could marry his daughter, but he would neither attend the ceremony nor give them his blessing. He and Mrs. Symmes went off to Cincinnati, and on 25 November a local justice of the peace united the young couple in the Symmes cabin.[20]

By December 1795, then, Harrison had accomplished everything he wanted: he had the wife of his dreams, with the approval of her fashionable, clever stepmother, who called him "a sensible[,] accomplished & I believe worthy young man," and the grudging neutrality of her influential father. Thanks to Wayne's protection, he was honored as a captain and as commandant of Fort Washington, although in fact he was not officially entitled to either distinction. The young couple had a house in the fort, "genteelly furnished *for this country*," as Susan Symmes put it, and worthy of the fine silver tea set the judge had recently ordered for Nancy, and were even able to reserve a special carpeted room for Susan Symmes to stay in whenever the judge was away on business. To add to Harrison's satisfaction, by early spring it was clear that Nancy was pregnant. As General Wilkinson jovially assured him, "To be auxiliary in forming an animated & intelligent being, is certainly a source of manly pride." Mrs. Symmes believed that Harrison was reading law books in his leisure hours, in preparation for leaving the service, but she was mistaken: he was reading military treatises on strategy and leadership, anticipating a successful and perhaps glorious career with the Legion, modeled to some extent on that of his friend James Wilkinson: frontier adventure enhanced by the presence of a well-bred, devoted wife and a few children. Meantime, he enjoyed crossing the parade ground where, four years earlier, he had been a lonely, neglected subaltern.[21]

Then the blow fell. Beginning in April, reports began reaching the West—first as rumors, then in letters and newspapers—that Congress, far from rewarding the Legion for its performance, had abolished it as of 31 October. On that date, it would revert to being the U.S. Army, and its four sublegions would shrink to two regiments. Few officers would be dismissed entirely, but many middle-level officers, majors and captains, would have to lose rank and take new positions. Politics was responsible: enemies of Washington's administration now controlled Congress and were determined to make punitive cuts in government. The war, they argued, was over; a large army was no longer needed.

Incredulity, then anger, spread through frontier posts at this "injury unprecedented," as Harrison called it. Bitter letters of resignation began appearing in Wayne's mail, from officers like Dr. Allison, Dr. Scott, the young Kentuckian William Clark, and John Thorp, the chief of artificers, who had been in service since 1776. For Harrison the news was a particularly ill-timed blow. "I have been for the past four years a Lieutenant," he reiterated to Wilkinson, "& but for the blunder of one of the Secretary [*sic*] I would have been a captain from the 6th July 1794." Now his promotion would be much longer in coming, and his whole future in the military was suddenly in question.[22]

By the time Wayne returned from Philadelphia in early July, Lieutenant Harrison had made up his mind. The general was on his way to Detroit, where the British had just surrendered their post and the United States needed to establish a strong presence, and needed the services of all his aides. Harrison, with Nancy's baby due in September, did not see how he could get away, and he wrote Wayne a letter to that effect, resigning as aide and adding, "The very illiberal treatment which I have met with from the government has determined me to abandon the profession of arms entirely in a short time."[23]

Doubtless Harrison meant this when he wrote it, but Wayne calmed him down. Before proceeding to the interior, the general had a pleasant visit with the Harrisons, and possibly the Symmeses as well. He assured Harrison that he need not resign as aide and that he could stay on as commandant of Fort Washington. Chagrined at his own lack of influence with Congress, Wayne was determined to see that his protégés were taken care of. Before leaving Fort Greenville for Detroit, he wrote perhaps his last letter to Harrison, stressing his "sincere friendship and Esteem" for the younger man. With backing like this, Harrison found it easy to remain at Fort Washington, where he and Nancy were at the center of such society as there was in Cincinnati. The amenities, rudimentary as they were—soldiers to fetch and carry, laundresses to do the wash—were comforting when Nancy had her baby, a daughter they named Elizabeth Bassett for Harrison's mother. Harrison was now officially commandant, Captain Pierce having departed on furlough in June.[24]

Jacob Burnet, a young lawyer and Princeton graduate from New Jersey who settled in Cincinnati in 1796 and rapidly became one of the Harrisons' numerous friends, recalled the impression that the fort, a "rude but highly interesting structure," made on an Easterner:

> It was composed of a number of strongly built, hewed log cabins, a story and a half high, calculated for soldiers' barracks. Some of them, more conveniently arranged and better finished, were intended for officers' quarters. They were so placed as to form a hollow square of

> about an acre of ground, with a strong blockhouse at each angle. It was built of large logs. . . . The Artificers' Yard was appended to the fort, and stood on the bank of the river, immediately in front. It occupied about two acres of ground, enclosed by small contiguous buildings, occupied as workshops and quarters for laborers. Within the enclosure, there was a large two-story frame house, familiarly called the "yellow house," which was the most commodious and best finished edifice in Cincinnati. . . . [I]mmediately behind the fort, Colonel Sargent, secretary of the Territory, had a convenient frame house and a spacious garden, cultivated with care and taste.[25]

Harrison was constantly reminded of how Fort Washington had changed since his first sight of it in November 1791. Militarily, it was no longer impressive. Now housing barely seventy residents, it seemed to one visiting French general that year "abandoned and useless" for martial purposes. The army was similarly transformed. The peace treaty with the Indians, together with recent treaties with England and Spain, had left the United States with no reason for a large army and had given Congress an excuse for its cuts. The few men left in the Ohio country were turning into a sort of frontier constabulary like the Royal Canadian Mounties of the next century, and the fort was on its way to becoming Cincinnati's civic center. In 1799, the year after Harrison's resignation, an Independence Day pageant was held there; the next year saw amateur theatricals. This new, reduced army held out little prospect of glory, or even excitement, except perhaps in the lower Mississippi Valley, near Spanish New Orleans. When the melancholy word of Wayne's death at a fort on the Great Lakes arrived in December 1796, it seemed the end of the heroic era.[26]

For Harrison, Wayne's death seemed a cue to quit the service, but, having taken on a family to support, he was no longer a free agent. He needed to exchange his commission for a post of equal status. Judge Symmes would have liked to see his son-in-law working as agent for the Symmes Purchase—from April on, he had been sending clients and parcels of land Harrison's way—but Harrison, despite his outgoing personality, had no interest whatever in sales. One constant throughout his life was an almost total ineptitude at the land business. Unlike Symmes's other son-in-law, Peyton Short (or most career Army officers in the Ohio country), Harrison got no thrill from showing a property to prospective buyers, working out clever deals, or dreaming of vast profits. He had also figured out that Judge Symmes, demanding but disorganized in his own dealings, would not be a good boss.

Casting about for alternatives, Harrison considered the role of merchant. It was a respectable occupation; Ben had been a merchant. Harrison tried it out in 1797 when, still in the army, he went into partnership with his friend James Findlay and Findlay's partner, James Smith. Together they bought a distillery near the fort, a popular spot. Over the next few years they sold a lot of whiskey, but the profit was surprisingly small. Harrison may already have been coming to the conclusion he articulated in a letter years later: "I never could succeed in the mercantile business even if I had capital to commence it. Such pursuits are neither congenial to my nature nor the habits of my life."[27]

There remained one other remote possibility, a post in the territorial government—remote because the government was very small and because Governor St. Clair was not particularly friendly to him. Nevertheless, Harrison felt he could do a good job: he was educated and serious about governance, and public service was in his family background. Harrison read constantly—in 1796, among others, a book by the Scottish historian Donald Robertson and the *Iliad;* in 1797 the English political philosopher Bolingbroke. Works like these may not now seem preparation for public office, but in eighteenth-century America they did. At the same time, he kept up contacts with friends in the East who could be useful with the Adams administration, which would make any appointment. Harrison's friend and neighbor Winthrop Sargent, with whom he frequently dined, had his eye on the possible governorship of the new territory likely to be set up on the lower Mississippi, in the lands around Natchez recently evacuated by the Spanish under the Treaty of San Lorenzo; if Sargent received the post, he promised to recommend Harrison as his successor. Late in November 1796, the two had dinner with Andrew Ellicott, President Washington's representative, who was on his way to Natchez to begin surveying the Spanish cession. Doubtless its administration was one of the subjects discussed.

Events over the next year kept the possibility in the back of Harrison's mind. His old comrade Solomon "Van" Rensselaer, on his way to take over a post on the lower Mississippi, stopped at Fort Washington for a visit. Harrison, if still single, probably would have sought an assignment there, but Nancy's delicate health and her father's attachment to her meant that he had to stay in the Northwest. He was now a captain, the long-deferred promotion having arrived in June, but his new rank was useful mainly to bolster his candidacy for civilian office. When Wilkinson went to Philadelphia in fall 1797 to shore up his own situation, he had a cordial interview with Adams and dropped Harrison's name in that connection.[28]

When the opportunity came, it was quick and unexpected, but Harrison was ready. In the spring of 1798, John Adams's nominee for governor of the newly created Mississippi Territory was rejected by a hostile Senate, and he sent in Sargent's name as a second choice. It was narrowly approved, 11 to 10. This happened 10 May; within days Sargent had written Philadelphia to suggest Harrison as his successor for the secretaryship of the Northwest Territory. Harrison wrote friends and mobilized supporters: his brother Carter, still in Congress, and Robert Goodloe Harper, now a congressman from South Carolina. Adams, whom he had never met, had heard his name from Wilkinson and thought of him favorably. Alexander Hamilton, who had powerful allies in the cabinet and in Congress and always trying to recruit bright young men for the government, had already offered to help him. With a good record, good connections, and strong recommendations, it all dropped into place, and by June Harrison knew he had the post. In his first political test, he had shown a good grasp of strategy, and seemed off to an auspicious start on his second career.[29]

In one way, however, his second career was markedly different from his first. He had become a soldier impelled by lofty ideals, national or even transnational, and a belief in his calling; he entered government out of need, driven by the imperatives of his Virginia upbringing to provide handsomely for his wife and family, hoping that the reading, the conscientiousness, the boyish self-confidence, and the winning personality that had obtained success for him in his military career would be equally effective in the new one. To a large degree, they were. The values and the vision that he helped, unreflectively, to implement in the Northwest would be those of the Virginia background he had initially rejected.

Afterword

When William Henry Harrison in later life described himself as a child of the Revolution, he meant it in a political context: that the time and the circumstances of his early life, in the middle of America's defining event, had given him a special access to authentic American heroism and values, and that voters could benefit from this by putting him in office. But, as he was probably aware, he was a child of the Revolution in many more senses than this one. In fact, one could call him a child of several interlocking revolutions.

For young Harrison, as for some other children of influential American families, the primary meaning of the Revolution was destruction and dislocation—a burned home, a shattered family, experience of terror, flight, and, subsequently, exile and a curtailed education. Accompanying these experiences, however, came a set of explanations about the significance of these hardships and the grandeur of the era in which they occurred. Like other children of influential American families (John Quincy Adams is a well-known example), Harrison grew up acutely aware of an obligation to develop ideals and attitudes appropriate to the greatness of the times he lived in. In Virginia, this feeling of obligation, in the context of the ongoing economic and social disruptions of the era, led Harrison and his peers to try one career plan and set of commitments after another, in search of a life that would be both workable and virtuous. To live up to the needs of the moment and the grand destiny they envisioned, many made adjustments in their thinking on disparate subjects: religion, slavery, and alcohol, to name three. Under the pressure of extraordinary events, they moved toward becoming "self-made men" in the sense studied by Daniel Walker Howe and Joyce Appleby.

The driving force of the American Revolution was the Enlightenment belief that communities had the right to govern themselves and a consequent duty to resist oppression by distant tyrants. Parallel to that revolution, Jay Fliegelman has pointed out, was another in the sphere of personal and family relations, which asserted that the parent-child bond was not a one-way chain of authority but a reciprocal relationship, in which each party had responsibilities toward the other. The new thinking of the era insisted that the parent-child relationship ought to be one of love and gratitude, rather than lordship and duty. Tested by this doctrine, Benjamin Harrison, absolute, sarcastic, and preoccupied, was a bad parent, whom his youngest son was right to resist. Like the hero of Charles Brockden Brown's 1799 novel *Arthur Mervyn,* in Daniel Cohen's perceptive interpretation, young Harrison searched his world for substitute fathers and found them in men like Wilkinson and Wayne; like Mervyn's, his was an experience "of personal transition in a profoundly transitional age."[1] For reasons that can be reconstructed only partially, William Henry came to reject Benjamin Harrison and the values he represented, and could feel in doing so that he, not his father, embodied Revolutionary virtue.

One can point, too, to a lesser sort of revolution in the area of sensibility. Harrison's generation stood at the beginning of the Romantic era, in which philosophers like Hegel and writers like Scott and Cooper and Byron would draw inspiration from the struggles of history. The battles of the past, perhaps especially those involving colorful and valiant fringe cultures, like the Celts, the barbarians, or aboriginal peoples, captured their imagination just as Rollin, and later the epic of the Indians of the Northwest, fascinated Harrison and others. Harrison was a reader, but it is impossible to know whether he read some single work that gave him this new angle of vision, or whether he picked it up largely on his own through hints and scraps in the authors he read. Whatever his path, he arrived at a view shared by many Americans of the next generation and explored by Roy Harvey Pearce.[2] To Harrison, as to his father, the Indians were savages; but to him they were also representatives of a culture endlessly interesting and worthy of study precisely because it was doomed to extinction.

One thing is certain: Harrison, with his sensibility, his ideals, and his personal history, was very different from most of the young Virginians who swarmed into the Ohio Valley after Independence. Typically, they came with slaves and surveyors, advance agents of Virginia planter culture. They had come to extend their dynasties; Harrison had come on a personal mission to escape the values of that culture, the one in which he had been raised. Their goals, very broadly speaking, were profit and family; Harrison's were national service and individual adventure.

This book has traced Harrison's rather spectacular success in realizing his goals. It ends with an irony, however. When in early manhood, the personal mission of his adolescence accomplished, he found and married the girl of his dreams, and he discovered that the army offered no answer to the problems facing a young married man. Remarkably indifferent throughout his life to his own comfort or status, Harrison was enough of a Virginian to feel that the status and comfort of his family were paramount.[3] To that end, he gave up his career as a warrior (or so he thought) and started over again, seeking security in the other area where he felt competent—government—and working toward a life that resembled his father's. He had many traits to assist him in that field: a charming optimism, an ability to relate to people, a smattering of education. These abilities, it turned out, would serve him well, allowing him to achieve some success in politics. Nevertheless, his whole career would be marked by the same rapid succession of triumphs and disappointments that characterized his early years. It also would show repeated traces of the impulsive idealism of those years. That it would climax in the presidency was an outcome oddly in keeping with his life's quick reversals, but one that neither he nor anyone who knew him well in 1798 could have foreseen.

Notes

Preface

1. Reginald Horsman, "William Henry Harrison: Virginia Gentleman in the Old Northwest," *Indiana Magazine of History* 96 (June 2000): 125–50.

1. An Ardent Ambition to Become a Soldier

1. On campaign biographies, see Scott E. Casper, *Constructing American Lives: Biography and Culture in Nineteenth-Century America* (Chapel Hill, N.C.: Univ. of North Carolina Press, 1999), 94–106, 263–69.

2. "Biographical Memoirs of Major General William Henry Harrison," *Port Folio,* 3rd series, 5 (Apr. 1815): 305–25. The writer of this article was very likely Charles Caldwell, then the editor of the Philadelphia-based literary and political magazine *Port Folio;* see Casper, *Constructing American Lives,* 41.

3. Casper, *Constructing American Lives,* 14. On the reading habits of William Henry Harrison (hereafter, WHH), see chapter 3 of this book.

4. WHH to Erastus Brooks, 20 July 1839, William Henry Harrison Correspondence, 1802–1815 and 1836–1841, NYHS (hereafter, WHH Correspondence, NYHS).

5. Ibid.; "Biographical Memoirs of Major General William Henry Harrison," 307.

6. The portrait is reproduced in Robert M. Owens, *Mr. Jefferson's Hammer: William Henry Harrison and the Origins of American Indian Policy* (Norman, Okla.: Univ. of Oklahoma Press, 2007), 157; for the engraving, see Fillmore Nortleet, *Saint-Memin in Virginia: Portraits and Biographies* (Richmond, Va.: Dietz Press, 1942), 109.

7. Nathaniel Harrison Diary, entry of 8 Sept. 1787, Robert Alonzo Brock Collection, Henry M. Huntington Library, CW (microfilm) ("Colo. Avery, Mr. Co[u]pland & Billy Harrison dined with me" quotation).

8. John Cleves Symmes to Judge Robert Morris, 22 June 1795, in *Intimate Letters of John Cleves Symmes,* ed. Beverley W. Bond (Cincinnati, Ohio: Historical and Philosophical Society of Ohio, 1956), 98; Isaac Darneille, quoted in Freeman Cleaves, *Old Tippecanoe* (Garden City, N.Y.: Doubleday and Co., 1939), 36; WHH to "Dear Brother" [Carter Bassett Harrison], 27 Nov. 1794, William Henry Harrison Papers, LC (hereafter, WHH Papers, LC).

9. WHH to Brooks, 20 July 1839, WHH Correspondence, NYHS.

10. The *Virginia Gazette,* 30 Mar., 30 Apr. 1791, mentions three clearances from Bermuda Hundred, on the James, for Philadelphia. *Virginia Gazette,* 30 Mar., 30 Apr. 1791. Thomas Lee Shippen came by sea from Philadelphia to Hampton in the same year (Thomas Lee Shippen to Dr. William Shippen, 3 Mar. 1791, Shippen Family Papers, LC). A Captain Crozier commuted regularly between the James River plantations and Philadelphia in the spring of 1790 (Nathaniel Harrison Diary, entries of 5, 30 Apr., 2 June 1790, CW) and also carried messages for planters (Eliza Dunbar to Eliza Shippen, 13 Nov. 1791, Shippen Family Papers, LC).

11. Benjamin Harrison VI (an older brother of WHH) calculated six days for a letter to go between Richmond and Philadelphia. Benjamin Harrison VI to Robert Morris, 23 Jan. 1788, Benjamin Harrison VI Letter Book, July 1787–Sept. 1789, Harrison, Benjamin, Mss. Collection, Patricia D. Klingenstein Library, NYHS, New York. Thomas Jefferson in 1790 estimated nine or ten days. *The Papers of Thomas Jefferson,* ed. Julian P. Boyd et al. (Princeton, N.J.: Princeton Univ. Press, 1950–), 18:65.

12. The city and its suburbs combined had a population of about 42,300 in the federal census of 1790.

13. John Pope, *A Tour through the Southern and Western Territories of the United States . . .* (Richmond, Va.: John Dixon, 1792), 100; Charles W. Turner, ed., "Letters (1790–1800) of John Johnston, Rockbridge Medical Student and Doctor," *Journal of the History of Medicine* 14 (Apr. 1959): 195; François Auguste René (vicomte de) Chateaubriand, *Travels in America,* trans. Richard Switzer (Lexington, Ky.: Univ. of Kentucky Press, 1969), 14–16.

14. *Moreau de St. Mery's American Journey, 1793–1798,* ed. Kenneth Roberts and Anna M. Roberts (Garden City, N.Y.: Doubleday and Co., 1947), 89, 257; Benjamin Davies, *Some Account of the City of Philadelphia* (Philadelphia, Pa.: Richard Folwell, 1794), 10; Ralph H. Brown, *Mirror for Americans* (1943; New York: Da Capo Press, 1968), 37, 40.

15. Roberts and Roberts, *Moreau,* 316–17, 363; American Philosophical Society, *Historic Philadelphia: From the Founding until the Early Nineteenth Century,* Transactions of the American Philosophical Society, vol. 43, pt. 1 (Philadelphia, Pa.: American Philosophical Society, 1953), 309–10; Chateaubriand, *Travels in America,* 14–16; William P. and Julia P. Cutler, *Life, Journals and Correspondence of Rev. Manasseh Cutler, LL.D.* (Cincinnati, Ohio: Robert Clarke and

Co., 1888), 1:262–63, 271–85; Richard L. Bushman, *The Refinement of America: Persons, Houses, Cities* (New York: Vintage Books, 1992), 157–59; J.-P. Brissot de Warville, *New Travels in North America,* ed. and trans. Durand Echeverria (Cambridge, Mass.: Belknap Press of Harvard University, 1964), 254–56; James Mease, *The Picture of Philadelphia* (Philadelphia, Pa.: B. and E. Kite, 1811), 25, 118–19; Billy G. Smith, *The "Lower Sort": Philadelphia's Laboring People, 1750–1800* (Ithaca, N.Y.: Cornell Univ. Press, 1980), 13; Pope, *Tour,* 100–103.

16. B. G. Smith, "*Lower Sort,*" 7–39; *Pennsylvania Gazette,* 29 June 1791.

17. Turner, "Letters," 195; William Cabell Bruce, *John Randolph of Roanoke* (New York: G. P. Putnam's Sons, 1922), 1:89, 91; Robert Dawidoff, *The Education of John Randolph* (New York: W. W. Norton and Co., 1978), 24–25, 313.

18. John Dandridge to John Hopkins, 27 Dec. 1791, 1 Jan. 1792, in "Letters of John Dandridge to John Hopkins," *William and Mary Quarterly* (hereafter, *WMQ*), 1st series, 20 (Jan. 1912): 156–58; Robert Carter to his children, Hill, Anne, Lucy, and Thomas Carter, Hampton, Va., 12–14 Oct. 1803, cont. 1, folder 13, Shirley Plantation Collection, CW.

19. George W. Corner, ed., *The Autobiography of Benjamin Rush,* Memoirs of the American Philosophical Society, vol. 25 (Princeton, N.J.: Princeton Univ. Press, 1948), 148; Cutler and Cutler, *Life,* 1:257; H. E. Scudder, ed., *Recollections of Samuel Breck* (London: Sampson Low, Marston, Searle, and Rivington, 1877), 203; Eleanor M. Young, *Forgotten Patriot: Robert Morris* (New York: Macmillan, 1950), 168–69, 171–76, 185, 189, 194–95; Clarence L. Ver Steeg, *Robert Morris, Revolutionary Financier* (Philadelphia, Pa.: Univ. of Pennsylvania Press, 1954), 37; Ellis P. Oberholtzer, *Robert Morris: Patriot and Financier* (New York: Macmillan, 1903), 271; Max Farrand, ed., *The Records of the Federal Convention of 1787,* rev. ed. (New Haven, Conn.: Yale Univ. Press, 1966), 3:91; Sarah Hall, "Reminiscences of Philadelphia," quoted in John R. Stilgoe, *Borderlands: Origins of the American Suburb, 1820–1939* (New Haven, Conn.: Yale Univ. Press, 1988), 121.

20. Cutler and Cutler, *Life,* 279–80; L. H. Butterfield, ed., *Letters of Benjamin Rush* (Princeton, N.J.: Princeton Univ. Press, 1951), 1: passim; *Autobiography of Benjamin Rush,* 18, 91; Robert E. Jones, "Portraits of Dr. Benjamin Rush, M.D., by His Contemporaries," *Antiques* 108 (July 1975), 94–113.

21. Charles Carter to Thomas Jefferson, 21 May 1791, in *Papers of Thomas Jefferson,* 20:474; Joseph Carson, *A History of the Medical Department of the University of Pennsylvania. . . .* (Philadelphia, Pa.: Lindsay and Blakiston, 1869), 96.

22. Lecture notes, John Peter Mettauer Papers, H-SC, Hampden-Sydney, Va.

23. "Biographical Memoirs of Major General William Henry Harrison," 310.

24. Henry Skipwith to Jefferson, 4 Sept. 1791, in *Papers of Thomas Jefferson,* 22:108.

25. Thomas Jefferson estimated that costs for a medical student in Edinburgh were a little less than those in Philadelphia. Thomas Jefferson to Charles Carter, 10 July 1791, in *Papers of Thomas Jefferson,* 20:613.

26. Butterfield, *Letters of Benjamin Rush,* 1:578, 610; Rush to Elizabeth Rush, 25 July 1791, *The Collector* 72, 685 (June 1949): 127. For Shippen, see John H. Powell, *Bring Out Your Dead* (Philadelphia, Pa.: Univ. of Pennsylvania Press, 1949), 32; and Ethel Armes, ed., *Nancy Shippen: Her Journal Book* (Philadelphia, Pa.: J. B. Lippincott Co., 1935), 24.

27. Barton's papers at the Historical Society of Pennsylvania contain many references to his interest in "the ancient works called, by me and by others, fortifications," during the early 1790s. Benjamin Barton to Joseph Banks, 26 May 1793, Benjamin Smith Barton Papers, 1778–1813, HSP. Barton had published on the subject in 1787. He corresponded with informants in the Western army, but WHH is not mentioned among them.

28. For a good summary of these pros and cons in a British setting, see Dorothy Porter and Roy Porter, *Patient's Progress: Doctors and Doctoring in Eighteenth-Century England* (Cambridge, UK: Polity Press, 1989), especially 26–27, 62–65, 117, 122, 137, 210–11. For the United States, and Virginia in particular, see Henry B. Shafer, *The American Medical Profession, 1783 to 1850,* Studies in History, Economics, and Public Law, no. 417 (New York: Columbia Univ. Press, 1936), 166–72; Wyndham D. B. Blanton, *Medicine in Virginia in the Eighteenth Century* (Richmond, Va.: Garrett and Massie, 1931), 207–8; George Tucker, *The Valley of Shenandoah* (New York: Charles Wiley, 1824), 2:149; and, for a good example from Virginia, James Walker to James T. Hubard, 6 Jan. 1797, Hubard Family Papers, 1741–1907, SHC.

29. Charles Rollin, *The Ancient History of the Egyptians, Carthaginians, Assyrians, Babylonians, Medes and Persians, Macedonians, and Grecians* (New York: Evert Duyckinck, 1812), 6:133.

30. James Elliot, *The Poetical and Miscellaneous Works of James Elliot* (Greenfield, Mass.: Thomas Dickman, 1798), 116.

2. An Education Manqué

1. Allen Kulikoff, *Tobacco and Slaves: The Development of Southern Cultures in the Chesapeake, 1680–1800* (Chapel Hill, N.C.: Univ. of North Carolina Press, 1986); Louis B. Wright, *The First Gentlemen of Virginia: Intellectual Qualities of the Early Colonial Ruling Class* (1940; Charlottesville, Va.: Dominion Books, 1964); Edmund Morgan, *Virginians at Home: Family Life in the Eighteenth Century* (Williamsburg, Va.: Colonial Williamsburg, 1952); Rhys Isaac, *The Transformation of Virginia, 1740–1790* (Chapel Hill, N.C.: Univ. of North Carolina Press, 1982); T. H. Breen, *Tobacco Culture: The Mentality of the Great Tidewater Planters on the Eve of Revolution*

(Princeton, N.J.: Princeton Univ. Press, 1985), quotes, 85, 89; Daniel Blake Smith, *Inside the Great House* (Ithaca, N.Y.: Cornell Univ. Press, 1980); David Hackett Fischer, *Albion's Seed* (New York: Oxford Univ. Press, 1989). The classic reference to patriarchs comes from William Byrd II's statement of his own power, quoted in Isaac, *Transformation of Virginia,* 39–40, with its comparison to the biblical patriarchs—"I have my Flocks and my Herds, my Bond-men, and Bond-women, and every Soart of trade amongst my own Servants, so that I live in a kind of Independence on everyone but Providence"; see also Isaac's accompanying discussion, 34–39.

2. Louis B. Wright explains the importance of the Roman classics, and shows how they related to planters' daily routine; see Wright, *First Gentlemen,* 14–15 and 58–59, respectively.

3. Fischer, *Albion's Seed,* 312–16.

4. D. B. Smith, *Inside the Great House,* 92–94; Wright, *First Gentlemen,* 14–15.

5. The planter's son was Alfred Lorrain, quoted in Joyce Appleby, ed., *Recollections of the Early Republic: Selected Autobiographies* (Boston, Mass.: Northeastern Univ. Press, 1997), 249; for some examples of intimacy between slaves and children of slaveholders, see *Journal & Letters of Philip Vickers Fithian, 1773–1774,* ed. Hunter D. Farish (Williamsburg, Va.: Colonial Williamsburg, 1943), 82, 83, 93–94. On the role of women as arbiters of appearance and conduct, see *Journal & Letters of Philip Vickers Fithian,* 160; Kulikoff, *Tobacco and Slaves,* 193–94; Elizabeth J. Ambler Carrington, "Old Virginia Correspondence," *Atlantic Monthly* 84 (Oct. 1899): 547; Tucker, *Valley of Shenandoah,* 2:73. On the influence of age mates, see Jack P. Greene, ed., *The Diary of Landon Carter of Sabine Hall, 1752–1778* (Charlottesville, Va.: Univ. Press of Virginia, 1965), 2:662, 664, 869, 900; and Phillip Hamilton, *The Making and Unmaking of a Revolutionary Family* (Charlottesville, Va.: Univ. of Virginia Press, 2003), 54–55.

6. On the general sequence of formal education, see Morgan, *Virginians at Home,* 12–17. On tutors, see D. B. Smith, *Inside the Great House,* 107–10; Wright, *First Gentlemen,* 133; *Journal & Letters of Philip Vickers Fithian,* passim; and W. Gordon McCabe, *Virginia Schools before and after the Revolution* (Charlottesville, Va.: Society of the Alumni of the University of Virginia, 1890), 33–34. For an example of an inadequate tutor, see *Diary of Landon Carter,* 2:668, 765. On the College of William and Mary, see Wright, *First Gentlemen,* 115; and Kulikoff, *Tobacco and Slaves,* 278. Johann David Schoepf, a European visiting Virginia in 1783, was struck by the boys' early assumption of adult roles: "A Virginia youth of fifteen years is already such a man as he will be at twice that age; at fifteen, his father gives him a horse and a negro, with which he riots about the country, attends every fox-hunt, horse-race, and cock-fight, and does nothing else whatever; a wife is his next and only care." Johann David Schoepf, *Travels in the Confederation,* ed. Alfred J. Morrison (Philadelphia, Pa.: W. J. Campbell, 1911), 1:95.

7. Clifford Dowdey, *The Great Plantation* (New York: Rinehart and Co., 1957), 97–104, 148–51; [W. G. Stanard,] "Harrison of James River," *Virginia Magazine of History and Biography* (hereafter, *VMHB*) 34:87–90. The quotation is from Kate M. Rowland, *Life of George Mason* (New York: G. P. Putnam's Sons, 1892), 2:77.

8. Howard W. Smith, *Benjamin Harrison and the American Revolution* (Williamsburg, Va.: Virginia Independence Bicentennial Commission, 1978), 43–73. On Colonel Harrison, see Lyon Gardiner Tyler, *Letters and Times of the Tylers* (Richmond, Va.: Whittet and Shepperson, 1884), 1:67. Harrison's property is enumerated in Jackson T. Main, "The One Hundred," *William and Mary Quarterly* (hereafter, *WMQ*), 3rd series, 11 (July 1964): 362, 364, 376. Isaac, *Transformation*, 109, discusses the importance of the rank of colonel.

9. Henry H. Wilson, "Benjamin Harrison, 5th, Signer of the Declaration of Independence, Governor of Virginia, etc.," James A. Green Papers, CHS, 4; Dowdey, *The Great Plantation*, 178, 216; Benjamin Harrison [V] to Robert Morris, 5 Sept. 1776, Emmet Collection, NYPL; Benjamin Harrison to Robert Morris, 8 Jan. 1777, in Edmund C. Burnett, ed., *Letters of Members of the Continental Congress* (Washington, D.C.: Carnegie Institution of Washington, 1921–36), 2:208; John Adams, *Autobiography*, and John Adams, diary, both quoted in Burnett, *Letters of Members of the Continental Congress*, quoted on 1:394n and 1:3, respectively; *Sanderson's Biography of the Signers of the Declaration of Independence*, ed. Robert T. Conrad (Philadelphia, Pa.: Thomas, Cowperthwait and Co., 1848), 785; Edmund Pendleton, quoted in *The Letters and Papers of Edmund Pendleton*, ed. David J. Mays, Virginia Historical Society Documents (Charlottesville, Va.: Univ. of Virginia Press, 1967), 2:479. Silas Deane of Connecticut, on first meeting Benjamin Harrison, described him as "an uncommonly large man . . . rather rough in his address and speech." Deane, quoted in Burnett, *Letters* of *Members of the Continental Congress*, 1:28. A portrait of Benjamin Harrison as a young man is on the cover of H. W. Smith, *Benjamin Harrison*.

10. D. B. Smith, *Inside the Great House*, 82–125—see especially 100, 124; Conrad, *Sanderson's Biography of the Signers*, 727; H. W. Smith, *Benjamin Harrison*, 47, 73, 82; Benjamin Harrison to George Washington, 26 Feb. 1789, in George Washington, *The Papers of George Washington: Presidential Series*, ed. W. W. Abbot (Charlottesville, Va.: Univ. Press of Virginia, 1987–), 1:345–46 ("Mrs. Harrison has been for a long time in a bad state of health"); Thomas Lee Shippen to Anne Shippen, 7 Nov. 1791, Shippen Family Papers, LC.

11. Benjamin Harrison's shipyard is repeatedly referred to in his wartime correspondence with Robert Morris, extensively quoted in *Catalogue No. 1183, The Confidential Correespondence of Robert Morris . . . to be sold Tuesday Afternoon and Evening, January 16, 1917, at 2:30 and 8 o'clock, Stan V. Henkels, Auction Commission Merchant.* His mills are mentioned in Charles Fleming

to William Davies, 10 Jan. 1781, in *Papers of Thomas Jefferson,* 4:329. Ben and Carter Harrison are discussed in [Stanard,] "Harrison of James River," 35: 89–93, although the account of Ben's marriages presented there is inaccurate; see also Benjamin Harrison, Benjamin Harrison VI Letter Book, July 1787–Sept. 1789, NYHS. On the shortage of tutors, see Hamilton, *Making and Unmaking,* 53–54; and McCabe, *Virginia Schools,* 29–31.

12. The sequence of the raid can be followed in the reports received by Governor Jefferson, in *Papers of Thomas Jefferson,* 4:258, 263, 297, 329. The flight of other planters' families is reported in Hamilton, *Making and Unmaking;* and St. George Tucker to Theodorick Bland, 21 Jan. 1781, in *The Bland Papers, Being a Selection from the Manuscripts of Colonel Theodorick Bland, Jr., of Prince George County, Virginia* (Petersburg, Va.: Edmund and Julian C. Ruffin, 1841–43), 2:55. A report of the Committee on Privileges and Elections in Virginia, in *Journal of the House of Delegates,* vol. 6, 3 Nov. 1785, summarizes the damage to Berkeley and ascribes it to both Arnold's raid and the subsequent invasion by Lord Cornwallis's forces in May 1781. A letter written in 1781 by John Banister to Colonel Bland (Letter 8, *The Bland Papers,* 2:63) expresses the Virginians' view that the acts of destruction committed by Arnold's troops were "always marked by personal animosity, and revenge, of long standing." (Bannister's letter does not mention Arnold by name, but the military context and his use of the adjective "personal" make the meaning unmistakable.) Colonel Harrison was particularly bitter about the destruction of the family portraits; see his comment in James A. Green, *William Henry Harrison: His Life and Times* (Richmond, Va.: Garret and Massie, 1941), 2. On Ben Harrison and Berkeley, see Dowdey, *The Great Plantation,* 298.

13. The Marquis de Chastellux visited Colonel Harrison in Richmond in April 1782, and much of this passage is based on his account. Francois-Jean, Marquis de Chastellux, *Travels in North America in the Years 1780, 1781 and 1782* (Chapel Hill, N.C.: Univ. of North Carolina Press, 1963), 2:428. The son who was assisting him was Ben, who lived next door and who seems to have handled a good deal of his father's correspondence (*Henkels Catalogue No. 1183, Correspondence of Robert Morris,* 20), perhaps because of his father's increasing disability, described later in this paragraph. According to a 1782 census reproduced in *Heads of Families at the First Census of the United States: Virginia* (Washington, D.C.: GPO, 1908), 118, Mrs. Harrison was with him, as was their daughter Sally and a niece, Anne Bassett, but WHH was absent. Two years later, however, the "Return of Inhabitants" for 1784, Richmond Common Hall Records, VSL, records that he was there with the other two young people. Presumably he was away studying in 1782. Billy's next documented school, Hampden-Sydney, was near his uncle Carter's home, and one of Carter's sons, Randolph Harrison, attended it during the same period; hence my suggestion that Carter H. Harrison had a part in directing Billy's

education. A descendant of Carter H. Harrison described him as "a man of literary attainments devoted to his books" who "carried on the instruction of his boys himself," though "a stern and harsh teacher." [Stanard,] "Harrison of James River," 34:207–10.

14. Benjamin Harrison VI to Robert Morris, 1 Oct., 7 Nov. 1788, Benjamin Harrison VI Letter Book, NYHS. For an example of a Virginia gentleman and contemporary of Benjamin Harrison who became an alcoholic in the modern sense, see Rodney M. Baine, *Robert Mumford: America's First Comic Dramatist* (Athens, Ga.: Univ. of Georgia Press, 1967), especially 55–56. For Harrison's loss of influence, see Mark A. Mastromarino, "'The Horrid Disposition of the Times': Charles City County, Virginia, and the American Revolution," in *Charles City County, Virginia: An Official History,* ed. James P. Whittenburg and John M. Coski (Salem, W.V.: Don Mills, 1989), 45.

15. Elizabeth Harrison's marriage was reported in the *Virginia Gazette* (Purdie), 5 May 1775. For Rickman's career, see Blanton, *Medicine in Virginia in the Eighteenth Century,* 248, 273, 280, 331; and Dowdey, The *Great Plantation,* 249. Rickman's death is mentioned in Elizabeth Farley to Thomas T. Byrd, 25 June 1783, Miscellaneous Mss., NYHS. On planters' selecting careers for their sons, see D. B. Smith, *Inside the Great House,* 93–95; on Harrison's doing so, see [Stanard,] "Harrison of James River," 35:89, 93.

16. The Presbyterian connection is sketched in John Luster Brinkley, *On This Hill* (Hampden-Sydney, Va.: Hampden-Sydney College, 1995), 4–5; the medical connection is suggested in Blanton, *Medicine in Virginia in the Eighteenth Century,* 92, 326–39; and Harry Toulmin, *The Western Country in 1793,* ed. Marion Tinling and Geoffrey Davies (San Marino, Calif.: Henry E. Huntington Library, 1948), 90. An example of what Colonel Harrison may have had in mind was the career of James Jones of Amelia County; Jones, a year older than WHH, graduated from Hampden-Sydney in 1790 and from Edinburgh in 1796. Alfred J. Morrison, *College of Hampden-Sidney—Dictionary of Biography, 1776–1825* (Hampden-Sydney, Va.: Hampden-Sydney College, 1921), 32.

17. H. W. Smith, *Benjamin Harrison,* 25–59; WHH to Robert Waln, 28 Oct. 1823, quoted in Green, *William Henry Harrison,* 476.

18. Hampden-Sydney College had two parts, with academy referring to its lower grades. In most biographies of WHH, the dates for his attendance at Hampden-Sydney are given as 1787–1790. The source for this statement is a *General Catalogue of the Officers & Students of Hampden-Sidney College, Virginia, 1776–1906* (Richmond, Va.: Whittet and Shepperson, 1908), which looks impressive but ultimately rests on no documentary evidence, given what the college's historian calls "the sorry state of the records." Brinkley, *On This Hill,* ix. In fact, there is no official documentation whatever of WHH's attendance at Hampden-Sydney. Three pieces of evidence, however, exist that bear on the

question: the statement in "Biographical Memoirs of Major General William Henry Harrison" that he entered at an unspecified age and left at age fourteen (i.e., in 1787); the torn 1786 exhibition program mentioned in the text, cited in Morrison, *Dictionary of Biography,* 52; and two entries in Dr. Francis J. Mettauer's 193-page ledger in the John Peter Mettauer Papers, H-SC. Herbert C. Bradshaw, a local historian, transcribed Mettauer's ledger in Appendix 3 of his *History of Hampden-Sydney College* (Durham, N.C.: Privately printed, 1976) in the belief that it supported the *General Catalogue*'s dates, but a comparison with Mettauer's manuscript shows that Bradshaw misread the date of one of the entries as "1789" rather than the actual date, 1785. (Other entries show clearly that Mettauer wrote his 9s differently from the figure taken by Bradshaw to be a 9 in this date. Moreover, it must be earlier than the 1787 entry, as shown by the fact that the 1785 amount is referred to in 1787 as remaining unpaid.)

Documentary evidence, therefore, places WHH at Hampden-Sydney in 1785 and 1787. These dates correspond with the *Port Folio* account (the earliest biography of WHH and one for which WHH himself furnished the material) and should be accepted as factual. Most likely, as suggested in the text, he entered the school at the expiration of his father's gubernatorial term in 1784.

The fact that WHH attended the school in his very early teens strongly suggests that he was studying in the academy, not in the collegiate division, a conclusion supported by the additional fact that after leaving Hampden-Sydney he entered Millfield Academy. Thus he belongs to the list of American presidents, beginning with Washington and ending with Truman, who had no college education at all.

19. Brinkley, *On This Hill,* 3–26, 30; William H. Foote, *Sketches of Virginia Historical and Biographical* (Philadelphia, Pa.: W. S. Martien, 1850–55), 1:405; Morrison, *Dictionary of Biography,* 50. Dabney Carr's attendance can be followed through letters, mostly from James Madison, in *Papers of Thomas Jefferson,* 7:598, 8:96, 9:39, 11:15, 11:402, and 15:157.

20. On John Blair Smith, see Brinkley, *On This Hill,* 28; Charles Grier Sellers, "John Blair Smith," *Journal of the Presbyterian Historical Society* 34 (Dec. 1956): 216–17; and Donald R. Come, "The Influence of Princeton on Higher Education in the South before 1825," *WMQ,* 3rd series, 2 (Oct. 1945): 372. The other faculty members after 1783 were Drury Lacy (for whom see Foote, *Sketches of Virginia,* 1:418, 491) and the unfortunate William Mahon, whose career is discussed in Brinkley, *On This Hill;* 64. According to William Hill (also quoted in Brinkley, *On This Hill,* 32), there were about eighty students in 1785. For a description, see Brinkley, *On This Hill,* 13; and Morrison, *Dictionary of Biography,* 288. Francis Asbury is quoted in Morrison, *Dictionary of Biography,* 60; James Mercer's comment is from a letter he wrote to James Madison, 19 May 1786, *The Papers of James Madison,* ed. Robert A. Rutland et al. (Chapel Hill, N.C.: Univ. of North Carolina Press, 1974–), 9:60.

21. Brinkley, *On This Hill,* 19; Wesley M. Gewehr, *The Great Awakening in Virginia, 1740–1790* (1930; Gloucester, Mass.: Peter Smith, 1965), 227–28. Randolph Harrison, born in 1769, evidently attended before 1786; see [Stanard,] "Harrison of James River," 35:210.

22. Information on the beginning of the winter term is in Brinkley, *On This Hill,* 16. The following works all illustrate the Virginia gentry's passion for horses and the eagerness of planters' sons like the Carters to ride as often and as far as possible: Schoepf, *Travels in the Confederation,* 45, 94–95; *Journal & Letters of Philip Vickers Fithian,* 46, 49, 64, 94, 227–28, 233, 250; Jane Carson, *Colonial Virginians at Play* (Williamsburg, Va.: Colonial Williamsburg, 1965), 103–4; and *Diary of Landon Carter,* 2:661–62, 664, 895–96, 900. Instances cited in Isaac, *Transformation,* 161–63, 169, suggest the importance of appearing mounted on horseback to the aggressive "gentry style." Following Isaac, I would argue that being able to appear unescorted in public on horseback was a central part of a Virginia youth's transition to manhood. The age at which this transition took place varied, no doubt, from family to family but seems usually to have been in the early teens (D. B. Smith, *Inside the Great House,* 84). Nine- or ten-year-olds sometimes rode horseback on their own farms (Bruce, *John Randolph,* 1:46, 2:155). Twelve-year-old Robert Bailey, in the family of a minor planter in Culpeper County, was allowed to ride to dancing school on Saturdays but not on any other occasion (Robert Bailey, *The Life and Adventures of Robert Bailey. . . .* [Richmond: J. and G. Cochran, 1822], 24). At fifteen, Landon Carter had a horse for his own full-time use (*Diary of Landon Carter,* 2:702–3), while at sixteen, Bob Carter rode freely within his family's plantation and occasionally with his family or tutor to church or on visits but went to dancing school in a carriage (*Journal & Letters of Philip Vickers Fithian,* 56, 68, 94). At the same age of sixteen, however, John Randolph could describe himself as "jaded with riding all over the country" and apparently had complete liberty of movement (Bruce, *John Randolph,* 1:100–101).

23. Bruce, *John Randolph,* 2:165, 415–20; John Hatchett, *Prince Edward County, Virginia: A Short Narrative of the Life of John Hatchett,* ed. Joseph D. Eggleston (Farmville, Va.: n.p., n.d.), 6, 8; Edward C. Carter II, ed., *The Virginia Journals of Benjamin Henry Latrobe* (New Haven, Conn.: Yale Univ. Press, 1977), 1:127, 142.

24. Bruce, *John Randolph,* 2:128, 530; Carter, *Virginia Journals,* 1:125; "The Journal of William Loughton Smith, 1790–1791," *Proceedings of the Massachusetts Historical Society* 51 (1917–18): 69.

25. A transcription of the program is in Morrison, *Dictionary of Biography,* 52. Morrison takes the name as referring to WHH.

26. The bill is in the John Peter Mettauer Papers, H-SC. I thank Dr. Frederick C. Skvara for his help in interpreting it. One of the medicines listed in it is kino, an astringent often used to assist the closure of a wound or incision.

27. Blanton, *Medicine in Virginia in the Eighteenth Century,* 386; Shafer, *American Medical Profession,* 24.

28. John Peter Mettauer Papers, H-SC; Tucker, *Valley of Shenandoah,* 2:105.

29. Alfred J. Morrison, *The College of Hampden-Sydney—Calendar of Board Minutes, 1776–1876* (Richmond, Va.: Hermitage Press, 1912), 30–31; Morrison, *Dictionary of Biography,* 288; Brinkley, *On This Hill,* 63; Chastellux, *Travels in North America,* 2:441; William Hill, *Autobiographical Sketches of Dr. William Hill. . . . ,* Historical Transcripts No. 4 (Richmond, Va.: Union Theological Seminary in Virginia, 1968), 7; Bradshaw, *History of Hampden-Sydney College,* 70.

30. Brinkley, *On This Hill,* 24n, 32, 64–65; Morrison, *Dictionary of Biography,* 295; Morrison, *Calendar of Board Minutes,* 30; Hill, *Autobiographical Sketches of Dr. William Hill,* 4–7; Foote, *Sketches of Virginia,* 1:415; Bradshaw, *History of Hampden-Sydney College,* 64–65.

31. Hill, *Autobiographical Sketches of Dr. William Hill,* 9, 107. The two principal accounts of this revival are in Hill, *Autobiographical Sketches,* 9–11; and in Foote, *Sketches of Virginia,* 1:414–24. They are not wholly independent of each other; Foote relied in part on Hill's recollections. Neither mentions WHH, but a comparison of the two accounts permits construction of a fairly detailed timetable for the first stirrings of religious enthusiasm in the area. Foote agrees with Hatchett (*Prince Edward County,* 6) that the revival began in 1787 and started outside the college, in Cumberland County, and spread later to Hampden-Sydney. Hill (*Autobiographical Sketches,* 9) places the meeting that Cary Allen attended in Cumberland during the Christmas holidays of 1786–87. On "enthusiasm," see Gewehr, *Great Awakening in Virginia,* 115–16, 153; and *Journal & Letters of Philip Vickers Fithian,* 96–97. The best modern account is in Iain Murray, *Revival and Revivalism: The Making and Meaning of American Evangelicalism, 1750–1858* (Edinburgh: The Banner of Truth Trust, 1994), 78–99.

32. Hill, *Autobiographical Sketches of Dr. William Hill,* 4, 42; Morrison, *Dictionary of Biography,* 78–79; Foote, *Sketches of Virginia,* 1:416–17. That Allen, Hill, and the others held their clandestine meetings in the woods, close to nature and away from the spaces authorized for religious activity, was very much in keeping with the pattern of romantic revivalism; see Isaac, *Transformation,* 301; and Thomas Coke, *Extracts of the Journals of the Rev. Dr. Coke* (London: G. Paramore, 1793), 69. The confrontation at Hill's room took place during the spring term of 1787 (Hill, *Autobiographical Sketches,* 10), a date supported by the statement of William Spencer, a convert during the early phase of the revival, that he accepted Christ on 17 May 1787, noted in his diary entry for 17 May 1790 (Diary of William Spencer, CW). Murray (*Revival and Revivalism,* 96) places the beginning of the revival in September, following Foote's dating (*Sketches of Virginia,* 1:414), but the weight of the evidence is against them.

33. WHH's treatment is in Dr. Mettauer's account book, John Peter Mettauer Papers, H-SC; his whereabouts in September are noted in the Nathaniel Harrison Diary, entries of 8, 24 Sept. 1787, CW (microfilm).

34. On Benjamin Harrison V's support for the Anglican Church, see James Madison to Thomas Jefferson, 9 Jan. 1785, in *Papers of Thomas Jefferson,* 7:597. The "greatest curse" quotation came from John Blair Smith to Madison, May 1785, in Rutland, *Papers of James Madison,* 8:282.

35. The prospectus for Millfield Academy is in the *Virginia Independent Chronicle,* 3 Oct. 1787. Burges's mention of room for "ten or twelve boarders" gives an idea of the size of the school. On Burges, see William Meade, *Old Churches, Ministers, and Families of Virginia* (Philadelphia, Pa.: J. B. Lippincott and Co., 1857), 1:308; *Virginia Gazette,* 17 Jan. 1777; G. McLaren Brydon, "The Wealth of the Clergy in Virginia," *Historical Magazine of the Protestant Episcopal Church* 22 (Mar. 1953): 94. WHH's attendance is also mentioned in Joseph B. Cheshire, ed., *Sketches of Church History in North Carolina* (Wilmington, N.C.: L. DeRosset Jr., 1892), 83–84; and *Proceedings of the 103d Annual Communication of the M. W. Grand Lodge of Ancient York Masons of Virginia. . . .* (Richmond, Va.: N.p., 1880), 377, 381, 390. Benjamin Drew, one of the other Millfield students mentioned in the latter source, has the same name as a fellow student of WHH at Hampden-Sydney in 1786 (Morrison, *Dictionary of Biography,* 52). If the similarity is not coincidental, it may provide a clue to the reason why Benjamin Harrison V sent WHH to this out-of-the-way academy.

3. Friend of Human Liberty

1. Blanton, *Medicine in Virginia in the Eighteenth Century,* 80–81, 207–8; James T. Hubard to George P. King, 6 Sept. 1794, Hubard Family Papers, SHC; Shafer, *The American Medical Profession,* 35–37.

2. *Sanderson's Biography of the Signers,* 723, 728; Benjamin Harrison V to George Washington, 26 Feb. 1789, Washington, *Washington Papers: Presidential Series,* 1:345–46; Benjamin Harrison V to Charles Carroll, 16 Feb. 1789, Society Collection, HSP; Benjamin Harrison V to William Pennock, 17 Feb. 1786, and Benjamin Harrison V to Thomas Willing, 18 Aug. 1789, both in Gratz Collection, HSP; *Virginia Independent Chronicle,* 12 Mar. 1788, 4 Mar. 1789; Thomas Willing Balch, *Willing Letters and Papers* (Philadelphia, Pa.: Allen, Lane, and Scott, 1922), 138–40.

3. Blanton, *Medicine in Virginia in the Eighteenth Century,* 326–39.

4. College of William and Mary, *A Provisional List of Alumni, Grammar School Students, Members of the Faculty, and Members of the Board of Visitors of the College of William and Mary in Virginia, from 1693 to 1888* (Richmond, Va.: Division of Purchase and Printing, 1941); *Sanderson's Biography of the Signers,* 728–29.

5. Samuel Mordecai, *Richmond in By-Gone Days* (Richmond, Va.: George M. West, 1856), 153, 182–84; *The Papers of John Marshall*, ed. Herbert A. Johnson et al. (Chapel Hill, N.C.: Univ. of North Carolina Press, 1974–), 1:386, 400; Richmond Personal Property Tax Lists, 1789–1798, VSL; Blanton, *Medicine in Virginia in the Eighteenth Century*, 30–40, 338; Harry M. Ward and Harold E. Greer Jr., *Richmond during the Revolution, 1775–1783* (Charlottesville, Va.: Univ. Press of Virginia, 1977), 16; Shafer, *The American Medical Profession*, 99–103; Daniel Drake, *Discourses Delivered by Appointment before the Cincinnati Medical Association. . . .* (Cincinnati: Moore and Anderson, 1852), 55.

6. Gerald W. Mullin, *Flight and Rebellion: Slave Resistance in Eighteenth-Century Virginia* (New York: Oxford Univ. Press, 1972), 137; Luigi Castiglioni, *Viaggio negli Stati Uniti dall' America Settentrionale fatto negli anni 1785, 1786, e 1787* (Milano: Stamperia di Giuseppe Marelli, 1790), 371; "Journal of William Loughton Smith," 65; *The Revolutionary Journal of Baron Ludwig Von Closen, 1780–1783*, ed. Evelyn M. Acomb (Chapel Hill, N.C.: Univ. of North Carolina Press, 1958), 186 ("much less beautiful" quotation); Robert Hunter Jr., *Quebec to Carolina in 1785–1786*, ed. Louis B. Wright and Marion Tinling (San Marino, Calif.: Huntington Library, 1943), 234 ("one of the dirtiest" quotation). According to Thomas Jefferson in 1789, the lower part of town was "so deserted, that you cannot get a person to live in a house there rentfree." Thomas Jefferson to William Short, 14 Dec. 1789, *Papers of Thomas Jefferson*, 16:26.

7. Benjamin Harrison VI to Robert Morris, 23 Jan., 8, 18 Aug. 1788; to Samuel Griffin, 6 Aug. 1788; to Robert Hare, 25 Nov. 1788; to James Mercer, 3 Aug. 1788; and to John S. Wills, 2 Mar. 1789, Harrison Letter Book, NYHS; Netti Schreiner-Yantis and Florene Speakman Love, comps., *The 1787 Census of Virginia* (Springfield, Va.: Genealogical Books in Print, 1987), 2:1092; fragment of account book, 1789, WHH Papers, LC; Ward and Greer, *Richmond during the Revolution, 1775–1783*, 133; [Stanard,] "Harrison of James River," 35:90.

8. *Virginia Gazette*, 13, 27 Oct. 1790; Eliza Ambler to Mildred Smith, [Feb.] 1785, in Carrington, "An Old Virginia Correspondence," 540; *Bulletin of the Virginia Historical Society*, no. 16; Schoepf, *Travels in the Confederation*, 64.

9. "Journal of William Loughton Smith," 65. This sort of enthusiasm for natural beauty, especially for hills and rocks, had become a standard theme in English writing by 1790; see, for example, Carl Paul Barbier, *Samuel Rogers and William Gilpin: Their Friendship and Correspondence* (London: Oxford Univ. Press), 1–7 and passim.

10. Reprinted in William Ogden Niles, comp., *The Tippecanoe Text-Book* (Baltimore, Md.: Duff Green, 1840), 69.

11. *Cincinnati Philanthropist*, 4 Feb. 1840, reprinted from the *Liberty Hall and Cincinnati Gazette*, Oct. or Nov. 1822; John McLean, Sketch of Rev. Philip Gatch (Cincinnati, Ohio: Swormstedt and Poe, 1854), 25; *Memorials Presented*

to the Congress of the United States of America, by the Different Societies Instituted for Promoting the Abolition of Slavery, &c., &c. (Philadelphia, Pa.: Francis Bailey, 1792), 29; Josiah Morrow, ed., "Tours into Kentucky and the Northwest Territory: Three Journals by the Rev. James Smith of Powhatan County, Va., 1783–1795–1797," *Ohio Historical and Archeological Quarterly* 16 (1907): 350.

12. WHH's statement (Niles, *The Tippecanoe Text-Book,* 69) said that he joined the Abolition Society at age eighteen. If taken literally, this means after his eighteenth birthday (9 Feb. 1791), or only two months before his departure for Philadelphia. This late date may well be correct—it fits with some of the possible reasons cited below (p. 49), and the short time between it and his departure underlines the promptness of Colonel Harrison's reaction. The society had been in existence since its formation in April 1790, also at a meeting in Richmond (*Pennsylvania Gazette,* 3 Feb. 1790), and since the summer of that year it had refused to admit slaveholders to membership, as Gatch said in his statement (Robert Pleasants to James Pemberton, 19 June 1790, Robert Pleasants Letter Book, Valentine Museum). Technically, then, WHH was ineligible for membership after inheriting the slave George early in 1791, unless he freed him. For Virginia slaveholders' unhappiness with slavery, see Chastellux, *Travels in North America,* 2:439; and Robert Pleasants to Patrick Henry, 1 Sept. 1790, Robert Pleasants Letter Book.

13. A large number of such documents from Virginia, assembled by genealogical researchers, can be found at the website www.freeafricanamericans.com. Several of these documents of possible relevance to WHH's story concern a Benjamin Drew of Southampton County, a Methodist who freed several slaves in 1792–1796 (Southampton County Deed Books, 7:276, 330, 475, 8:299). See chapter 2, note 35, for more on Benjamin Drew.

14. Thad W. Tate Jr., *The Negro in Eighteenth-Century Williamsburg,* Williamsburg Research Studies (Williamsburg, Va.: Colonial Williamsburg, 1965), 227–29; Jay Worrall Jr., *The Friendly Virginians: America's First Quakers* (Athens, Ga.: Iberian Publishing Co., 1994), 243; Charles T. Nall, ed., "A Letter from Petersburg, Virginia, Jan. 10, 1789," *VMHB* 82 (Apr. 1974): 147; Lewis C. Gray, *History of Agriculture in the Southern United States to 1860* (1932; Gloucester, Mass.: Peter Smith, 1958), 2:617; Stephen B. Weeks, *Southern Quakers and Slavery,* Johns Hopkins University Studies in History and Political Science, extra volume, 15 (Baltimore, Md.: Johns Hopkins Press, 1896), 212–13.

15. Bruce, *John Randolph of Roanoke,* 1:104–5; Robert Carter to his children, 12–14 Oct. 1803, Shirley Plantation Collection, CW. Isaac (*The Transformation of Virginia,* 309–10) usefully distinguishes between the two springs of antislavery feeling in Virginia.

16. Winthrop D. Jordan, *White over Black: American Attitudes toward the Negro, 1550–1812* (Chapel Hill, N.C.: Univ. of North Carolina Press, 1968),

341; Morgan, *Virginians at Home,* 54–64; Kulikoff, *Tobacco and Slaves,* 393; Mullin, *Flight and Rebellion,* 51, 80–81; *Journal & Letters of Philip Vickers Fithian,* 169–70, 177.

17. W. D. Jordan, *White over Black,* 159–62; Chastellux, *Travels in North America,* 2:585; *Virginia Journals of Benjamin Henry Latrobe,* 1:225.

18. David Brion Davis, *The Problem of Slavery in Western Culture* (Ithaca, N.Y.: Cornell Univ. Press, 1966), 356–64; W. D. Jordan, *White over Black,* 366–72. Jordan (*White over Black,* 369–70n66) gives a list of antislavery articles of this kind published in the 1790s and after. Several were from the Philadelphia periodical *American Museum,* which circulated freely in Virginia and to which WHH's master, Andrew Leiper, subscribed.

19. WHH to Brooks, 20 July 1839, WHH Correspondence, NYHS.

20. *Memorials Presented to the Congress,* 29; Diary of William Spencer, 13 June, 27 July 1790, CW. In general, on this topic, see Cynthia L. Lyerly, *Methodism and the Southern Mind, 1770–1810* (New York: Oxford Univ. Press, 2006).

21. Gewehr, *Great Awakening in Virginia,* 168–73; Murray, *Revival and Revivalism,* 79–80, 94.

22. Diary of Rev. William Spencer, 27 July 1790, CW; Minton Thrift, *Memoir of the Rev. Jesse Lee* (New York: N. Bangs and T. Mason, 1823), 78–80; Gewehr, *Great Awakening in Virginia,* 242–43; Thomas Coke, *Extracts of the Journals of the Rev. Dr. Coke* (London: G. Paramore, 1793), 33.

23. Will of Elizabeth Harrison Edmondson, 3 May 1790, in Charles City County Will Book, 1789–1808, VSL. The Virginia records of manumissions in these years have been compiled, and neither WHH's name nor that of the slave George appears in them. Possibly he took the slave to Pennsylvania with him and freed him there.

24. Gary B. Nash and Jean R. Soderlund, *Freedom by Degrees: Emancipation in Pennsylvania and Its Aftermath* (New York: Oxford Univ. Press, 1791), 144–46. For a similar transaction by Benjamin Rush in 1788, see David Freeman Hawke, *Benjamin Rush: Revolutionary Gadfly* (Indianapolis, Ind.: Bobbs-Merrill, 1971), 361–62. The documents collected on the website www.freeafricanamericans.com show that the practice was common in Virginia in the 1780s and 1790s as well. Nash and Soderlund (*Freedom by Degrees,* 173–87) discuss in detail how this manumission-plus-indenture system worked in Philadelphia and its environs; in Indiana Territory, of course, conditions were substantially different. For Harrison's later practice, see Owens (*Mr. Jefferson's Hammer,* 68, 113, 240), who advances a different interpretation: that WHH valued slave ownership as a way of validating his status in the Northwest. On WHH's indignation, see Cleaves, *Old Tippecanoe,* 253–54; and Niles, *The Tippecanoe Text-Book,* 69.

4. The Grand Gesture

1. J. T. Scharf and Thompson Westcott, *The History of Philadelphia* (Philadelphia, Pa.: L. H. Everts and Co., 1884), 1:461, 467–68; "Observations on the Weather and Diseases for the Month of June, 1791," *American Museum* 10 (July 1791): 5–6; *Pennsylvania Gazette,* 6 July 1791.

2. *Moreau de St. Méry's American Journey,* 269; *The Journal of William Maclay,* ed. Kenneth R. Bowling and Helen E. Veit (Baltimore, Md.: Johns Hopkins Univ. Press, 1988), 365; cf. the account of Benjamin Harrison in *Journal & Letters of Philip Vickers Fithian,* 256–57. WHH's "Biographical Memoirs of Major General William Henry Harrison," 310, states that Edmund Randolph, "on being appointed secretary of state," offered WHH a place in his office. The statement cannot be right as it stands; it appears in the part of the narrative dealing with the summer of 1791, whereas Randolph was not appointed secretary of state until late 1793, at a time when WHH was well ensconced in the army and not looking for other work. Presumably what WHH meant was that Randolph offered to help him find a position in the federal service, perhaps in the State Department. (Randolph himself had no employees at that time; there was an attorney general, but no Department of Justice. See Bruce, *John Randolph of Roanoke,* 1:75.)

3. Tucker gives a fictional description of visiting Virginians' activities in Philadelphia (*Valley of Shenandoah,* 2:247–51); on the City Tavern, see American Philosophical Society, *Historic Philadelphia,* 322–24; and James Monroe to Thomas Jefferson, 26 Nov. 1790, in *Papers of Thomas Jefferson,* 18:30. Some idea of the centrality of drinking to Virginia male social life can be gathered from the fact that a party of five gentlemen, after dinner on an ordinary Sunday afternoon, consumed three bottles of Madeira and two bowls of toddy (*Journal & Letters of Philip Vickers Fithian,* 38). On WHH's drinking, see Rudolph Marx, *The Health of the Presidents* (New York: G. P. Putnam's Sons, 1960), 128. On Randolph, see Hugh A. Garland, *The Life of John Randolph of Roanoke* (1855; New York: Johnson Reprint Corporation, 1968), 59–60, corrected by Rufus B. Griswold, *The Republican Court, or American Society in the Days of Washington* (New York: D. Appleton and Co., 1854), 266n; and Bruce, *John Randolph of Roanoke,* 1:82, 89, 91, 111.

4. *New Letters of Abigail Adams,* ed. Stewart Mitchell (Boston, Mass.: Houghton Mifflin Co., 1947), 77; Robert C. Alberts, *The Golden Voyage: The Life and Times of William Bingham, 1752–1804* (Boston, Mass.: Houghton Mifflin Co., 1969), 161, 212–13; *Journal & Letters of Philip Vickers Fithian,* 232; Elizabeth Powel to Bushrod Washington, 22 June 1785, Powel Family Papers, HSP. Harper in 1791 was an agent employed to sell stock in one of the four Yazoo land companies; Morris and Nicholson of Philadelphia were involved in buying the land. Harper's job kept him in Philadelphia for a few

months. Joseph W. Cox, *Champion of Southern Federalism: Robert Goodloe Harper of South Carolina* (Port Washington, N.Y.: Kennikat Press, 1972), 25.

5. *Pennsylvania Gazette,* June–Aug. 1791, passim. American apprehension about the course of the French Revolution is apparent in, for example, Washington to Lafayette, 28 July 1791, in which Washington comments, "The tumultuous populace of large cities are ever to be dreaded" (*Washington Papers: Presidential Series,* 8:378). On the course of events in Saint-Dominque, see C. L. R. James, *The Black Jacobins* (New York: Vintage Books, 1963), 82–86; while for the American reaction, see Thomas Jefferson to Martha Jefferson Randolph, 24 Mar. 1791, *Papers of Thomas Jefferson,* 19:604. The Indian campaign is described in greater detail in chapter 7.

6. WHH's dating of the interview is in his letter to Brooks, 20 July 1839, WHH Correspondence, NYHS. I followed Henry Lee's movements through the following letters: Lee to John Fitzgerald, 16 June 1791, Henry Lee Papers, LC; Thomas Jefferson to James Madison, 27 July, 3 Aug. 1791, *Papers of Thomas Jefferson,* 20:682, 715; and Lee to Alexander Hamilton, 12 Aug. 1791, *Papers of Alexander Hamilton,* ed. Harold C. Syrett et al. (New York: Columbia Univ. Press, 1961–87), 9:31–32. Cleaves (*Old Tippecanoe,* 7) erroneously identifies "Lee" as Richard Henry Lee, who was never governor of Virginia and who, moreover, was no particular friend of the Harrisons; see *Papers of Thomas Jefferson,* 2:16–17.

7. For fuller data on Henry Lee, see Charles Royster, *Light-Horse Harry Lee and the Legacy of the American Revolution* (New York: Alfred A. Knopf, 1981), 30, 59–82; Thomas Boyd, *Light-horse Harry Lee* (New York: Charles Scribner's Sons, 1931), passim; and Washington to Henry Knox, 1 Apr. 1791, in *Washington Papers: Presidential Series,* 8:37. An applicant for a commission commonly relied on the backing of some powerful person, as WHH did with Lee; Richard Chandler, another Virginian who applied in 1792 for a post in the Rifle Corps, had recommendations from Secretaries Randolph and Jefferson. They were evidently less potent than Lee, however: after a year, Chandler was still waiting for a commission (Chandler to Anthony Wayne, 12 Sept. 1793, Anthony Wayne Papers, HSP).

8. Charles Caldwell, *Autobiography,* ed. Harriot W. Warner (Philadelphia, Pa.: Lippincott, Grambo, and Co., 1855), 205.

9. On slaves at Berkeley, see the 1791 will of Benjamin Harrison, in [Stanard,] "Harrison of James River," *VMHB* 34:84–86; and cf. Dowdey, *The Great Plantation,* 271. On slave attendants, see Dawidoff, *Education of John Randolph,* 98; Dumas Malone, *Jefferson the Virginian* (Boston, Mass.: Little, Brown and Co., 1948), 64; *Journal & Letters of Philip Vickers Fithian,* 53, 104; and Tucker, *Valley of Shenandoah,* 1:171. On formality in planters' behavior, see Tucker, *Valley of Shenandoah,* 2:8; and *Journal & Letters of Philip Vickers Fithian,* 54, 64. Smith (*Inside the Great House,* 89) refers to the disciplining of slaves as giving planters' sons "command experience."

10. Thomas Jefferson, *Notes on the State of Virginia* (1785; New York: W. W. Norton and Co., 1954), 162; Kulikoff, *Tobacco and Slaves,* 389.

11. Neither of WHH's own accounts of obtaining his commission mentions an interview with Washington, but several early biographies did so; see, for example, [Isaac R. Jackson], *The Life of William Henry Harrison (of Ohio)....* (Philadelphia, Pa.: W. Marshall and Co., 1840), 19, 22; and Charles S. Todd and Benjamin Drake, *Sketches of the Civil and Military Services of William Henry Harrison* (Cincinnati, Ohio: U. P. James, 1840), 13. Harrison's own version is in "Biographical Memoirs of Major General William Henry Harrison," 309–10. Knox's statement of policy was in a letter to Anthony Wayne, quoted in Richard C. Knopf, ed., *Anthony Wayne: A Name in Arms* (Pittsburgh, Pa.: Univ. of Pittsburgh Press, 1960), 110; cf. Alan D. Gaff, *Bayonets in the Wilderness: Anthony Wayne's Legion in the Old Northwest* (Norman, Okla.: Univ. of Oklahoma Press, 2004), 66. The description of Washington at this time is from *The Journal of William Maclay,* 364.

12. The Gilbert Stuart portrait of Morris is reproduced in Young, *Forgotten Patriot: Robert Morris,* frontispiece. Particulars about the Army are from various sources. The size is noted in Francis B. Heitman, *Historical Register and Dictionary of the United States Army* (Washington, D.C.: GPO, 1903), 2:561; the reputation of the men, in Samuel Hildreth, *Pioneer History* (Cincinnati, Ohio: H. W. Derby and Co., 1848), 41; their pay, in James R. Jacobs, *The Beginning of the U.S. Army, 1783–1812* (Princeton, N.J.: Princeton Univ. Press, 1947), 77. On the officers, see chapter 9 of this book and sources cited there.

13. Lockwood Barr, "Joseph Strong, M.D., Yale 1788," *Yale Journal of Biology and Medicine* 13 (Mar. 1941): 441; James Elliot, *Poetical and Miscellaneous Works,* 202.

14. Young, *Forgotten Patriot: Robert Morris,* 202–4; Robert Morris to Timothy Pickering, 12 June 1792, O'Reilly Collection, NYHS.

15. On recruiting, see Norman W. Caldwell, "The Enlisted Soldier at the Frontier Post, 1790–1814," *Mid-America: An Historical Review* 37 (Oct. 1955): 195; Gaff, *Bayonets in the Wilderness,* 37ff; and "An Eighteenth-Century Recruiting Poster," ed. Julian P. Boyd, *PMHB* 60 (Apr. 1936): 186–88, as well as the letter from George Washington to William Darke, 7 Apr. 1791, in *Washington Papers: Presidential Series,* 8:70–71, and the letter from Erkuries Beatty to John Armstrong, 24 Apr. 1791, in Charles Cist, *The Cincinnati Miscellany* (Cincinnati, Ohio: C. Clark, Printer, 1845–46), 1:150. Also, cf. the personal accounts in John Robert Shaw, *An Autobiography of Thirty Years, 1777–1807* (Athens, Ohio: Ohio Univ. Press, 1992), 87; and "A Picture of the First United States Army: The Journal of Captain Samuel Newman," ed. Milo M. Quaife, *Wisconsin Magazine of History* 2 (Sept. 1918): 46. A set of recruiting instructions from 1792 can be found in the Anthony Wayne Papers, HSP. For an ensign's uniform, see A. B. Gardner, "The Uniforms of the American Army," *Magazine of American History* 1 (Aug. 1877): 79–484.

5. Parallel Lives

1. "Letters of the Byrd Family," *VMHB* 38 (Jan. 1930): 51–63; Meade, *Old Churches, Ministers, and Families,* 1:318–20. Samuel Tyler, a respected Charles City lawyer to whom Byrd entrusted his incomplete cases when he left for the Ohio country in 1795, was likely his teacher (Tyler to Byrd, 3 Sept. 1794, Charles Willing Byrd Papers, Lilly Library, Indiana University). The following contemporary sources place Byrd in the James River area in the period 1788–90: Benjamin Harrison Jr. to Mary Willing Byrd, 13 Sept. 1788, Benjamin Harrison VI Letter Book, July 1787–Sept. 1789, NYHS; Nathaniel Harrison Diary, entries of 8 May 1789, 25–26 Jan., 16 May, and 7 Nov. 1790, CW (microfilm).

2. "Will of Colonel William Byrd 3rd," *VMHB* 9 (July 1901): 85; Chastellux, *Travels in North America,* 2:430.

3. Charles W. Byrd to Nancy Byrd, 26 June 1796, Charles Willing Byrd Papers, Lilly Library, Indiana University ("ills and mortifications" quotation). The traditional account of Byrd's early life is in Nelson W. Evans's article "Charles Willing Byrd," *The "Old Northwest" Genealogical Quarterly* 11 (Jan. 1908): 1–6.

4. Evans, "Charles Willing Byrd," 6–8; Stephen J. Stein, "The Conversion of Charles Willing Byrd to Shakerism," *Filson Club History Quarterly* (Oct. 1982): 398–99; William S. Byrd, *Letters from a Young Shaker,* ed. Stephen J. Stein (Lexington, Ky.: Univ. Press of Kentucky, 1985), 154; Charles W. Byrd to Nancy Byrd, 26 June 1796; Benjamin Harrison Jr. to Charles W. Byrd, 22 Aug. 1794; and Elizabeth Powel to Charles W. Byrd, 28 Feb. 1800, all in Charles Willing Byrd Papers, Lilly Library, Indiana University.

5. Ann Byrd to Charles W. Byrd, 5 Jan., 20 Nov. 1795; William Byrd to Charles W. Byrd, 20 June 1795, all in Charles Willing Byrd Papers, Lilly Library, Indiana University; Benjamin Harrison Jr. to Robert Hare, 18 Sept. 1788, Benjamin Harrison VI Letter Book, July 1787–Sept. 1789, NYHS.

6. For the Harrison family of Brandon, see [Stanard,] "Harrison of James River," *VMHB* 34 (Oct. 1926): 386–87; for the house, see Paul Wilstach, *Tidewater Virginia* (Indianapolis, Ind.: Bobbs-Merrill, 1929), 129–31. For "I'm very happy" quotation, see Tucker, *Valley of Shenandoah,* 2:100.

7. Nathaniel Harrison Diary, entry of 19 Mar. 1790, CW (microfilm). The identifications of the persons designated by initials only are mine, based on knowledge of the Harrison family.

8. "The Daingerfield Family," *WMQ,* 1st series, 9:189.

9. For Daingerfield's military service, see Heitman, *Historical Register;* Gaff, *Bayonets in the Wilderness,* 117; and General orders, 22 Aug. 1793, and Edward Miller to Anthony Wayne, 26 Oct., 5 Nov. 1793, both in the Anthony Wayne Papers, HSP. Further references are in chapter 14 of this book. Daingerfield resigned on 30 Nov. 1794. In 1799, at the time of the quasi war with France, he

again enlisted briefly. The rest of his career is sketched in F. L. Brockett, *The Lodge of Washington* (Alexandria, Va.: G. H. Ramey and Son, 1899), 126.

10. For the name "Billy," see *The Journal of John Harrower,* ed. Edward Miles Riley (Williamsburg, Va.: Colonial Williamsburg, 1963), 121.

11. Ibid., xx.

12. Hamilton, *Making and Unmaking of a Revolutionary Family,* 73–75, 84–85; Tucker, quoted in Robert McColley, *Slavery and Jeffersonian Virginia* (Urbana, Ill.: Univ. of Illinois Press, 1964), 45; George Washington to George Steptoe Washington, 5 Dec. 1790, in *Washington Papers: Presidential Series,* 7:32.

13. Cynthia A. Kierner, *Scandal at Bizarre* (New York: Palgrave Macmillan, 2004), 14–15, 19–25, 29; Alan Pell Crawford, *Unwise Passions* (New York: Simon and Schuster, 2000), 50; Bruce, *John Randolph of Roanoke,* 1:49, 73, 104–5.

14. Bruce, *John Randolph of Roanoke,* 1:82.

15. Ibid., 1:42–43, 56, 73–75, 89–91; 2:323–25; Dawidoff, *Education of John Randolph,* 92–93, 212–13; Davis, *Intellectual Life,* 113.

16. Robert Carter to his children, 12 Oct. 1803; Bishop James Madison to Robert Carter, 17 June 1799; Carter Berkeley to Robert Carter, 11 Apr. 1800, 9 Nov. 1804; all in Shirley Plantation Collection, CW.

17. Robert Carter to his children, 12 Oct. 1803, Shirley Plantation Collection, CW. Carter's journal for November 1801 narrates his contacts with Philadelphia physicians and vividly shows his excitement at urban society, its charitable institutions, and its intellectual stimulation. His certificate as a founding member of the American Linnean Society, January 1803; his diploma from June of the same year; and his will, written in August and September 1805, are also in the CW library.

18. Rhys Isaac, "Stories and Constructions of Identity: Folk Tellings and Diary Inscriptions in Revolutionary Virginia," in *Through a Glass Darkly: Reflections on Personal Identity in Early America,* ed. Ronald Hoffman, Mechal Sobel, and Fredrika Teute (Chapel Hill, N.C.: Univ. of North Carolina Press, 1997), 222; Roy F. Baumeister, *Identity: Cultural Change and the Struggle for the Self* (New York: Oxford Univ. Press, 1986), 192.

19. Baumeister, *Identity,* 251: "Values are acquired during the process by which society teaches its members how to think and act (e.g., child-rearing patterns, schools, initiations)." Jay Fliegelman has written at length on the experience of American sons facing the fact that their fathers' guidance had been mistaken or hurtful; see Jay Fliegelman, *Prodigals & Pilgrims: The American Revolution against Patriarchal Authority, 1750–1800* (Cambridge, UK: Cambridge Univ. Press, 1982), 36, 39–40, 187–88, 275. Particularly interesting in light of WHH's experience is Fliegelman's characterization (p. 36) of "parental tyranny" as treated in eighteenth century novels: "the unwillingness to acknowledge a child's reason and the rights it confers, the unwillingness to distinguish between childhood and adolescence or young adulthood. . . . Such

tyranny usually takes one of several forms: denying a child a proper education, arranging a marriage for 'familial aggrandizement,' unjustly denying a child an inheritance, or irrationally preferring one child to another; in short, infringements of filial liberty or independence."

20. Daniel Walker Howe, *Making the American Self: Jonathan Edwards to Abraham Lincoln* (Cambridge, Mass.: Harvard Univ. Press, 1997), 8.

21. Joseph F. Kett's excellent discussion of adolescent conversion in *Rites of Passage* (New York: Basic Books, 1977), 62–85, which focuses on New England and the Northern states, is not quite relevant here for that reason: in a Puritan society, a young person's conversion involved a reconciliation with society's values; in the formalist Anglican society of the Chesapeake, however, it involved a confrontation with social values.

22. Jesse Lee (*Memoir,* 96) recognized that some of the conversions in the Southside Virginia revival of the 1780s were not lasting: "Not a few who professed to be cleansed, have become again polluted. The cup of joy and peace, from whence they could once drink with pleasure, they have dashed from their lips." For more details from Gunderson, see note 1 on p. 190.

23. On reading for moral and even occupational guidance, see David D. Hall, "Books and Reading in Eighteenth-Century America," in *Of Consuming Interests: The Style of Life in the Eighteenth Century,* ed. Cary Carson, Ronald Hoffman, and Peter J. Albert, 367–68, Perspectives on the American Revolution (Charlottesville, Va.: Univ. Press of Virginia, 1994). Meyer Reinhold refers to "the tireless and purposeful reading by early Americans of the Classics as a repository of timeless models for guidance in republicanism and private and civic virtue." Meyer Reinhold, ed., *The Classick Pages: Classical Reading of Eighteenth-Century Americans* (University Park, Pa.: American Philological Association, 1975), 2. On Rollin, see Reinhold, *Classick Pages,* 157–63 (the quote is on 158); and Joseph F. Kett and Patricia A. McClung, "Book Culture in Post-Revolutionary Virginia," in *Proceedings of the American Antiquarian Society* 94 (1984): 130–34. William Gribbin's comment in "Rollin's Histories and American Republicanism" (*WMQ,* 3rd series, 29 [Oct. 1972]: 615) is thought-provoking: "Rollin's histories were more than didactic. They were meant to forge a new order of things by molding impressionable readers into Christian rebels against their times." John Randolph was much impressed by Rollin, and frequently recommended the book in his old age (Davis, *Intellectual Life,* 112).

24. For an example of WHH's instant recall and use of Rollin's account as a guide, see his 1810 proposal for militia training in Indiana Territory, in William Henry Harrison, *Messages and Letters of William Henry Harrison,* ed. Logan Esarey, Indiana Historical Collections, vols. 8–9 (Indianapolis, Ind.: Indiana Historical Commission, 1922), 1:404–5. On reading and imagination, see Arnold M. Ludwig, *How Do We Know Who We Are? A Biography of the Self* (New York: Oxford Univ. Press, 1997), 105.

6. Introduction to the Ohio Country

1. For the practice of reassigning newly enlisted officers and men to existing companies, see, for example, "The Journal of Captain Samuel Newman," 46; Gaff, *Bayonets in the Wilderness,* 53; and the military accounts for 1793 in the John Pratt Papers, CSL. Robert Gunderson portrays WHH as leading his men to Pittsburgh alone, but the sources he cites do not support this contention, nor his statement that WHH arrived on 12 October. Robert G. Gunderson, "William Henry Harrison: Apprentice in Arms," *Northwest Ohio Quarterly* 65 (Winter 1993): 3–4. For the movements of the four companies in late 1791, see the correspondence of the secretary of war, Henry Knox, in *American State Papers* (Washington, D.C.: Gales and Seaton, 1832), 4:182, 192; and that of General Arthur St. Clair in William Henry Smith, comp., *The St. Clair Papers* (1882; New York: Da Capo Press, 1971), 2:247. For the date of WHH's arrival at Fort Washington, see chapter 7, note 1.

2. Cist, *The Cincinnati Miscellany,* 1:174, contains Knox's orders to Captain John Armstrong, 26 Apr. 1791. Haskell probably followed the same route. The date of arrival at Pittsburgh is from Smith, *St. Clair Papers,* 2:247. William Eaton's company left Philadelphia 21 September of the following year and arrived at Pittsburgh 22 October (Gaff, *Bayonets in the Wilderness,* 53).

3. The Philadelphia-Lancaster road is described in Mease, *Philadelphia,* 347. Norman W. Caldwell ("Enlisted Soldier," 195–204) examines the makeup of the early American army; contemporary views of soldiers are from Elliot, *Poetical and Miscellaneous Works,* 202; and Henry M. Brackenridge, *Recollections of Persons and Places in the West* (Philadelphia, Pa.: James Kay, Jun., and Brother, 1834), 16. For a glimpse of the actual marching order on the way west, see "Detachment Orders Trenton June 28th 1793" in the John Pratt Papers, CSL.

4. "Mrs. Mary Dewees's Journal from Philadelphia to Kentucky, 1787–1788," *PMHB* 28 (Apr. 1904): 182; "Journal of Captain Samuel Newman," 45; John W. Jordan, "Notes of a Journey from Philadelphia to New Madrid, Tennessee, 1790," *PMHB* 36, no. 2 (1912): 209; Shaw, *Autobiography of Thirty Years,* 119–20.

5. To estimate the rate of march, see "Journal of Captain Samuel Newman" and "Report of Capt. James Stephenson," 26 Nov. 1792, both in Anthony Wayne Papers, HSP. For a description of military routine, see "Mrs. Mary Dewees's Journal," 133; Brown, *Mirror,* 199–200; "Journal of Captain Samuel Newman," 46, 48; Shaw, *Autobiography of Thirty Years,* 89–91; Elliot, *Poetical and Miscellaneous Works,* 122–23; and Paul A. W. Wallace, *Thirty Thousand Miles with John Heckewelder* (Pittsburgh, Pa.: Univ. of Pittsburgh Press, 1958), 235–36. On north of Ireland settlers, see Harry Emerson Wildes, *Anthony Wayne* (New York: Harcourt, Brace, and Co., 1941), 354. (The whole passage in which this citation occurs should be compared with this chapter.)

6. Thaddeus Harris, in Brown, *Mirror,* 197; Elliot, *Poetical and Miscellaneous Works,* 122; C. Caldwell, *Autobiography,* 215.

7. "Mrs. Mary Dewees's Journal," 184; Samuel Hildreth, "Early Emigration," *American Pioneer* 2 (Mar. 1843): 123–24; S. Wilkeson, "Early Recollections of the West," *American Pioneer* 2 (Apr. 1843): 161–62; James Bowman, "Redstone Old Fort," *American Pioneer* 2 (Feb. 1843): 63; Wallace, *Thirty Thousand Miles,* 236; "Memoirs of Benjamin Van Cleve," ed. Beverley W. Bond, *Ohio Historical and Philosophical Society Publications* 17 (Jan. 1922): 12.

8. Hildreth, "Early Emigration," 113, 117, 129.

9. "Memoirs of Benjamin Van Cleve," 12–13; "Journal of Colonel John May, of Boston, Relative to a Journey to the Ohio Country, 1789," *PMHB* 45 (Apr. 1921): 111; "Mrs. Mary Dewees's Journal," 187; "Journal of Captain Samuel Newman," 50; Hildreth, "Early Emigration," 121; Elliot, *Poetical and Miscellaneous Works,* 125; Francis Baily, *Journal of a Tour in Unsettled Parts of North America in 1796 & 1797,* ed. Jack D. L. Holmes (Carbondale, Ill.: Southern Illinois University, 1969), 47.

10. Wallace, *Thirty Thousand Miles,* 237; Elliot, *Poetical and Miscellaneous Works,* 128–29; "Journal of Captain John May," 113; Jordan, "Notes of a Journey," 209; "Mrs. Mary Dewees's Journal," 287.

11. Hildreth, "Early Emigration," 121; "Journal of Captain Samuel Newman," 57; Wallace, *Thirty Thousand Miles,* 260.

12. On Benjamin Harrison and New Englanders, see, for example, his letter of 8 Jan. 1777 to Robert Morris on the subject of moving Congress back to Philadelphia, quoted in Burnett, *Letters of Members of the Continental Congress,* 2:208: "I am told the Yankeys are against it, if so we go not, they Rule us absolutely as the Grand Turk does in his own Dominions"; and the assessment by Benjamin Rush (*Autobiography,* 152), a fellow delegate to the Continental Congress: "He had strong state prejudices, and was very hostile to the leading characters from the New England States." See William B. Skelton, *An American Profession of Arms: The Army Officer Corps, 1784–1861,* Modern War Studies (Lawrence, Kans.: Univ. Press of Kansas, 1992), for an excellent summary of the aristocratic ideal current among American officers (53–56) and for Rush's view of the status of a gentleman (225). The heartache of an officer who was forced to defend his status as a gentleman can be inferred from a letter from Lieutenant Nathaniel Huston to his commander, Anthony Wayne, 26 Dec. 1792 (Anthony Wayne Papers, HSP). Huston, whose family were artisans, was aware of "jealousy in the breast of many officers on the ground that I am not a proper person to be in the Service as an officer—I have been told Sir, by Lieutenant [Daniel of St. Thomas] Jeniver that I was no gentleman & such were the Sentiments of a number of other officers." On duelling in Virginia, see Ferdinand-Marie Bayard, *Travels of a Frenchman in Maryland and Virginia. . . . ,* ed. and trans. Ben C. McCary (Ann Arbor,

Mich.: Edwards Brothers, 1950), 100. WHH's early views are in a letter to A. B. Howell, 7 Apr. 1838, in the *Cincinnati Daily Gazette.* For further discussion of duelling and the military code of honor, see chapter 12 and its notes.

13. "Dr. Saugrain's Note-Books, 1788," ed. Eugene F. Bliss, *Proceedings of the American Antiquarian Society,* n.s., 19:236; *The Indian Captivity of O. M. Spencer,* ed. Milo M. Quaife, The Lakeside Classics (Chicago, Ill.: R. R. Donnelley and Sons, 1917), 15:7; Wallace, *Thirty Thousand Miles,* 239–42; Baily, *Journal,* 49; "Journal of Captain Samuel Newman," 51–56; "Mrs. Mary Dewees's Journal," 86; Van Cleve, "Journal," 28; Ebenezer Denny journal, in Smith, *St. Clair Papers,* 2:254–58; *American Museum* 10 (Nov. 1791), 207; Lewis Condict, "Journal of a Trip to Kentucky in 1795," *Proceedings of the New Jersey Historical Society,* n.s., 4 (1919): 113–14.

14. "Journal of Captain Samuel Newman," 56; Neville B. Craig, *The History of Pittsburgh* (Pittsburgh, Pa.: John H. Mellor, 1851), 211; Isaac Craig, "Fort Lafayette at Pittsburgh," *American Historical Record* 2 (1873): 497–503. John Nevill's "Account of provisions issued at or near Pittsburgh," 1791, in William Duer Papers, NYHS, records that the troops encamped on the northwest bank of the Allegheny.

15. Daniel Story to Winthrop Sargent, 22 Oct. 1791, Winthrop Sargent Papers, MHS. Nevill's account, just referred to, records that Haskell's company arrived 8 October and stayed encamped opposite Pittsburgh through 25 November; the exact dates in his accounts are unreliable, but they do give an idea of the length of the company's stay. See also Knox's reports to Congress, *American State Papers,* 4:184, 216. For the Indian attacks, see Neville B. Craig, *Pittsburgh,* 211; *Calendar of Virginia State Papers,* 5:400; and Hildreth, *Pioneer History,* 303–4. For evidence that October was a season of low water, see Baily, *Journal,* 54; Wallace, *Thirty Thousand Miles,* 222; and Balthasar H. Meyer et al., *History of Transportation in the United States before 1860* (1917; Gloucester, Mass.: Peter Smith, 1948), 97. John Nevill, in a letter to William Duer (25 Aug. 1791 [William Duer Papers, NYHS]), mentions the low water at that time.

16. On Pittsburgh, see Brackenridge, *Recollections,* 14, 77; C. Caldwell, *Autobiography,* 221. For more detailed information on St. Clair's Defeat, see chapter 7, below, and notes 23 and 24 in this chapter. On WHH's arrival in Cincinnati, see WHH to Brooks, 20 July 1839, WHH Correspondence, NYHS; Green, *William Henry Harrison,* 29; Cleaves, *Old Tippecanoe,* 9–10; Gunderson, "William Henry Harrison," 4. Smith, *St. Clair Papers,* 2:262, gives the date St. Clair's defeated army reached Fort Washington. In support of their contention that WHH arrived 8 November, Cleaves and Gunderson offer a distorted interpretation of the 1831 speech, arguing that WHH camped at Peter Cox's cabin on 21 November because it was on the road to Fort Hamilton. But although, as James McBride notes, Peter Cox was slain by Indians on the Hamilton road, his cabin was definitely in Cincinnati, as the speech

states. James McBride, *Pioneer Biography,* Ohio Valley Historical Series, no. 4 (Cincinnati: Robert Clarke and Co., 1869), 1:147–48, 2:271.

17. Gunderson suggests that twelve days was a typical travel time from Pittsburgh to Cincinnati. Actually, the time varied. At low water in late spring, summer, or early fall, it could be that long or longer, while at high water, in spring or late fall, a good passage could be made in five to seven days. In late 1791, at what was called low water, a boat reached Cincinnati from Wheeling in eleven days. Gunderson, "William Henry Harrison," 4; Beverley W. Bond, *The Civilization of the Old Northwest* (New York: Macmillan Co., 1934), 354–55; "Memoirs of Benjamin Van Cleve," 39–40; Elliot, *Poetical and Miscellaneous Works,* 132–35; Pope, *Tour,* 18; George Croghan to Isaac Craig, 1 July 1792, *PMHB* 14:202; Jordan, "Notes of a Journey," 211–12.

18. Robert R. Jones, *Fort Washington at Cincinnati, Ohio* (Cincinnati, Ohio: Society of Colonial Wars in the State of Ohio, 1902), 25, shows that the practice of assigning a small guard to accompany shipments down the river had been standard since 1790. John Nevill's accounts in the William Duer Papers, NYHS, give a general picture of trade on the river.

19. Seymour Dunbar, *A History of Travel in America* (Indianapolis, Ind.: Bobbs-Merrill Co., 1915), 2:284–86; *A Journal of the Adventures of Matthew Bunn* (Providence, R.I.: Matthew Bunn, 1796), 3; Brackenridge, *Recollections,* 17; "Memoirs of Benjamin Van Cleve," 39–40. On the crew of eight, see John Nevill to William Duer, 25 Aug. 1791, William Duer Papers, NYHS.

20. "Mrs. Mary Dewees's Journal," 191–95; Wallace, *Thirty Thousand Miles,* 223–24, 291; "Dr. Saugrain's Note-Books," 235; *Journal of Capt. Daniel Bradley,* ed. Frazier E. Wilson (Greenville, Ohio: Frank H. Jobes and Son, 1935), 9; "John D. Shane's Copy of Needham Parry's Diary of Trip [*sic*] Westward in 1794," ed. Lucien Beckner, *The Filson Club History Quarterly* 22 (Oct. 1948): 229–30.

21. WHH's fascination with Indian culture and behavior, to be discussed more fully in later chapters, makes it likely that his attitude toward the Indians themselves was not one of automatic enmity. His father, as governor of Virginia, had worked for a policy of negotiation rather than confrontation with the tribes of the West, arguing to the governor of North Carolina that the "Indian has his national rights as well as a white man and the latter, having his mind cultivated and enlarged by civilization and education, is called on by every Tie of Humanity and Justice to support them in those rights." Smith, *Benjamin Harrison,* 64–65; quote from Henry H. Wilson, "Benjamin Harrison, 5th, Signer of the Declaration of Independence, Governor of Virginia, etc.," 14, James A. Green Papers, CHS.

22. Richard H. Kohn, *Eagle and Sword* (New York: Free Press, 1975), 91–95; Wiley Sword, *President Washington's Indian War: The Struggle for the Old Northwest, 1790–1795* (Norman, Okla.: Univ. of Oklahoma Press, 1975), 7,

117–43; Dale Van Every, *Ark of Empire* (New York: William Morrow and Co., 1963), 190–207; Richard White, *The Middle Ground: Indians, Empires, and Republics in the Great Lakes Region, 1650–1815* (Cambridge, UK: Cambridge Univ. Press, 1991), 436–40, 452–53; R. Douglas Hurt, *The Ohio Frontier: Crucible of the Old Northwest, 1720–1830* (Bloomington, Ind.: Indiana Univ. Press, 1996), 95–105.

23. Hurt, *The Ohio Frontier,* 105–11. For the Indian-British connection, see Sword, *President Washington's Indian War,* 20–21; Gaff, *Bayonets in the Wilderness,* 70; and Kohn, *Eagle and Sword,* 95. White (*Middle Ground,* 454) argues that British domination of the Indians was a consequence of the massive American attacks in 1790 and 1791. Harmar's return through Pittsburgh is mentioned in Smith, *St. Clair Papers,* 2:251–52.

24. Hurt, *The Ohio Frontier,* 111; Kohn, *Eagle and Sword,* 109–11. William O. Odom carefully analyzes the mission of the expedition. William O. Odom, "Destined for Defeat: An Analysis of the St. Clair Expedition of 1791," *Northwest Ohio Quarterly* 65 (Spring 1993): 68–77.

25. Wallace, *Thirty Thousand Miles,* 226; "Journal of Colonel John May," 137; *Journal of Capt. Daniel Bradley,* 13; Elliot, *Poetical and Miscellaneous Works,* 133; Hildreth, *Pioneer History,* 276, 326; Waldeurard Meulette, "Gallipolis," *American Pioneer,* 2:182–87; Gaff, *Bayonets in the Wilderness,* 18.

26. Smith, *St. Clair Papers,* 2:254–58, 269; Gaff, *Bayonets in the Wilderness,* 112.

7. Aftermath of a Disaster

1. David A. Simmons, *The Forts of Anthony Wayne* (Fort Wayne, Ind.: Historic Fort Wayne, 1977), 4–6; R. R. Jones, *Fort Washington,* 14–17; *The Indian Captivity of O. M. Spencer,* 32–33.

2. WHH to Brooks, 20 July 1839, WHH Correspondence, NYHS; Green, *William Henry Harrison,* 30; Shaw, *Autobiography of Thirty Years,* 160.

3. "Return of killed wounded & missing," 17 Nov. 1791, and "Return of Ordinance, Military & other Stores, lost on the fourth of November, 1791," n.d., Winthrop Sargent Papers, MHS; WHH to Brooks, 20 July 1839, WHH Correspondence, NYHS; Arthur St. Clair to [?], 17 Nov. 1791, St. Clair Papers, Ohio Historical Society; Green, *William Henry Harrison,* 28; Smith, *St. Clair Papers,* 2:269–71; Odom, "Destined for Defeat," 81–83; "Diary of St. Clair's Disastrous Campaign," *American Pioneer* 2 (Mar. 1843): 137; Danske Dandridge, *George Michael Bedinger: A Kentucky Pioneer* (Charlottesville, Va.: Michie Co., 1909), 152–53.

4. WHH to Brooks, 20 July 1839, WHH Correspondence, NYHS. WHH's impression is from a speech he gave in 1833, reproduced in *Celebration of the Forty-fifth Anniversary of the First Settlement of Cincinnati and the Miami*

Country, on the 26th Day of December, 1833, by Natives of Ohio (Cincinnati, Ohio: Shreve and Co., 1834), 25. "Mere trifle" is John Shaw's phrase, from his *Autobiography*, 124. On Peter Cox, see McBride, *Pioneer Biography*, 1:147–48.

5. *American Museum* 11, Appendix 3, p. 2; Winthrop Sargent, Orderly Book, 11, 18 Nov., 1 Dec. 1791, Winthrop Sargent Papers, MHS; WHH to Brooks, 20 July 1839, WHH Correspondence, NYHS; Kohn, *Eagle and Sword*, 114–15; Van Every, *Ark of Empire*, 236–41; Ebenezer Denny journal, in Smith, *St. Clair Papers*, 2:255–56; "The Journal of Captain Samuel Newman," 61–73; "Diary of St. Clair's Disastrous Campaign," 137; Francis Paul Prucha, *The Sword of the Republic: The United States Army on the Frontier, 1743–1846* (London: Collier-Macmillan, 1969), 25; Odom, "Destined for Defeat," 81–90.

6. Sword (*President Washington's Indian War*, 176–89) gives a vivid, thorough description. See also Gaff, *Bayonets in the Wilderness*, 3–8; and Hurt, *Ohio Frontier*, 114–18. Richard Butler's death is described in Gaff, *Bayonets in the Wilderness*, 57.

7. McBride, *Pioneer Biography*, 2:184; A. E. Jones, *Extracts from the History of Cincinnati. . . .* (Cincinnati: Cohen and Co., 1888), 64; *The Correspondence of John Cleves Symmes*, ed. Beverley W. Bond (New York: Macmillan Co., 1926), 150–57; Charles Cist, *Sketches and Statistics of Cincinnati in 1859* (Cincinnati: N.p., 1859), 101–2; Smith, *St. Clair Papers*, 2:267–69; Gaff, *Bayonets in the Wilderness*, 10.

8. WHH to Brooks, 20 July 1839, WHH Correspondence, NYHS. WHH did not identify the captain by name in his account, but it is probable that he was referring to Joseph Brock. Assuming that the captain was a Virginian, he would to have been one of the four who commanded the Virginia levies in the battle—Van Swerengen, Darke, Hannah, and Brock. (Cleaves, *Old Tippecanoe*, 10, errs in supposing the unnamed officer a regular army captain, as does Green, *William Henry Harrison*, 25, in calling him a captain of militia.) Of the four possibilities, two can be eliminated quickly: Van Swerengen was killed in the battle and Darke was wounded so badly that he remained at Fort Jefferson throughout November ("Consolidated Pay Roll," Post Revolutionary War Collection, National Archives; Smith, *St. Clair Papers*, 2:270. Of the two remaining, Brock lived nearer to the Harrisons and seems slightly more likely to have been the man. If he was, however, the story of his encounter with WHH has an ironic sequel; he enlisted in the regular forces only four or five months later, returned to the West, and fought creditably alongside WHH in the later campaigns against the Indians (Gaff, *Bayonets in the Wilderness*, 36, 304–8).

9. WHH to Brooks, 20 July 1839, WHH Correspondence, NYHS. On WHH's sometimes incongruous cheerfulness as an older man, see, for example, Cleaves, *Old Tippecanoe*, 291, 323, 334.

10. Joseph R. Riling, *Baron Von Steuben and His Regulations* (Philadelphia, Pa.: Ray Riling Arms Book Co., 1966), 3–4, 11–25, 141. An espontoon

is described in H. Henry Lumpkin's *From Savannah to Yorktown* (Columbia, S.C.: Univ. of South Carolina Press, 1981), 151, 158.

11. The march to Fort Hamilton does not appear in the letter to Brooks but is recounted in most of the early biographies, for example, "Biographical Memoirs of Major General William Henry Harrison," 312, and Todd and Drake, *Sketches of the Civil and Military Services*, 14. Jacob Burnet adds the detail that junior officers always traveled on foot. He also maintains that WHH marched not only to Fort Hamilton but to Fort Jefferson, fifty miles farther into the interior. Other sources, however, do not corroborate this assertion; probably Burnet's memory was playing him tricks, as it often did. Jacob Burnet, "Letters Relating to the Early Settlement of the Northwestern Territory," Transactions of the Historical and Philosophical Society of Ohio, part 2, 1 (Cincinnati, Ohio: George W. Bradbury and Co., 1839), 23.

12. Simmons, *The Forts of Anthony Wayne*, 7–9; McBride, *Pioneer Biography*, 1:152; Henry Montgomery, *The Life of Major-General William Henry Harrison* (Philadelphia, Pa.: Porter and Coates, 1852), 50.

13. Smith, *St. Clair Papers*, 2:269, 271, 274; George A. Katzenberger, *Major David Ziegler* (Columbus, Ohio: F. J. Heer Printing Co., 1912), 38, 44–45. Henry Howe gives the lyrics of the ballad; Brackenridge recalled having heard it in Pittsburgh as early as 1792 or 1793. Henry Howe, *Historical Collections of Ohio* (Cincinnati: Henry Howe, 1852), 136; Brackenridge, *Recollections*, 73.

8. The First Regiment

1. Samuel Newman's reference to "ye bloods of ye 1st. U. S. Regt." ("Journal of Captain Samuel Newman," 64) suggests that the unit was known for its carousing. Other sources making the same point include the reminiscences of Jacob Burnet, quoted in Charles F. Goss, *Cincinnati, The Queen City* (Cincinnati, Ohio: S. J. Clarke Publishing Co., 1912), 1:66; "Dr. Daniel Drake's Memoir of the Miami Country, 1779–1794 (An Unfinished Manuscript)," ed. Beverley W. Bond, *Ohio Historical and Philosophical Society Quarterly* 18 (Apr. 1923): 86; James Wilkinson to Henry Knox, 13 Mar. 1792, and Winthrop Sargent to Henry Knox, 13 Mar. 1792, both in Henry Knox Papers, MHS; and Knopf, *Wayne: A Name in Arms*, 88, 94. Zeigler's early career is given in Katzenberger, *Major David Ziegler*, 5. For a description of Beatty, see Knopf, *Wayne: A Name in Arms*, 163; and Joseph M. Beatty Jr., ed., "Letters of the Four Beatty Brothers of the Continental Army, 1774–1794," *Pennsylvania Magazine of History and Biography* 44 (July 1920): 193, 263, passim. On Smith, see chapter 10 of this book. The illiteracy of some officers is mentioned in James Wilkinson to Jeremiah Wadsworth, 18 Sept. 1792, quoted in James R. Jacobs, *Tarnished Warrior: Major-General James Wilkinson* (New York: Macmillan Co., 1938), 123. For the officers' service before 1791, see Prucha, *The Sword of the Republic*, 22.

2. The description of WHH's physical appearance as ensign rests on the sources cited in chapter 1 and on the eyewitness description of him at age forty given in Green, *William Henry Harrison,* 464. Anthony Wayne, in a letter written three years later (quoted in Knopf, *Wayne: A Name in Arms,* 449), refers to a "very unpleasant dispute that [had] long subsisted" between WHH and Marks without giving details of its origin, but it may well have been identical to the "dispute in rank" referred to in a letter from Marks to his patron, Secretary Thomas Jefferson (10 Jan. 1792, *Papers of Thomas Jefferson,* 23:33). WHH's commission, direct from the president, bore the date of 15 August; Marks, as explained in the editors' note, was appointed to fill a slot made vacant in October by a promotion. The distinction was important because the officer with the earlier commission had seniority, making him eligible for promotion to lieutenant first. The "very irregular" quotation is from Martha Jefferson Carr to Thomas Jefferson, 3 Dec. 1787, Thomas Jefferson Papers, Small Library, UVa.

3. This story is also from WHH's letter to Erastus Brooks, 20 July 1839, WHH Correspondence, NYHS. It resembles literary narratives of knighthood before his time and of the American frontier after it, but there is small likelihood of literary influence here; probably it reflects the actual workings of all-male groups where prestige is based on some sort of prowess. WHH did not mention David Strong by name, but he was the first captain to receive a promotion to major, hence the most senior, and his son Elijah, six years WHH's senior, was appointed a "conditional ensign" on 15 July 1793 (general orders, Anthony Wayne Papers, HSP). Basic data on the family is to be found in the Strong Family Papers at the Cincinnati Historical Society (CHS). Knox, in a memo to George Washington dated 2 Mar. 1792 (Henry Knox Papers, MHS), described David Strong as "a plain, brave man, but without any considerable abilities." Jacob Burnet (quoted in Goss, *Cincinnati, The Queen City,* 1:66) recalled Strong as one of the very few early officers who were not "hard drinkers," while John Armstrong (Captain John Armstrong to Winthrop Sargent, 17 Mar. 1792, Winthrop Sargent Papers, MHS) seems to show that his colleagues esteemed him. On Marks's ignorance of tactics, see Hastings Marks to Thomas Jefferson, 10 Jan. 1792, *Papers of Thomas Jefferson,* 23:33.

4. WHH to Brooks, 20 July 1839, WHH Correspondence, NYHS.

5. Henry A. and Kate B. Ford, *History of Hamilton County, Ohio* (Cleveland, Ohio: L. A. Williams and Co., 1881), 334–35; "Dr. Daniel Drake's Memoir," 86; Winthrop Sargent to Arthur St. Clair, 19 Jan. 1793, in Clarence E. Carter, ed., *The Territorial Papers of the United States* (Washington. D.C.: GPO, 1934), 3:401; *Journal of Philip Vickers Fithian,* 52–53.

6. Thomas R. Hay and M. R. Werner, *The Admirable Trumpeter: A Biography of General James Wilkinson* (Garden City, N.Y.: Doubleday, Doran and Co., 1941), 1–6, 74, 84, 109, 218; Brackenridge, *Recollections,* 49; James R. Jacobs, *Tarnished Warrior: Major-General James Wilkinson* (New York:

Macmillan Co., 1938), 114, 118; James Wilkinson to Harry Innes, 29 Feb., 12 June 1792, Harry Innes Papers, LC.

7. Jacobs, *Tarnished Warrior,* 116; "Winthrop Sargent's Diary while with General St. Clair's Expedition Against the Indians," *Ohio Archeological and Historical Quarterly* 33 (July 1924): 272; Winthrop Sargent to Arthur St. Clair, 5 Feb. 1792, Winthrop Sargent Papers, MHS; John Cleves Symmes to Jonathan Dayton, 17 Jan. 1792, in Bond, *Correspondence,* 159.

8. McBride, *Pioneer Biography,* 1:30–35; A. E. Jones, *Extracts from the History of Cincinnati. . . .* (Cincinnati, Ohio: Cohen and Co., 1888), 104; Rush, *Autobiography,* 302; Winthrop Sargent to Arthur St. Clair, 5 Feb. 1792, Winthrop Sargent Papers, MHS. There is some variation in the sources as to numbers of troops and departure date; Gaff, *Bayonets in the Wilderness,* 11–12, has slightly different figures.

9. *Journal of Capt. Daniel Bradley,* 36–37; Carter, *Territorial Papers,* 2:364.

10. Jacobs, *Beginning of the U.S. Army,* 141–42; James Wilkinson to John Armstrong, 19 Mar. 1792, in Cist, *Miscellany,* 1:210–20; *Journal of Capt. Daniel Bradley,* 39; James Wilkinson to Winthrop Sargent, 9, 16, 19 Mar. 1792, Winthrop Sargent Papers, MHS; Winthrop Sargent to Lt. Col. Oliver Spencer, 9 Mar. 1792, in Carter, *Territorial Papers,* 3:367. For a detailed description of the building of Fort Hamilton, see the extensive footnote in Smith, *St. Clair Papers,* 2:292–93n; Fort St. Clair was of similar construction.

11. WHH to Thomas P. Chilton, 17 Feb. 1834, printed in *Cincinnati Daily Gazette,* 10 May 1834. This experience did much to create WHH's lifelong conviction that he was "suited to exposure and hardship" (Cleaves, *Old Tippecanoe,* 286). Harrison recalled the weather as being cold and severe, but Wilkinson's boast of having built a sturdy fort in only six days' time (Hay and Werner, *The Admirable Trumpeter,* 112) suggests that if the weather was favorable for building, it cannot have been as bad as WHH remembered. The speedy march to the site and back likewise implies that the road was not too wet, while one settler's memory that spring came early that year implies that while it may have been cold, the weather probably wasn't really bitter (*The Indian Captivity of O. M. Spencer,* 36–37).

12. Cist, *Miscellany,* 1:210; WHH to Brooks, 20 July 1839, WHH Correspondence, NYHS; B. H. Pershing, "Winthrop Sargent," *Ohio Archeological and Historical Quarterly* 35 (Oct. 1926): 589–90, 598.

13. James Wilkinson to Anthony Wayne, 1 Nov. 1792, Anthony Wayne Papers, HSP; and Henry Knox to George Washington, 2 Mar. 1792; James Wilkinson to David Zeigler, 9 Mar. 1792; David Zeigler to James Wilkinson, 10 Mar. 1792; and James Wilkinson to Henry Knox, 13 Mar. 1792, all in Henry Knox Papers, MHS.

The generally black reputation as an intriguer that Wilkinson acquired in the early nineteenth century has led to distortions both great and small of the American history in which he appears. An early historian of Cincinnati (Goss, *Cincinnati, The Queen City*, 2:10) maintained, for instance, that Zeigler was ousted from command of Fort Washington, and subsequently from the army, by Wilkinson's scheming. The truth is that Zeigler yielded command to Wilkinson because the latter outranked him; see Katzenberger, *Major David Ziegler*, 31–32. His subsequent resignation was apparently a gesture he made during a dispute over his conduct as an officer. He did not expect it to be accepted, and, according to another officer, was "mortified" when it was. Ebenezer Denny to Winthrop Sargent, 23 May 1792, Winthrop Sargent Papers, MHS. According to Wilkinson, Zeigler's resignation was accepted because of his drunkenness and insubordination—see Jacobs, *Beginning of the U.S. Army*, 142, and Cist, *Miscellany*, 1:233. There is no other evidence to support Wilkinson's charge, but in light of the First Regiment's reputation its veracity seems all too probable. None of Zeigler's contemporaries who mentioned the affair seemed to think an injustice had been done.

14. Jacobs, *Tarnished Warrior*, 4–7, 82–83. WHH's claim (in his "Biographical Memoirs of Major General William Henry Harrison") that sometime in 1792 Wilkinson prevented his transfer contains few particulars. Wilkinson's action must have taken place early in his command, however, since presumably he was countermanding an order by one of the previous commanders. The fort in question was probably Fort Jefferson, commanded until 1 Mar. by Captain Joseph Shaylor—"I fear that Shaylor has depreciated," Anthony Wayne wrote James Wilkinson (7 July 1792, Anthony Wayne Papers, HSP). It is difficult to see what other fort it could have been. Major John F. Hamtramck at Fort Knox, Captain Thomas Cushing at Fort St. Clair after 24 Mar., Captain John Armstrong at Fort Hamilton, and Captain David Strong at Fort Jefferson after 1 Mar. were all respected and sober men. Information is scant regarding Forts Steuben and Franklin (the smaller posts farther up and down the Ohio), but they seem unlikely choices in any case. Fort Jefferson, however, definitely needed reinforcement in Jan. 1792, since Captain Montfort and his company had just left it for Fort Washington (David Zeigler to Winthrop Sargent, 7 Jan. 1792, Winthrop Sargent Papers, MHS). WHH's account in the *Port Folio* ends with a warm, heartfelt tribute to Wilkinson.

15. *The Indian Captivity of O. M. Spencer*, 33.

9. Cincinnati

1. Goss, *Cincinnati, The Queen City*, 1:82; Cist, *Cincinnati in 1859*, 131; Dudley Woodbridge to Winthrop Sargent, Oliver J. Spencer to Winthrop Sargent, both 10 Mar. 1792, Winthrop Sargent Papers, MHS.

2. *Indian Captivity of O. M. Spencer*, 36.

3. The number of houses in the village in 1792 is a matter of surprising

uncertainty. WHH and O. M. Spencer remembered 40 cabins at most; John Heckewelder, who was there in July 1792, noted more than 200; and Daniel Drake gave figures that seem to add up to at least 150. WHH to Brooks, 20 July 1839, WHH Correspondence, NYHS; *The Indian Captivity of O. M. Spencer,* 31. John Heckewelder, quoted in Wallace, *Thirty Thousand Miles,* 269; "Dr. Daniel Drake's Memoir," 76–78, 87–90. The disparity is too great to ascribe to observational error. I have decided to follow Heckewelder and Drake, whose notations were closer in time, rather than WHH and Spencer, whose recollections probably had a slight romantic tendency to exaggerate the loneliness of the settlement. Heckewelder is the only source to record that the cabins, however many they were, were painted red.

"Dr. Daniel Drake's Memoir," 77–78, focuses on the early Jersey settlers, but a short list of early pioneers surviving and still living in Cincinnati in 1832 suggests that Pennsylvania and Virginia, in addition to New Jersey, contributed important contingents. "Cincinnati Pioneers," *Bulletin of the Ohio Historical and Philosophical Society* 20 (Apr. 1962): 148–49. On other details, see McBride, *Pioneer Biography,* 1:112, 291; Cist, *Miscellany,* 1:199; "Dr. Daniel Drake's Memoir," 78–79; Wallace, *Thirty Thousand Miles,* 269–70; Ford and Ford, *History of Hamilton County,* 334; Bond, *Civilization,* 317; and [John S. Williams], "Our Cabin; or, Life in the Woods," *American Pioneer* 2 (Oct. 1843): 445.

4. Cist, *Cincinnati in 1859,* 149, 154; "Dr. Daniel Drake's Memoir," 88–89; Goss, *Cincinnati, The Queen City,* 1:67; Winthrop Sargent to the Judges of the Territory, 30 Aug. 1790, in Carter, *Territorial Papers,* 3:330.

5. Wallace, *Thirty Thousand Miles,* 269–70; "Memoirs of Benjamin Van Cleve," 21; Goss, *Cincinnati, The Queen City,* 2:218, 272. The phrase "bite, ballock, and gouge" was used by George Greive, an early translator of the Marquis de Chastellux's travels in Virginia (Chastellux, *Travels,* 2:601); such sources as "Captivity of Israel Donelson," *American Pioneer* 1 (Dec. 1842): 426, show that the same practices were common in the Ohio Valley. On the houses of early Cincinnati, see Cist, *Cincinnati in 1859,* 41; Cist, *Miscellany,* 2:65; Jacob Burnet, *Notes on the Early Settlement of the Northwestern Territory* (Cincinnati, Ohio: Derby, Bradley, and Co., 1847), 33–34 and note; and Wilkinson to Harry Innes, 7 June 1792, Harry Innes Papers, LC.

Winthrop Sargent's house and "spacious garden" are mentioned in Burnet, *Notes,* 34. The house must have been built some time between May 1791, when Sargent was living in the fort, and March 1793, when John Armstrong stayed in it; the spring of 1792 seems the most plausible time. Winthrop Sargent to Judge Turner, 19 June 1791, in Carter, *Territorial Papers,* 3:334; John Armstrong to Winthrop Sargent, 11 Mar. 1793, Winthrop Sargent Papers, MHS.

6. Goss, *Cincinnati, The Queen City,* 1:76, 470–72; McBride, *Pioneer Biography,* 1:149; A. E. Jones, *Extracts from the History of Cincinnati,* 51–52; Wallace, *Thirty Thousand Miles,* 270.

7. The first definite evidence of WHH's lifelong fascination with the Indian mounds is from the summer of 1793, just after he returned to Cincinnati from the East, but it seems reasonable to suppose that it began during his earlier stay in 1791–92. WHH, *Discourse on the Aborigines* (Cincinnati: Cincinnati Express, 1838), 12–13. For Winthrop Sargent, the first evidence is his letter in 1794 to Dr. Benjamin Barton, later printed in *Transactions of the American Philosophical Society* 4 (1799): 177–81, which seems to reflect an established interest. Dr. Richard Allison, the chief medical man of the Western army, also had an interest in archeology; see Virginius C. Hall, "Richard Allison, Surgeon to the Legion," *Bulletin of the Historical and Philosophical Society of Ohio* 9 (Oct. 1951): 291. Sargent and WHH became acquainted in 1792; by June of that year Sargent was already writing to his superiors on WHH's behalf, and by 1796 they were, in WHH's phrase, "sworn friends." Winthrop Sargent to Henry Knox, 9 June 1792, in Carter, *Territorial Papers,* 2:400; WHH to James Wilkinson, 17 June 1796, WHH Papers, LC. The details in this paragraph are from Sargent's letter to Barton, but Sargent also wrote papers for the American Academy of Arts and Sciences in Boston, as mentioned in the sketch of his life in the *Dictionary of American Biography;* see also Josiah Priest, *American Antiquities and Discoveries in the West,* 4th ed. (Albany, N.Y.: Hoffman and White, 1834), 136–37, 174–75.

8. Burnet, *Notes,* 434–35; Robert Clarke, *The Pre-Historic Remains Which Were Found on the Site of the City of Cincinnati, Ohio. . . .* (Cincinnati, Ohio: Robert Clarke, 1876), 5–11.

9. WHH's literary interests kept him in touch with what was going on in American letters. Perhaps he was already aware when he went west that the earthworks were becoming a topic of interest to American writers. Early writings about them can be followed in Robert Silverberg's excellent *Mound Builders of Ancient America: The Archeology of a Myth* (Greenwich, Conn.: New York Graphic Society, 1968). Silverberg (*Mound Builders,* 76) categorizes WHH's views, expressed in his later writings, as "basically romantic." His interest was not that of a modern archeologist; he worked the Indians' history into the classical past he had learned from Rollin, describing the era before the advent of the British and Americans as the Indians' age of Saturn, a reference to the "Saturnia regna" of Virgil's *Eclogues.* Alan Borer, "William Henry Harrison and the Rhetoric of History," *Northwest Ohio Quarterly* 68 (1996): 119. Barton, in a letter to Joseph Banks (26 May 1793, Benjamin Smith Barton Papers, 1778–1813, HSP), referred to "the ancient works called, by me and by others, fortifications."

10. *Correspondence of John Cleves Symmes,* 149, 161; Gaff, *Bayonets in the Wilderness,* 14. There are two versions of the Bartle-Pasteur incident: Cist, *Cincinnati in 1859,* 133–34; and Goss, *Cincinnati, The Queen City,* 1:65, which is less accurate. The battle in front of McMillan's house is narrated in William McMillan to Winthrop Sargent, 16 Feb. 1792, Winthrop Sargent Papers, MHS.

11. Dudley Woodbridge to Winthrop Sargent, 6 July 1792; Oliver J. Spencer to Winthrop Sargent, 10 Mar. 1792; R. J. Meigs to Withrop Sargent, 20 Mar. 1792, all in Winthrop Sargent Papers, MHS; *Journal of Capt. Daniel Bradley,* 41; "Dr. Daniel Drake's Memoir," 89.

12. Bond, *Civilization,* 37–41; Van Every, *Ark of Empire,* 244–50; Kohn, *Eagle and Sword,* 117–23. For a sample of pro-peace, anti-Western sentiment, see "Serious Hints on a Very Serious Subject," *American Museum* 11 (Jan. 1792): 37–38.

13. Paul C. Wilson Jr., *A Forgotten Mission to the Indians: William Smalley's Adventures among the Delaware Indians of Ohio* (Galveston, Tex.: N.p., 1965), 11–14; Gaff, *Bayonets in the Wilderness,* 15–16; James Wilkinson to Harry Innes, 10 May, 7 June 1792, Harry Innes Papers, LC.

14. Cist, *Miscellany,* 1: 233; Wilkinson to Innes, 10 May 1792; John Brown to Harry Innes, 13 Apr. 1792, Harry Innes Papers, LC; Gaff, *Bayonets in the Wilderness,* 22–24; Prucha, *The Sword of the Republic,* 28–29.

15. John Pratt to Winthrop Sargent, 18 Mar. 1791, Winthrop Sargent Papers, MHS, is a fair example of officers' dissatisfaction. Katzenberger, *Major David Ziegler,* 33–34, offers an actual instance of an officer's going into trade. On the Indian prisoners, see "Dr. Daniel Drake's Memoir," 87; and James Wilkinson to Henry Knox, 6 July 1792, Anthony Wayne Papers, HSP.

16. Hay and Werner, *The Admirable Trumpeter,* 112–13; Jacobs, *Tarnished Warrior,* 125.

17. My account of this incident and the ensuing legal controversy comes from four letters: James Wilkinson to Winthrop Sargent, 2 June 1792, Winthrop Sargent Papers, MHS, a long explanation of the whole affair which includes the text of the 11 May order; and Winthrop Sargent to Wilkinson, 4 June 1792, Winthrop Sargent to John Cleves Symmes, 4 June 1792, and Winthrop Sargent to Henry Knox, 9 June 1792, all in Carter, *Territorial Papers,* 3:376–77, 3:377, and 2:400, respectively. A variant tradition of uncertain origin, in Goss, *Cincinnati, The Queen City,* 1:83, has WHH settling the affair himself by surrendering to the authorities and being confined to McHenry's tavern for twenty-four hours as punishment; but nothing in the letters cited above suggests that the controversy was ever resolved in any definite fashion, at least not by 9 June—and Harrison left for the East on 12 or 13 June.

18. Winthrop Sargent's comment about "young men" in his letter to Henry Knox, 9 June 1792, Carter, *Territorial Papers,* 2:400, did not specify the behavior he was commenting on. Probably it did not refer to the original flogging, which was a simple misunderstanding of orders. Although he may have meant the ten lashes meted out to the other man, I think it likely he was referring to WHH's attitude with regard to the writ.

19. Jacobs (*Beginnings of the U.S. Army,* 146) is surely correct in supposing that Wilkinson sent WHH to the East to get him out of the way. A later letter

from Wilkinson to Anthony Wayne (17 Sept. 1792, Anthony Wayne Papers, HSP) suggests that he expected him back by the end of the summer.

10. Anthony Wayne Takes Over

1. Bond, *Civilization of the Old Northwest,* 354; Wallace, *Thirty Thousand Miles,* 267–68; Baily, *Journal of a Tour,* 54; "Memoirs of Benjamin Van Cleve," 40.

2. Archer B. Hulbert, *The Ohio River* (New York: G. P. Putnam's Sons, 1906), 228–29; Dunbar, *A History of Travel,* 1:281–82; Charles Prentiss, *The Life of the Late Gen. William Eaton* (Brookfield, Mass.: E. Merriam and Co., 1813), 19.

3. Anthony Wayne to James Wilkinson, 7 July 1792, Anthony Wayne Papers, HSP; James Wilkinson to Harry Innes, 7, 12 June 1792, Harry Innes Papers, LC; Jacobs, *Tarnished Warrior,* 84, 157–58; Prentiss, *Eaton,* 18; *Journal of Capt. Daniel Bradley,* 14; "John D. Shane's Copy of Needham Parry's Diary," 229; Hay and Werner, *The Admirable Trumpeter,* 45, 65, 112–13.

4. Wallace, *Thirty Thousand Miles,* 264; Wildes, *Anthony Wayne,* 34. The Savage portrait of Wayne is in Glenn Tucker, *Mad Anthony Wayne and the New Nation* (Harrisburg, Pa.: Stackpole Books, 1973), frontispiece. Anthony Wayne to "Ensign Harrison," 3 July 1792; Anthony Wayne to James Wilkinson, 7 July 1792, Anthony Wayne Papers, HSP.

5. Samuel Hodgdon to Winthrop Sargent, 3 July 1792, Winthrop Sargent Papers, MHS; Henry Knox to Anthony Wayne, in Knopf, *Wayne: A Name in Arms,* 33, 35; Wildes, *Anthony Wayne,* 350–51; *Virginia Gazette,* 11 Dec. 1788; and *Autobiography of Benjamin Rush,* 307, give some idea of the fantastic tales about the Ohio Valley heard and repeated by Easterners.

6. "Memoirs of Benjamin Van Cleve," 39.

7. WHH to Thomas P. Chilton, 17 Feb. 1834, in *Cincinnati Daily Gazette,* 10 May 1834; Anthony Wayne to Major Joseph Ashton, 3 July 1792; general orders, 22 Dec. 1792, 6 Oct. 1793, all in Anthony Wayne Papers, HSP; Anthony Wayne to Henry Knox, in Knopf, *Wayne: A Name in Arms,* 58; Wildes, *Anthony Wayne,* 357–58; Craig, "Fort Lafayette," 497–503; "Journal of Captain Samuel Newman," 45, 47, 48; *American Museum,* 9, Appendix III (The gazette): 39; Ebenezer Denny to Winthrop Sargent, 27 July 1792, Winthrop Sargent Papers, MHS; Shaw (*Autobiography of Thirty Years,* 91) used the term "Hell-street" in describing another army town, Carlisle, in 1785, but no doubt it or something similar was current in Pittsburgh seven years later.

8. Van Every, *Ark of Empire,* 246; Tucker, *Mad Anthony Wayne and the New Nation,* 225; "General Wayne's Orderly Book," 377–82. On the new organization of the army, see Kohn, *Eagle and Sword,* 124.

9. Wildes, *Anthony Wayne,* 261, 321, 332; Carl Binger, *Revolutionary Doctor: Benjamin Rush, 1746–1813* (New York: W. W. Norton and Co., 1966), 157; James Wilkinson to Anthony Wayne, 17 Sept. 1792, Anthony Wayne Papers, HSP.

10. Anthony Wayne to Rufus Putnam, 6 Aug. 1792, Anthony Wayne Papers, HSP; *American State Papers,* 4:237; Gaff, *Bayonets in the Wilderness,* 18, 80–81.

11. Knopf, *Wayne: A Name in Arms,* 97; Kohn, *Eagle and Sword,* 146; *Journal of Capt. Daniel Bradley,* 42, 44; *Indian Captivity of O. M. Spencer,* 41–44; Wallace, *Thirty Thousand Miles,* 268, 271–72, 274; Cist, *Cincinnati in 1859,* 70; J. Gilman to Winthrop Sargent, 26 June 1792, Winthrop Sargent Papers, MHS; Anthony Wayne to Col. David Shepherd, 26 July 1792; Anthony Wayne to Wilkinson, 31 July 1792, Anthony Wayne Papers, HSP; Gaff, *Bayonets in the Wilderness,* 61.

12. Wildes, *Anthony Wayne,* 359–60; Gaff, *Bayonets in the Wilderness,* 70. Some sample reports of British participation are *Journal of Capt. Daniel Bradley,* 44; "Sargent's Diary," 273; and Knopf, *Wayne: A Name in Arms,* 56. For Wayne's thinking, see Knopf, *Wayne: A Name in Arms,* 74, 79, 98; and Ebenezer Denny to Winthrop Sargent, 27 July 1792, in Winthrop Sargent Papers, MHS.

13. Richard C. Knopf, "Crime and Punishment in the Legion, 1792–1793," *Bulletin of the Historical and Philosophical Society of Ohio* 14 (July 1965): 232–38; Norman W. Caldwell, "The Enlisted Soldier," 202; Gaff, *Bayonets in the Wilderness,* 60, 62–64; Clarence M. Burton, ed., "General Wayne's Orderly Book," *Michigan Pioneer and Historical Collections* 34 (1904): 358–59, 370–71, and passim. For discipline in the army before Wayne, see Shaw, *Autobiography of Thirty Years,* 118, 120; Hildreth, *Pioneer History,* 141; and "Journal of Captain Samuel Newman," 45, 48, 52.

14. Knopf (*Wayne: A Name in Arms,* 118) allows for an approximation of the number of soldiers. Wayne's orders are in Burton, "General Wayne's Orderly Book," 377–82.

15. My estimate of Ballard Smith's character is drawn from several small incidents. He seems to have written Wilkinson some sort of indiscreet letter in July 1792, for which he later apologized (Carter, *Territorial Papers,* 2:412). Then followed the incident related in this chapter. Smith was restored to command in May 1793, but removed again in October of that year for drunkenness (Knopf, *Wayne: A Name in Arms,* 280; Gaff, *Bayonets in the Wilderness,* 161–62; Henry DeButts to Edward Butler, 15 Oct. 1793, Anthony Wayne Papers, HSP).

16. The Smith-Bedinger feud is described in Wildes, *Anthony Wayne,* 376; Gaff, *Bayonets in the Wilderness,* 65; and cf. Burton, "General Wayne's Orderly Book," 389. The biography of Bedinger by a descendant (Dandridge, *George Michael Bedinger,* 106) confirms his propensity for stepping on the toes of older army officers during his brief service. It does not appear that he had been a street singer or anything of the sort, though Wildes seems to believe Smith's charge that he had been; probably it was just a wild term of abuse that had occurred to Smith.

17. Wildes, *Anthony Wayne,* 376–77; Burton, "General Wayne's Orderly Book," 391, 396; Captain Thomas T. Underwood, "A Journal of Wayne's Campaign," Mss. 16U, 121, Lyman C. Draper Manuscripts, State Historical Society of Wisconsin.

18. Ensign Charles Hyde, quoted in Gaff, *Bayonets in the Wilderness,* 53. The recollections of WHH as an officer are those of William Wiseman, in Cist, *Cincinnati in 1859,* 103; and John Johnston, in Cist, *Miscellany,* 2:297. Both date from a time after WHH became famous, and one is tempted to dismiss their praise as conventional on that account, but their emphasis on his peaceful and sympathetic qualities is unusual in the case of a martial figure, and probably reflects reality. For another example of an officer exploiting a private, see Shaw, *Autobiography of Thirty Years,* 122.

19. Burton, "General Wayne's Orderly Book," 395; Ensign Charles Hyde, quoted in Gaff, *Bayonets in the Wilderness,* 53; Knopf, "Crime and Punishment in the Legion," 236; Neville Craig, *The History of Pittsburgh,* 237–41; Wildes, *Anthony Wayne,* 379.

20. Knopf, *Wayne: A Name in Arms,* 101; Tucker, *Mad Anthony Wayne and the New Nation,* 17–18; Wildes, *Anthony Wayne,* 367–68; Underwood, "A Journal of Wayne's Campaign," Mss. 16U, 122, Lyman C. Draper Manuscripts, State Historical Society of Wisconsin; *Pittsburgh Gazette,* 27 Apr. 1793; Neville B. Craig, *History of Pittsburgh,* 215.

21. Orders of 27, 28 Nov. 1792, Anthony Wayne Papers, HSP; Knopf, *Wayne: A Name in Arms,* 142. The list of supplies was suggested by Winthrop Sargent's "Return of Ordinance, Military & other Stores . . . ," Winthrop Sargent Papers, MHS. The Legion had to wait some time in November until the Ohio River was high enough for it to embark (Knopf, *Wayne: A Name in Arms,* 121). According to Wayne, the river was still fairly low at the time of the move (Knopf, *Wayne: A Name in Arms,* 137–38); John Heckewelder, however, reported it as high at Marietta on 28 November (Wallace, *Thirty Thousand Miles,* 291). The order of 10 September calls WHH an ensign; that of 15 October calls him a lieutenant (Burton, "General Wayne's Orderly Book," 381, 396). He evidently received his promotion between these dates. According to Heitman, *Historical Register,* the promotion was dated from 2 June 1792; but that dating was, of course, retroactive.

11. Legionville and a Trip East

1. Wildes, *Anthony Wayne,* 368. A sketch of the camp is reproduced in Gaff, *Bayonets in the Wilderness,* 77.

2. Knopf, *Wayne: A Name in Arms,* 138, 147, 150, 152; S. J. Burr, *The Life and Times of William Henry Harrison* (New York: L. W. Ransom, 1840), 38; Barr, "Joseph Strong, M.D.," 438; Underwood, "A Journal of Wayne's

Campaign," Mss. 16U, 121, Lyman C. Draper Manuscripts, State Historical Society of Wisconsin; Gaff, *Bayonets in the Wilderness,* 76; Wildes, *Anthony Wayne,* 369.

3. *Pittsburgh Gazette,* 27 April 1793; Jacobs, *Beginnings of the U.S. Army,* 130–40.

4. William B. Skelton, *An American Profession of Arms: The Army Officer Corps, 1784–1861,* Modern War Studies (Lawrence, Kans.: Univ. Press of Kansas, 1992), 36–37.

5. See chapters 8 and 9 of this book.

6. Skelton, *American Profession,* 37–39.

7. Riling, *Baron Von Steuben,* 3–4; Cleaves, *Old Tippecanoe,* 36.

8. WHH to "Dear Brother," 27 Nov. 1794, WHH Papers, LC.

9. WHH to Brooks, 20 July 1839, WHH Correspondence, NYHS. A family memoir by Catharina V. R. Bonney (*A Legacy of Historical Gleanings* [Albany, N.Y.: J. Munsell, 1875], 2:94–97, 129) enables one to track Van Rensselaer's movements with some precision. Not until later is WHH mentioned in his correspondence. The development of his close friendship with WHH, however, probably began at Legionville, when the two were stationed together for a couple of months. They were together again during the summer and fall campaign of 1793. On Van Rensselaer's personality, see Gaff, *Bayonets in the Wilderness,* 208.

10. WHH to A. B. Howell, 7 April 1838, in *Cincinnati Daily Gazette,* 19 May 1838; Wildes, *Anthony Wayne,* 389. Dixon Ryan Fox briefly describes the importation of the duel to America in the 1770s and stresses its military context. D. R. Fox, "Culture in Knapsacks," *Quarterly Journal of the New York State Historical Association* 11 (Jan. 1930): 42. For the basic rules, see the "twenty-six commandments," formalized in 1777, of the Irish code duello, "from which all other codes (in the English language) have been written or made." Ben C. Truman, *The Field of Honor* (New York: Fords, Howard, and Hulbert, 1884), 48–53.

11. Wildes, *Anthony Wayne,* 389; Prentiss, *William Eaton,* 15–17; Skelton, *American Profession,* 53–56. There are accounts of several duels in Underwood, "A Journal of Wayne's Campaign" (Mss. 16U, Lyman C. Draper Manuscripts, State Historical Society of Wisconsin), for the first half of 1793. For Wayne's attitude, see Underwood, "A Journal," 16U126; and Burton, "General Wayne's Orderly Book," 433. Gaff discusses friction among the officers at Legionville (*Bayonets in the Wilderness,* 78 and 99–101).

12. WHH to A. B. Howell, 7 April 1838, in *Cincinnati Daily Gazette,* 19 May 1838; Joseph Strong to John Pratt, 14 May 1793, John Pratt Papers, CSL. For some literate criticisms of duelling that WHH may have read, see "Thoughts on Duelling" and "Directions for the Improvement of the Rising Generation," both in *American Museum* 6 (Sept. 1789): 281–82, 240–41; and "Cursory Thoughts

on Duelling," *American Museum* 9 (Jan. 1791): 20–21. A college oration is probably a fair sample of the produelling argument. Francis Hopkinson, "On Duelling," in *The Miscellaneous Essays and Occasional Writings of Francis Hopkinson, Esq.* (Philadelphia, Pa.: T. Dobson, 1792), 2:24–33.

13. As early as December, Wayne was "intolerant" about leaves of absence and turned down requests for them from several officers (Wildes, *Anthony Wayne,* 376, 483). In January and again in March, he complained to Knox in particular about the shortage of subalterns (Knopf, *Wayne: A Name in Arms,* 177, 197; cf. Gaff, *Bayonets in the Wilderness,* 102–3). For his health, see Anthony Wayne to William Heyman, 28 Dec. 1792, Anthony Wayne Papers, HSP; and Gaff, *Bayonets in the Wilderness,* 79–80. His attitude toward WHH is discussed further below. No document states that WHH's leave was for the purpose of escorting Ann Wilkinson, but in May he was at Pittsburgh in her company (see below), and the connection is evident.

Elizabeth Harrison died in 1792 (*Sanderson's Biography of the Signers,* 727), some time after 24 September, when Thomas Lee Shippen wrote his father that everyone was well at Berkeley (Shippen Family Papers, LC). No source I have seen gives an exact date.

14. William Brown diary, in Thomas Speed, *The Wilderness Road,* Filson Club Publications, no. 2 (Louisville, Ky.: John P. Morton and Co., 1886), 55–62; Bayard, *Travels of a Frenchman,* 67; Archer B. Hulbert, *Historic Highways of America,* vol. 12, *Pioneer Roads and Experiences of Travelers* (Cleveland, Ohio: Arthur H. Clark Co., 1904), 48–62.

15. Deed, WHH to Carter B. Harrison, 23 February 1793, WHH Papers, LC; WHH to Carter B. Harrison, 27 Nov. 1794, WHH Papers, LC; Benjamin Harrison VI Account Book, VHS; *Sanderson's Biography of the Signers,* 728–29; Richmond Personal Property Tax Returns, 1793, VSL; Stanard, "Harrison of James River," 35:90; Dowdey, *The Great Plantation,* 281.

For the transaction with Ben, there are two documents with differing dates and amounts: WHH to Benjamin Harrison, 5 Mar. 1793, WHH Papers, LC; and same to same, 9 Mar. 1793, Deed Book 4, Charles City County Court House. They seem to refer to the same transaction, and I have no explanation for the discrepancies; but it seems rash to assert, as Gunderson does ("Apprentice in Arms," 12–13), that the transaction shows WHH as lacking in business acumen. Much of the Berkeley land was valued at a low rate, and Colonel Harrison had tried unsuccessfully to sell it a few years earlier; there is no way to state with confidence how much his son's inheritance was worth. What the transaction clearly shows, as Gunderson concedes, is that WHH wanted to sever his ties with Virginia.

16. Edward Carrington to Winthrop Sargent, 10 Mar. 1793, Winthrop Sargent Papers, MHS ("promising young Gentleman" quotation). There is good reason to suppose that Daingerfield and WHH traveled together from

Philadelphia to Pittsburgh a few months later; see below. On Charles Harrison, see Stanard, "Harrison of James River," 34:386.

17. WHH to Carter B. Harrison, 27 Nov. 1794, WHH Papers, LC; Edward Carrington to Winthrop Sargent, 10 Mar. 1793, Winthrop Sargent Papers, MHS.

18. Tench Coxe to Benjamin Harrison, 21 July 1793, Tench Coxe Papers, HSP.

19. WHH to "Dear Brother," 27 Nov. 1794, WHH Papers, LC; Mary Morris to Gouverneur Morris, 9 June 1791, Gouverneur Morris Papers, 1768–1816, CU.

20. WHH to "Dear Brother," 27 Nov. 1794, WHH Papers, LC. The Stuart portrait is reproduced in Randolph W. Church, "James Markham Marshall," *Virginia Cavalcade* 13 (Spring 1964): 23. Not enough is known of WHH's early romantic involvements to make any judgments about his style of wooing, but it may be relevant that in his courtship of Anna Symmes, who became his wife, he again had to deal with the opposition of her family, or, more precisely, her father (Cleaves, *Old Tippecanoe,* 24–25).

21. Church, "James Markham Marshall," 22–29. His arrival in Philadelphia is noted in Thomas Jefferson to John Wayles Eppes, 12 May 1793, *Papers of Thomas Jefferson,* 26:7.

22. These plans and departures are best followed in Isaac Craig, "Major Isaac Craig: Extracts from His Letter-Books While Quartermaster at Fort Pitt, 1791–1804," in *Historical Register: Notes and Queries, Historical and Genealogical. . . .* (Harrisburg, Pa.: L. S. Hart, 1883–84). The series begins at vol. 1, p. 290, and runs in episodes through vol. 2. From 10 May on, Major Isaac Craig at Fort Fayette was in "hourly" expectation of Mrs. Wilkinson's arrival at Pittsburgh, but she did not arrive until 13 May or later. Posey was expected 22 May. Craig does not state that the two parties arrived together, but they, with WHH, descended the river together beginning 28 May, and it seems plausible, for the reasons given in the text, that they may have wished to travel together. Craig, "Major Isaac Craig: Extracts from His Letter-Books," 2:134–35, 136, 161. WHH, who knew members of both parties, would have made the arrangement. The dates conjectured assume that the journey by coach took two weeks or so. Posey, who had served under Daingerfield's father in the Revolution, is described in John Thornton Posey, *General Thomas Posey: Son of the American Revolution* (East Lansing, Mich.: Michigan State Univ. Press, 1992), 31, 144. His commission was docketed at the War Department on 2 May (Posey, *General Thomas Posey,* 155). On Wilkinson sons, see Jacobs, *Tarnished Warrior,* 159. Despite Gaff (*Bayonets in the Wilderness,* 117), Daingerfield was not Posey's son-in-law; he was a member of his family only in the military sense.

12. The March into the Woods

1. WHH to "Dear Brother," 27 Nov. 1794, WHH Papers, LC; "Major Isaac Craig," 2:161.

2. Wilkinson was at Marietta the day before his wife's party left Pittsburgh. James Wilkinson to Anthony Wayne, 27 May 1793, Anthony Wayne Papers, HSP; "Major Isaac Craig," 2:161; Posey, *General Thomas Posey*, 133.

3. Gaff, *Bayonets in the Wilderness*, 115, 128.

4. Brackenridge, *Recollections*, 19; Gaff, *Bayonets in the Wilderness*, 114–15; *Cist's Weekly Advertiser*, 8 Oct. 1845; Underwood, "A Journal of Wayne's Campaign," Mss. 16U, 125, Lyman C. Draper Manuscripts, State Historical Society of Wisconsin; Burton, "General Wayne's Orderly Book," 443; Kohn, *Eagle and Sword*, 146, 150; Van Every, *Ark of Empire*, 268–69, 273–85. "God of War" was a fairly common usage; for an example, see James Wilkinson to John Armstrong, 29 April 1792, reprinted in Cist, *Miscellany*, 1:233.

5. Wallace, *Thirty Thousand Miles*, 274; James Wilkinson to Harry Innes, 18 May, 14, 23, 29 June, Harry Innes Papers, LC. For orders that concern WHH, see those of 9 July, 12 Aug., and 13 Aug., Anthony Wayne Papers, HSP; and Burton, "General Wayne's Orderly Book," 461. The order of 12 August says only that orders given by the aides in the commander's name "are to be obeyed with promptitude" and does not refer to WHH by name, but it is clearly a response to an incident of some kind, being issued only one day before the order appointing him as "second Aid de Camp" and stating that he was "to be respected accordingly." Perhaps Wayne had been using WHH as an aide even before 12 August, despite his official line position.

6. Messages and Letters of William Henry Harrison, 2:746. For the heavy paperwork in the Legion, see the stationery allotments in Burton, "General Wayne's Orderly Book," 359–60.

7. WHH to Thomas P. Chilton, 17 Feb. 1834, in *Cincinnati Daily Gazette*, 10 May 1834; Gaff, *Bayonets in the Wilderness*, 125; Goss, *Cincinnati*, 2:171–72; *Cist's Advertiser*, 17 Dec. 1845.

8. Sargent left for the East 5 Aug. (Winthrop Sargent to Anthony Wayne, 25 July 1793, Anthony Wayne Papers, HSP). He and WHH may not have seen each other again for some time, as WHH and the Legion had moved into the interior by the time Sargent returned in 1794.

My characterization of Charles Harrison rests on two facts, both in Stanard, "Harrison of James River," 34:386: his death in a duel in 1796, and his father's career as the most military of the Harrisons. WHH's 1794 letter to Carter (WHH Papers, LC) contains several references to other Virginians in the Legion: a Mr. Bowman, whom Ben knew; two Edmondsons, connected with the Charles City County family of that name; and, of course, Tinsley and Balfour. In August, William Daingerfield showed up and was assigned to the Second Sub-Legion (general orders, 22 Aug. 1794, Anthony Wayne Papers, HSP). On Van Rensselaer, see James Wilkinson to Anthony Wayne, 16 Aug. 1793, Anthony Wayne Papers, HSP; on Scott, see Gaff, *Bayonets in the Wilderness*, 156; on Joseph Phillips, see Goss, *Cincinnati*, 2:217.

9. WHH, in later life, apparently boasted occasionally of his sexual prowess as a young man. Young Salmon Chase described his humor as "earthy"; William L. Marcy, a political opponent to be sure, understood that his talk was replete with "obscene stories, thoroughly intent with the spirit of lechery" (Borer, "William Henry Harrison," 119–20). In other words, his conversation made the same impression on Northerners of a Yankee background as his father's had on John Adams.

10. WHH to A. B. Howell, 7 April 1838, in *Cincinnati Daily Gazette,* 16 May 1838. WHH did not name Drake's opponent, but Wayne's order for a general court-martial to consider Guion's charges against Drake obviously refers to the same incident. General orders, 7 July 1793, Anthony Wayne Papers, HSP; cf. Gaff, *Bayonets in the Wilderness,* 124–25.

11. Knopf, *Wayne: A Name in Arms,* 449.

12. WHH, *Discourse on the Aborigines,* 12; Burton, "General Wayne's Orderly Book," 463; Burnet, *Notes,* 434–35.

13. Knopf, *Wayne: A Name in Arms,* 266; Ford and Ford, *Hamilton County,* 334; Underwood, "A Journal of Wayne's Campaign," Mss. 16U, 128, Lyman C. Draper Manuscripts, State Historical Society of Wisconsin; Wildes, *Anthony Wayne,* 369; Gaff, *Bayonets in the Wilderness,* 134.

14. For problems in Cincinnati, see Burton, "General Wayne's Orderly Book," 429; and Green, *William Henry Harrison,* 35. The letters reprinted in Bonney, *A Legacy of Historical Gleanings,* 106, give a glimpse of society in Lexington.

15. Knopf, *Wayne: A Name in Arms,* 270; Gaff, *Bayonets in the Wilderness,* 148–49; Jacobs, *Beginnings of the U.S. Army,* 158.

16. Knopf, *Wayne: A Name in Arms,* 273, 276; Green, *William Henry Harrison,* 37; McBride, *Pioneer Biography,* 2:15; *Journal of Capt. Daniel Bradley,* 21. The number three thousand includes the Kentucky militia with the Legion; cf. Gaff, *Bayonets in the Wilderness,* 151.

17. Wallace, *Thirty Thousand Miles,* 271–72; WHH, *Discourse on the Aborigines,* 42, 51; Wildes, *Anthony Wayne,* 393, 398; McBride, *Pioneer Biography,* 2:18; Gaff, *Bayonets in the Wilderness,* 149–50; Paul A. Hutton, "Williams Wells: Frontier Scout and Indian Agent," *Indiana Magazine of History* 74 (Sept. 1978): 184–93.

18. Wildes, *Anthony Wayne,* 395; John Bakeless, *Lewis & Clark* (New York: William Morrow and Co., 1947), 37–40; Knopf, *Wayne: A Name in Arms,* 274. On Clark's mission, see Gaff, *Bayonets in the Wilderness,* 142–43.

19. Knopf, *Wayne: A Name in Arms,* 276; cf. Cist, *Cincinnati in 1859,* 25–26; *Journal of Capt. Daniel Bradley,* 52; and *St. Clair Papers,* 2:327. James Wilkinson, in a letter to Harry Innes, 3 Oct. 1793 (Harry Innes Papers, LC), made an explicit comparison to St. Clair's campaign; doubtless the same idea was in the minds of many people.

20. Richard C. Knopf, ed., "Two Journals of the Kentucky Volunteers, 1793 and 1794," *Filson Club History Quarterly* 27 (July 1953): 251; Erna Risch, *Quartermaster Support of the Army: A History of the Corps, 1775–1939* (Washington, D.C.: Office of the Quartermaster General, 1962), 106; Ford and Ford, *Hamilton County*, 334. The full number of companies in the Legion was fifty-six, fourteen to each sublegion (Burton, "General Wayne's Orderly Book," 372–76), but no record I have seen states precisely how many marched with Wayne in October, and I have been purposely vague.

21. Journal of John M. Scott, 7 Oct. 1793, quoted in Cist, *Miscellany*, 2:55; Jacobs, *Tarnished Warrior*, 131.

22. McBride, *Pioneer Biography*, 2:113–15; Cist, *Miscellany*, 2:55; General orders, 29 Aug. 1793, Anthony Wayne Papers, HSP. For an example of the sort of message WHH carried, see Knopf, "Two Journals of the Kentucky Volunteers," 252.

23. Knopf, "Two Journals of the Kentucky Volunteers," 251–52; Daniel Drake, *Notices Concerning Cincinnati* (Cincinnati, Ohio: John W. Browne and Co., 1810), 28; Cist, *Miscellany*, 2:55.

24. "Journal of Capt. Daniel Bradley," 54; Knopf, *Wayne: A Name in Arms*, 276; Gaff, *Bayonets in the Wilderness*, 161.

25. Cist, *Miscellany*, 2:55.

26. Ibid.; *Journal of Capt. Daniel Bradley*, 55; Gaff, *Bayonets in the Wilderness*, 162–63; Burnet, *Notes*, 160; Underwood, "A Journal of Wayne's Campaign," Mss. 16U, 130, Lyman C. Draper Manuscripts, State Historical Society of Wisconsin.

27. Wildes, *Anthony Wayne*, 401; Cist, *Miscellany*, 2:56; Knopf, *Wayne: A Name in Arms*, 27, 280; John H. Powell, *Bring Out Your Dead* (Philadelphia, Pa.: Univ. of Pennsylvania Press, 1949), passim; Caleb Swan to Winthrop Sargent, 22 Nov. 1793, Winthrop Sargent Papers, MHS.

28. Cist, *Cincinnati in 1859*, 84–86; Knopf, *Wayne: A Name in Arms*, 280; Knopf, "Two Journals of the Kentucky Volunteers," 251–55; Gaff, *Bayonets in the Wilderness*, 171–72.

29. Knopf, *Wayne: A Name in Arms*, 280; Thomas Cushing to John Pratt, 2 Nov. 1793, John Pratt Papers, CSL. There were three controlling factors in the decision, according to Kohn (*Eagle and Sword*, 155): the lateness of the season, low supplies, and the fact that the Legion was still under strength.

13. Nerves

1. Knopf, "Two Journals of the Kentucky Volunteers," 255–58; Thomas Cushing to John Pratt, 2 Nov. 1793, John Pratt Papers, CSL; Gaff, *Bayonets in the Wilderness*, 172–73; Knopf, *Wayne: A Name in Arms*, 284; Wallace, *Thirty Thousand Miles*, 156; Arthur St. Clair to Alexander Hamilton, in *St. Clair Papers*, 2:318.

2. Simmons, *The Forts of Anthony Wayne*, 12–13; *Journal of Capt. Daniel Bradley*, 30; Elliot, *Poetical and Miscellaneous Works*, 138. Early construction of the fort can be followed through documents in the Anthony Wayne Papers, HSP; Knopf, *Wayne: A Name in Arms*, 283; and "General Wayne's Orderly Book," 498. Underwood, "A Journal of Wayne's Campaign" (Mss. 16U, 130, Lyman C. Draper Manuscripts, State Historical Society of Wisconsin), supplies the sequence of building, although its date for completion of 10 November is clearly wrong. Dates in the Underwood diary are uniformly unreliable; 10 December, however, is a plausible emendation.

3. On officers' wives, see J. Pierce to John Pratt, 26 June 1794, John Pratt Papers, CSL. On Rebecca Strong, see Hall, "Richard Allison," 288. Details of daily life at a comparable military post are given in Richard C. Knopf, ed., "A Surgeon's Mate at Fort Defiance: The Journal of Joseph Gardner Andrews for the Year 1795," *Ohio Archeological and Historical Quarterly* 66 (Jan. 1957): 55–86; see also *Journal of Capt. Daniel Bradley*, 43. On standard practice for the location of latrines, see Wilkinson's orders in Gaff, *Bayonets in the Wilderness*, 92.

4. Quoted in Gaff, *Bayonets in the Wilderness*, 156.

5. Wildes, *Anthony Wayne*, 403–5; Knopf, *Wayne: A Name in Arms*, 282; Prentiss, *William Eaton*, 19–20; Hay and Werner, *The Admirable Trumpeter*, 118; Gaff, *Bayonets in the Wilderness*, 164; Thomas Cushing to Jeremiah Wadsworth, 15 Mar. 1794, Joseph Trumbull Papers, CSL. Both George Washington and William Eaton noted Wayne's susceptibility to flattery; see Prucha, *The Sword of the Republic*, 28–29; and Prentiss, *William Eaton*, 19–20.

6. The fullest account of the clash between Wayne and the contractors is in Wildes, *Anthony Wayne*, 399–402 (see also Paul David Nelson, *Anthony Wayne: Soldier of the Early Republic* [Bloomington, Ind.: Indiana Univ. Press, 1985], 246, 249), but it needs to be supplemented by Carl A. Brettschneider's article "Some of the Personalities and Problems of Supply Affecting the Indian Campaign of 1792–1794," which uses the Otho H. Williams Papers in the Maryland Historical Society and gives the same story from the contractors' point of view (*Bulletin of the Historical and Philosophical Society of Ohio* 9 [Oct. 1951]: 299–318). There is ample warrant for believing that Wayne's demands were unreasonable. The journey was, in fact, arduous and dangerous. James Wilkinson's letter of 30 November to Anthony Wayne (in Hay and Werner, *The Admirable Trumpeter*, 118) mentions the difficulty of the roads, while William Stanley notes both the bad roads and the danger from Indians. William Stanley, "The Diary of Major William Stanley, 1790–1810," ed. L. Belle Hamlin, *Ohio Historical and Philosophical Society Quarterly* 14 (Apr. 1919): 22. (Stanley was one of the few merchants whom Wayne allowed up to sell whiskey; for mention of others, see Underwood, "A Journal of Wayne's Campaign," Mss. 16U, 136, Lyman C. Draper Manuscripts, State Historical

Society of Wisconsin; and "Memoirs of Benjamin Van Cleve," 42.) An account of one Indian attack was printed in the first newspaper to be published in the region, the *Centinel of the North-West Territory,* 18 Jan. 1794. Brettschneider ("Personalities and Problems," 302–4, 308–9) points out that the road could have been better and the journey safer had Wayne been willing to detail more men for escort and maintenance. However, Wayne was to some degree a victim of government policy; as Kohn points out (*Eagle and Sword,* 153), the restriction on offensive movements in the summer of 1793 had prevented him from building the roads he needed north of Cincinnati.

Elliott and Williams themselves, and Major Cushing among the officers, were inclined to fix the blame for Wayne's excessive demands on Quartermaster General O'Hara, Wayne's intimate friend, whom Cushing called an "artful, designing knave" out to defraud the government (Cushing to Jeremiah Wadsworth, 15 Mar. 1794, Joseph Trumbull Papers, CSL; see also Brettschneider, "Personalities and Problems," 311–12). Certainly, Wilkinson had some justification for counseling the contractors not to take Wayne's urgings too seriously if he believed, as he may have done, that the commander was acting arbitrarily on the basis of O'Hara's bad advice.

7. Thomas Cushing to John Pratt, 2 Nov. 1793, John Pratt Papers, CSL; letter of Lieutenant Campbell Smith, quoted in Brettschneider, "Personalities and Problems," 315; James Wilkinson to Jeremiah Wadsworth, 12 Mar. 1794, Thomas Cushing to same, 15 Mar. 1794, both in Joseph Trumbull Papers, CSL. Wayne's papers for November–December 1793 are full of requests for leave (Anthony Wayne Papers, HSP).

8. Wildes, *Anthony Wayne,* 403–6; John Mills to John Pratt, 4 Dec. 1793, Isaac Guion to same, 22 Dec. 1793, and Thomas Cushing to same, 13 Jan. 1794, all in John Pratt Papers, CSL. A small example of Wayne's obsession is the password and countersign he ordered for 3 January 1794, as recorded in the Anthony Wayne Papers, HSP: "Parole Resignation Countersign Pusillanimous."

9. James Wilkinson to Harry Innes, 14 June, 23 Oct. 1793, Harry Innes Papers, LC; Wildes, *Anthony Wayne,* 389; W. E. Blue to Anthony Wayne, 11 Jan. 1794, Anthony Wayne Papers, HSP.

10. In the years after 1794, WHH was one of the very few officers in the West to stay on good terms with both generals; in 1798 he was able, when the occasion required, to produce testimonials from both (Goebel, *William Henry Harrison,* 38–39). Nevertheless, his surviving correspondence suggests that he was on more intimate terms with Wilkinson in these years than with Wayne; compare his letter to Wayne, 30 Nov. 1795, with Wilkinson's to him, 2 Apr. 1796, both in WHH Papers, LC.

11. Nelson, *Anthony Wayne,* 449–51. Extreme examples of the tendency to demonize Wilkinson are John Hyde Preston, *A Gentleman Rebel: The Exploits of Anthony Wayne* (New York: Farrar and Rinehart, 1930), 296–300; and

Timothy M. Rusche, "Treachery within the United States Army," *Pennsylvania History* 65 (Autumn 1998): 478–91. Wildes (*Anthony Wayne,* 401–2) makes the charge about the contractors.

12. Jacobs, *Tarnished Warrior,* 133; Anthony Wayne to James Wilkinson, 22 Dec. 1793, Anthony Wayne Papers, HSP.

13. Knopf, *Wayne: A Name in Arms,* 297; Underwood, "A Journal of Wayne's Campaign," Mss. 16U, 133–34, Lyman C. Draper Manuscripts, State Historical Society of Wisconsin; Burton, "General Wayne's Orderly Book," 502; McBride, *Pioneer Biography,* 2:119; Green, *William Henry Harrison,* 40; Gaff, *Bayonets in the Wilderness,* 185–86. Gunderson ("Apprentice in Arms," 27) errs in saying that neither WHH nor Wayne mentioned the expedition to Fort Recovery "either in correspondence or memoirs"; on the contrary, see Anthony Wayne to James Wilkinson, 22 Dec. 1793, and same to Captain Alexander Gibson, 26 Dec. 1793, both in Anthony Wayne Papers, HSP, which both mention it.

14. Major John H. Buell, quoted in Gaff, *Bayonets in the Wilderness,* 187.

15. Underwood, "A Journal of Wayne's Campaign," Mss. 16U, 133, Lyman C. Draper Manuscripts, State Historical Society of Wisconsin; *Centinel of the North-West Territory,* 13 Dec. 1793; WHH, *Discourse on the Aborigines,* 51. Collins's mission can be followed in Anthony Wayne to Joseph Collins, 30 Dec. 1793, and Anthony Wayne to Charles Scott, 4 Jan. 1794, both in Anthony Wayne Papers, HSP; Knopf, *Wayne: A Name in Arms,* 298; Gaff, *Bayonets in the Wilderness,* 187; and *Centinel of the North-West Territory,* 11 Jan. 1794. The adventurous Vermonter Captain William Eaton subsequently took over Collins's mission and completed it successfully: Anthony Wayne to Thomas Posey, 12 Jan. 1794, Anthony Wayne Papers, HSP; Prentiss, *William Eaton,* 20.

16. *Journal of Capt. Daniel Bradley,* 59; Thomas Cushing to Jeremiah Wadsworth, 15 Mar. 1794, Joseph Trumbull Papers, CSL; John M. Scott to John Pratt, 12 Jan. 1794, and John Mills to same, 12 Jan. 1794, both in John Pratt Papers, CSL; Knopf, *Wayne: A Name in Arms,* 299–300; Gaff, *Bayonets in the Wilderness,* 188–89; Anthony Wayne to James Wilkinson, 13 Jan. 1794, Anthony Wayne Papers, HSP. Sword (*President Washington's Indian War,* 296) mentions a "lone Delaware warrior" as the emissary, but all the primary sources I have seen describe a party of four. On George White Eyes, see Wildes, *Anthony Wayne,* 409–10; *A Journal of the Adventures of Matthew Bunn* (Providence, R.I.: The Author, 1796), 18–19; Hay and Werner, *The Admirable Trumpeter,* 168; and Ruth L. Woodward and Wesley Frank Craven, eds., *Princetonians, 1784–1790* (Princeton, N.J.: Princeton Univ. Press, 1991), 442–51. Hutton, "William Wells," 194, states that the peace embassy was a response to Wells's freeing an Indian captive.

17. The document issuing whiskey to the Indians, transcribed in John Heise, Catalogue #2467, n.d., American Antiquarian Society, gives a date of

4 January; but 14 January, the date of the Indians' departure, must be correct. On the Indians' dress and appearance, see Wallace, *Thirty Thousand Miles,* 52–53; Charles Johnston, *A Narrative of the Incidents Attending the Capture, Detention, and Ransom of Charles Johnston. . . .* (New York: J. and J. Harper, 1827), 72–73; C. A. Weslager, *The Delaware Indian Westward Migration* (Wallingford, Pa.: Middle Atlantic Press, 1978), 129–30; and Gaff, *Bayonets in the Wilderness,* 189; and compare with Heckewelder's account of their garb at a peace treaty, in Wallace, *Thirty Thousand Miles,* 283–84. According to John M. Scott to John Pratt, 12 Jan. 1794 (John Pratt Papers, CSL), Dr. Allison sat in on the talks with the Indians; presumably other members of Wayne's staff, including WHH, did so too.

18. Anthony Wayne to James Wilkinson, 13 Jan. 1794, Anthony Wayne Papers, HSP; *Journal of Capt. Daniel Bradley,* 59; Thomas Cushing to Jeremiah Wadsworth, 15 Mar. 1794, Joseph Trumbull Papers, CSL; and John Mills to John Pratt, 12 Jan. 1794, and John M. Scott to same, 12 Jan. 1794, both in John Pratt Papers, CSL.

19. Knopf, *Wayne: A Name in Arms,* 202–5; WHH, *Discourse on the Aborigines,* 42. Confusingly, Big Tree was often called Stiff Knee as well: a letter in Knopf, *Wayne: A Name in Arms,* 203, refers to "Stiff Knee (alias) Big Tree." In the two accounts of his quest and suicide, WHH refers to him as Stiff Knee, Wayne as Big Tree. The primary evidence is so divided that I cannot say which name was in more common usage; I have chosen Big Tree arbitrarily.

14. Toward a Showdown

1. *Journal of Capt. Daniel Bradley,* 9; Alta H. Heiser, *West to Ohio* (Yellow Springs, Ohio: Antioch Press, 1954), 41; Gaff, *Bayonets in the Wilderness,* 130–31; Knopf, "The Journal of Joseph Gardner Andrews for the Year 1795," 62, 79. No document states exactly where WHH was on 9 February, but it is certain that he was at or near Fort Greenville. By his own account, he was present at the time of Big Tree's suicide in late January; and on 19 February, at the fort, he countersigned a provision return for a party of three men from Fort Recovery (WHH Papers, IHS).

2. Oliver Ormsby to Anthony Wayne, 2 Feb. 1794, and Daniel Bradley to Anthony Wayne, 10 Mar. 1794, both in Anthony Wayne Papers, HSP. See also the letters from DeButts of early 1794, one written from Philadelphia on 31 January and one from Fort Hamilton on 13 February (Anthony Wayne Papers, HSP). Note that other officers often referred to Harrison as "Mister," not "Lieutenant," possibly because he had a staff position rather than a line command.

3. Anthony Wayne to James Wilkinson, 7, 18 Feb., 14 Apr. 1794, and James Wilkinson to Anthony Wayne, 19 Feb., 14, 30 Apr. 1794, all in Anthony Wayne Papers, HSP. On Indian attack, see Gaff, *Bayonets in the Wilderness,* 196.

4. James Wilkinson to Harry Innes, 10 Feb. 1794, Harry Innes Papers, LC; Nelson, *Anthony Wayne,* 257.

5. John Armstrong to Anthony Wayne, 13 Apr., 18 June 1794, Anthony Wayne Papers, HSP.

6. William Daingerfield to Anthony Wayne, 30 Jan., Anthony Wayne to Daingerfield, 17 Apr., and Anthony Wayne to Captain Alexander Gibson, 17 Apr. 1794, all in Anthony Wayne Papers, HSP.

7. *History of Van Wert and Mercer Counties, Ohio* (Wapakoneta, Ohio: R. Sutton and Co., 1882), 292, 301; Frazer E. Wilson, *History of Darke County, Ohio. . . .* (Milford, Ohio: Hobart Publishing Co., 1914), 42–43; Knopf, *Wayne: A Name in Arms,* 300; Anthony Wayne to Thomas Posey, 18 Jan., Anthony Wayne to Major William McMahon, 28 Feb., and Alexander Gibson to Anthony Wayne, 21 Feb., 23 Mar. 1794, all in Anthony Wayne Papers, HSP.

8. Anthony Wayne to McMahon, 28 Feb., and Anthony Wayne to Wilkinson, 14 Mar. 1794, Anthony Wayne Papers, HSP; Underwood, "A Journal of Wayne's Campaign," Mss. 16U, 126, Lyman C. Draper Manuscripts, State Historical Society of Wisconsin. Gaff (*Bayonets in the Wilderness,* 209–10) has a full account of Miller's capture and interrogation. For the background on relations with Britain, see Forrest McDonald, *Alexander Hamilton* (New York: W. W. Norton and Co., 1979), 289–91; and Thomas Lewis to Anthony Wayne, 18 Mar. 1794, Anthony Wayne Papers, HSP.

9. Anthony Wayne to Alexander Gibson, 19 Mar., and Alexander Gibson to Anthony Wayne, 20 Mar., 11 May, 14 May, 24 June 1794, all in Anthony Wayne Papers, HSP; Gaff, *Bayonets in the Wilderness,* 233–34.

10. Underwood, "A Journal of Wayne's Campaign," Mss. 16U, 127, 129, Lyman C. Draper Manuscripts, State Historical Society of Wisconsin; WHH's letter of 7 Apr. 1838 to A. B. Howell (in *Cincinnati Daily Gazette,* 19 May 1838) alludes to a duel that changed his mind about the custom, in which the dying loser forgave the winner. This was evidently the Dunn-Blue encounter in July; see Gaff's thorough account in *Bayonets in the Wilderness* (255–56), which also gives a vivid and interesting account of duels earlier in 1794, including the Huston-Bradshaw affair (199–200). On WHH and Marks, see WHH to James Wilkinson, 13 May 1796, WHH Papers, IHS; and Knopf, *Wayne: A Name in Arms,* 449.

11. Knopf, *Wayne: A Name in Arms,* 326; Gaff, *Bayonets in the Wilderness,* 211–12; and Thomas Doyle to Anthony Wayne, 26 Feb., 4 Mar., 26 Apr. 1794; Anthony Wayne to William Winston, 24, 30 Mar.; Anthony Wayne to William McMahon, 22 Apr.; Anthony Wayne to Elliott and Williams, 22 Apr.; and Anthony Wayne to James Wilkinson, 13 May 1794, all in Anthony Wayne Papers, HSP.

12. Nelson, *Anthony Wayne,* 257–58; Knopf, *Wayne: A Name in Arms,* 335; Anthony Wayne to John Belli, 26 May 1794, Anthony Wayne Papers, HSP; cf. other letters under that date.

13. By far the best description of the battle and the Indians' intentions, using Canadian as well as American sources, is in Gaff, *Bayonets in the Wilderness,* 240–53. See also Sword, *President Washington's Indian Wars,* 273–77; Underwood, "A Journal of Wayne's Campaign," Mss. 16U, 127–28, Lyman C. Draper Manuscripts, State Historical Society of Wisconsin; Richard C. Knopf, ed., "A Precise Journal of General Wayne's Last Campaign," *Proceedings of the American Antiquarian Society* 64 (1955): 301; and Burton, "General Wayne's Orderly Book," 523.

14. Sword, *President Washington's Indian Wars,* 273; Alexander Gibson to Anthony Wayne, 7, 30 June 1794, Anthony Wayne Papers, HSP.

15. Harry M. Ward, *Charles Scott and the "Spirit of '76"* (Charlottesville, Va.: Univ. Press of Virginia, 1988), 136, 139; Sword, *President Washington's Indian Wars,* 271, 276. Another reason for the Indians' rapid dispersal was a shortage of provisions (hence the slaughtered horses) and gunpowder. The best assessment of the significance of the engagement is White, *The Middle Ground,* 466–67.

16. Ward, *Charles Scott,* 140–42.

15. Consummation

1. For a descriptive report from Fort Greenville in midsummer, see Elliott, *Poetical and Miscellaneous Works,* 143; for officers' gardens, cf. Skelton, *An American Profession of Arms,* 41–42. My sources for the Fallen Timbers campaign are John Cooke, "General Wayne's Campaign in 1794 & 1795," *American Historical Record* 2:311–16 (a journal of Captain John Cooke of the 4th Sub-Legion); "William Clark's Journal of General Wayne's Campaign," *Mississippi Valley Historical Review,* 1:418–44; Knopf, "A Precise Journal of General Wayne's Last Campaign" (whose author is unknown); Dwight L. Smith, ed., "From Greene Ville to Fallen Timbers," *Indiana Historical Society Publications* 16, no. 3 (1952): 249–326 (which was written either by James Wilkinson under a fictitious persona or by someone very close to him); Underwood, "A Journal of Wayne's Campaign," Mss. 16U, Lyman C. Draper Manuscripts, State Historical Society of Wisconsin; and Nathaniel Hart, journal of Gen. Anthony Wayne's expedition, Mss. 5U, 96–99, also in Lyman C. Draper Manuscripts, State Historical Society of Wisconsin. Henry Bowyer's "Daily Journal of Wayne's Campaign" is reprinted in Burton, "General Wayne's Orderly Book," 539–64, and I have used that edition.

2. Burton, "General Wayne's Orderly Book," 540; Cooke, "General Wayne's Campaign in 1794 & 1795," 312; "William Clark's Journal," 420; Knopf, "A Precise Journal of General Wayne's Last Campaign," 281; Gaff, *Bayonets in the Wilderness,* 266.

3. Smith, "From Greene Ville to Fallen Timbers," 251–53; Knopf, "A Precise Journal of General Wayne's Last Campaign," 280. Gaff's *Bayonets in the Wilderness* (268) gives several quotes vividly describing the "Black Swamp" country.

4. Anthony Wayne to Alexander Gibson, 3 July 1794, Anthony Wayne Papers, HSP; Smith, "From Greene Ville to Fallen Timbers," 253–60; John Sugden (*Blue Jacket: Warrior of the Shawnees* [Lincoln, Neb.: Univ. of Nebraska Press, 2000], 130–32) explains the importance of the towns at Grand Glaize.

5. Burton, "General Wayne's Orderly Book," 540; "William Clark's Journal," 421; Smith, "From Greene Ville to Fallen Timbers," 259, 261; Knopf, "A Precise Journal of General Wayne's Last Campaign," 281–82; Wilson, *History of Darke County,* 1:101. (This is one of several explanations for Wayne's nickname; none seems authoritative.)

6. Anthony Wayne to Isaac Wayne, 10 Sept. 1794, Anthony Wayne Papers, HSP; Burton, "General Wayne's Orderly Book," 541; "William Clark's Journal," 422; Smith, "From Greene Ville to Fallen Timbers," 262; Knopf, "A Precise Journal of General Wayne's Last Campaign," 282 and note; Gaff, *Bayonets in the Wilderness,* 274. Sword (*President Washington's Indian War,* 281–82) considers the incident probably premeditated; Gaff (*Bayonets in the Wilderness,* 389–90) ridicules the idea, but it is worth noting that several officers at the time, not merely later historians, seriously entertained the possibility.

7. "William Clark's Journal," 422; Bonney, *A Legacy of Historical Gleanings,* 1:101; Smith, "From Greene Ville to Fallen Timbers," 265. Underhill's post was initially called Fort Randolph, then Fort Adams; see Simmons, *The Forts of Anthony Wayne,* 14–15; and Gaff, *Bayonets in the Wilderness,* 275–76.

8. "William Clark's Journal," 422–423; Smith, "From Greene Ville to Fallen Timbers," 263–68.

9. Cooke, "General Wayne's Campaign in 1794 & 1795," 313–14; Burton, "General Wayne's Orderly Book," 543; Knopf, "A Precise Journal of General Wayne's Last Campaign," 285. Nathaniel Hart heard 10 August that one of the volunteers had found $800 in bank notes in the ruins (Hart, journal of Gen. Anthony Wayne's expedition, Mss. 5U, 97, Lyman C. Draper Manuscripts, State Historical Society of Wisconsin); cf. Dwight L. Smith, *With Captain Edward Miller in the Wayne Campaign in 1794* (Ann Arbor, Mich.: William L. Clements Library, 1965), 4.

10. "William Clark's Journal," 424. Although Clark's journal found constant fault with Wayne's decisions, it should not be dismissed; the opinions of a man who would jointly command the great Mississippi-Missouri expedition ten years later and who was, moreover, a younger brother of the great frontier fighter George Rogers Clark deserve to be taken seriously. See "William Clark's Journal," 423–24, 426, on Wayne's health and mental state as well, along with Smith, "From Greene Ville to Fallen Timbers," 278–79, 281, 283. On morale, see Burton, "General Wayne's Orderly Book," 542, 544; and Knopf, "A Precise Journal of General Wayne's Last Campaign," 284, 286, 288.

11. Cooke, "General Wayne's Campaign in 1794 & 1795," 314; Smith, "From Greene Ville to Fallen Timbers," 275–77.

12. Smith, "From Greene Ville to Fallen Timbers," 277–82; Smith, *With Captain Edward Miller,* 6.

13. "William Clark's Journal," 426–27; Smith, *With Captain Edward Miller,* 6; Cleaves, *Old Tippecanoe,* 21.

14. Burton, "General Wayne's Orderly Book," 545; "William Clark's Journal," 427–28; Knopf, "A Precise Journal of General Wayne's Last Campaign," 289–90.

15. Knopf, "A Precise Journal of General Wayne's Last Campaign," 290–91; Smith, "From Greene Ville to Fallen Timbers," 288–90; Cooke, "General Wayne's Campaign in 1794 & 1795," 316.

16. Gunderson, "William Henry Harrison: Apprentice in Arms," 18–19. In his account to John Brown of the action, Wilkinson asserted that neither he nor Hamtramck had received a single order from Wayne during the battle and implied that Wayne gave none. "General James Wilkinson's Narrative of the Fallen Timbers Campaign," ed. M. M. Quaife, *Mississippi Valley Historical Review* 16 (June 1929): 84–85. However, Wilkinson was frequently away from his post and may have missed a good deal of what went on. For the continuation of the action, see Smith, *With Captain Edward Miller,* 7; Burton, "General Wayne's Orderly Book," 545; Cooke, "General Wayne's Campaign in 1794 & 1795," 316; "William Clark's Journal," 428–29; "A Precise Journal of General Wayne's Last Campaign," 290–91; Hart, journal of Gen. Anthony Wayne's expedition, Mss. 5U, 100, Lyman C. Draper Manuscripts, State Historical Society of Wisconsin; and Bonney, *Legacy of Historical Gleanings,* 2:134. The general account in Sword, *President Washington's Indian War,* 299–305, is a useful synthesis with which I disagree on a few details. See also Gaff, *Bayonets in the Wilderness,* 301–13.

17. Smith, "From Greene Ville to Fallen Timbers," 295; "William Clark's Journal," 430–432; Knopf, *Wayne: A Name in Arms,* 343.

18. Underwood, "A Journal of Wayne's Campaign," Mss. 16U, 131, Lyman C. Draper Manuscripts, State Historical Society of Wisconsin; Bonney, *Legacy of Historical Gleanings,* 1:102–3; WHH to "Dear Brother," 23 Nov. 1794, WHH Papers, LC. WHH places Edmondson's death some hours after the battle, but Wilkinson or whoever wrote "From Greene Ville to Fallen Timbers," 302, stated that it was days later.

19. Underwood, "A Journal of Wayne's Campaign," Mss. 16U, 130, Lyman C. Draper Manuscripts, State Historical Society of Wisconsin.

16. The End of the Dream

1. Wayne to Knox, 12 Nov. 1794, in Knopf, *Wayne: A Name in Arms,* 362. For the return march, see Gaff, *Bayonets in the Wilderness,* chap. 28, "End of a Successful Campaign."

2. WHH to "Dear Brother," 27 Nov. 1794, WHH Papers, LC; Gaff, *Bayonets in the Wilderness,* 362. For the identity of the unnamed young woman as Hetty Morris, see chapter 11. Clearly, if she was already promised to James Marshall, it would have been an embarrassment for her to continue receiving love letters from an officer in the Indian wars.

3. Oath of Bartholemew Shaumburgh, 29 Jan. 1796, Anthony Wayne Papers, HSP. Wayne's early peace feelers are described in Sword, *President Washington's Indian Wars,* 316.

4. Sword, *President Washington's Indian Wars,* 316–19; Jonathan Alder, *A History of Jonathan Alder: His Life and Captivity with the Indians,* ed. Larry Nelson (Akron, Ohio: Univ. of Akron Press, 2002), 116–17. The colorful quote is from a New England newspaper, cited in Gaff, *Bayonets in the Wilderness,* 365.

5. Hutton, "William Wells," 204.

6. The tangled Robert Newman story and Wayne's fury at Wilkinson can be followed in Paul David Nelson, *Anthony Wayne,* 273–74; Knopf, *Wayne: A Name in Arms,* 373–77, 383; and Gaff, *Bayonets in the Wilderness,* 269–73. On Wilkinson's furlough, see Wildes, *Anthony Wayne,* 437; and an uncompleted letter (vol. 43), Anthony Wayne Papers, HSP, written by Wayne in October 1795 to an unknown recipient.

7. Knopf, *Wayne: A Name in Arms,* 390, 394, 408; William Clark to Fanny Clark O'Fallon, 9 May 1795, in William Clark, *Dear Brother: Letters of William Clark to Jonathan Clark,* ed. James J. Holmberg (New Haven, Conn.: Yale Univ. Press, 2002), 271; WHH to Wayne, 13 Apr. 1796, Dreer Collection, HSP. For background on Scott, see Gaff, *Bayonets in the Wilderness,* 153.

8. On the heavy rains, see A. Kirkpatrick to Wayne, 6 Apr. 1795, Anthony Wayne Papers, HSP; and Winthrop Sargent, Journal, 1–22 Apr. 1795, Winthrop Sargent Papers, Ohio Historical Society (hereafter, OHS) (microfilm), Reel 4, Box 4, Folder 5. Data on Sargent's mistress is in the enciphered passages of Sargent's Journal for February 1795. On young men and matrimony, see Ellen K. Rothman, *Hands and Hearts: A History of Courtship in America* (Cambridge, Mass.: Harvard Univ. Press, 1987), 51, 57ff. On WHH's sexual prowess in youth, see William L. Marcy, quoted in John Niven, *Martin Van Buren and the Romantic Age of American Politics* (New York: Oxford Univ. Press, 1983), 473. A list of American male travelers who commented with interest on Indian females' sexual freedom would include Christopher Gist, whose journal is quoted in Greve, *Centennial History of Cincinnati,* 63; Jonathan Alder, in Larry Nelson, *Jonathan Alder,* 101; and James Elliott, in *Poetical and Miscellaneous Works,* 178.

9. On the physical and commercial aspects of Lexington, see the accounts of two travelers who were there in 1795, Condict, "Journal of a Trip to Kentucky in 1795," 120; and Thomas Chapman, "Journal of a Journey through the United States, 1795–6," *The Historical Magazine* 5 (June 1869): 363; and also Charles

Staples, *The History of Pioneer Lexington, 1779–1806* (1939; Lexington, Ky.: Univ. Press of Kentucky, 1996), 74, 94–95, 104, 105. Bernard Mayo is excellent on the social tone. Bernard Mayo, "Lexington: Frontier Metropolis," in *Historiography and Urbanization: Essays in American History in Honor of W. Stull Holt* (1941; Port Washington, N.Y.: Kennikat Press, 1968), 21–42, especially 24–25. Both Condict and Chapman met Peyton Short; see their accounts, and the short sketch by L. Belle Hamlin, in *The Quarterly Publication of the Historical and Philosophical Society of Ohio* 5 (Jan.–Mar. 1907): 3. Short's prosperity was to some degree a front; he was so much in debt that he felt himself "ruined," as appears from his letter to his former business partner James Wilkinson, 15 Aug. 1795 (James Wilkinson Letters, Chicago Historical Society). On Maria Symmes Short, see Susan Livingston Symmes to Sarah Livingston Jay, 13 Mar. 1796, John Jay Papers, Columbia University.

10. Beverley W. Bond, "John Cleves Symmes, Pioneer," in *Correspondence of John Cleves Symmes*, 1–24; Winthrop Sargent, Journal, 21 Aug. 1794, Winthrop Sargent Papers, OHS (microfilm); Susan Livingston Symmes to Sarah Livingston Jay, 13 Mar. 1796, John Jay Papers, Columbia University.

11. John Cleves Symmes to Robert Morris [of New Jersey], 22 June 1795, in *Correspondence of John Cleves Symmes*, 98.

12. Marks to Wayne, 17 May 1795; General Orders, 18 May 1795, both in Anthony Wayne Papers, HSP; William Clark to Fanny Clark O'Fallon, 9 May [*sic*] 1795, in Holmberg, *Dear Brother*, 271.

13. Sword, *President Washington's Indian Wars*, 316–30, gives a good account of the treaty and the peace overtures leading up to it. A detailed account, giving the text of several speeches on both sides and much other information, is Frazer E. Wilson's 78-page booklet, *Around the Council Fire* (1945; Mt. Vernon, Ind.: Windmill Publications, 1990). For an excellent reading of the outward behavior and inner motivations of the participants, see Andrew R. L. Cayton, "'Noble Actors' upon 'the Theatre of Honour': Power and Civility in the Treaty of Greenville," 235–69, in *Contact Points: American Frontiers from the Mohawk Valley to the Mississippi, 1750–1830*, ed. Cayton and Fredrika J. Teute (Chapel Hill, N.C.: Univ. of North Carolina Press, 1998). The quote is from William Clark to Fanny Clark O'Fallon, 1 June 1795, in Holmberg, *Dear Brother*, 273–74.

14. Heiser, *West to Ohio*, 24, 40–41, 51; Elliott, *Poetical and Miscellaneous Works*, 140; David Barrow diary, Draper Mss. 12CC171; Wilson, *Around the Council Fire*, 25–26, 30–34. Notations at the bottom of the Clark letters previously cited suggest that they were carried to Kentucky by family slaves.

15. Wilson, *Around the Council Fire*, 39–42; Harvey Lewis Carter: *The Life and Times of Little Turtle: First Sagamore of the Wabash* (Urbana, Ill.: Univ. of Illinois Press, 1987), 148–49. Carter notes that his description is based not on an eyewitness account but on a later painting. On WHH's acquaintance

with chiefs, see WHH, *Discourse on the Aborigines,* especially 21–22, 24–25, 28–30, 35, 39–41, in which WHH makes frequent comparisons of aboriginal history with classical history and alludes to his conversations with some chiefs; and Borer, "William Henry Harrison and the Rhetoric of History," 119, 121.

16. Knopf, *Wayne: A Name in Arms,* 447–52.

17. WHH's talk with Wayne, described in this paragraph, is entirely undocumented but must have taken place prior to the wedding, 25 November, for all the arrangements to have fallen into place so fast; his letter to Wayne of 30 November 1795 (WHH Papers, LC) assumes the general's previous knowledge of Nancy Symmes's name and circumstances, and a residence in Fort Washington. As for the date of the wedding, it is obvious that if it had truly been "a run away match," as Symmes described it in a letter to Silas Condict, 28 Feb. 1796 (*Intimate Letters,* 103), the best time for it would have been during his absence between mid-August and early November. Instead, WHH and Nancy waited for his return to North Bend. Symmes described it that way to indicate that he did not endorse it. For Wayne's tight restrictions on Wilkinson's command, see Timothy Pickering to Anthony Wayne, 24 Oct. 1795, in Knopf, *Wayne: A Name in Arms,* 466–67.

18. Receipt to Charles Brown, 31 Aug. 1795, WHH Papers, LC; Cleaves, *Old Tippecanoe,* 24; Susan Livingston Symmes to Sarah Livingston Jay, 13 Mar. 1796, John Jay Papers, Columbia University.

19. William Cooper, "Notices of Big Bone Lick," *The Monthly American Journal of Geology and Natural Science* 1 (Sept. 1831): 159–61; Willard R. Jillson, "The Big Bones of Northern Kentucky," *Register of the Kentucky State Historical Society* 33 (July 1935): 183. The best modern source on the site is Stanley Hedeen, *Big Bone Lick: The Cradle of American Paleontology* (Lexington, Ky.: Univ Press of Kentucky, 2008). That WHH himself never mentioned the episode publicly is no argument against its veracity; he may have hesitated to do so, believing that excavating and losing a quantity of important specimens added nothing creditable to his record. It is hard to disagree. Others in Cincinnati were also investigating the site; Judge George Turner was there before 1797, when he wrote the American Philosophical Society a short report (*Transactions of the American Philosophical Society* 4 [1799]: 510–18); conceivably his investigation and Harrison's were somehow related. The New York gentlemen who related the story did not recall Harrison's telling them the intended recipient of the bones, but one wonders if his identity might be related to Thomas Jefferson's telling a correspondent in 1796, "I have been in daily expectation of recieving [*sic*] some other bones of the newly discovered animal" (Thomas Jefferson to Benjamin S. Barton, 10 Oct. 1796, *Papers of Thomas Jefferson,* 29:192).

20. Symmes to Robert Morris, 22 June 1795, 2 Mar. 1796, *Intimate Letters,* 82, 98; Greve, *Centennial History,* 403. The bitterness of the scene is evident

from WHH's letter to Susan Livingston Symmes, 13 Dec. 1795 (WHH Papers, IHS). A persistent local tradition, which Cleaves (*Old Tippecanoe*, 25) accepts, was that the wedding took place not at the Symmes home but in a nearby cabin (Heiser, *West to Ohio*, 54); John and Susan Symmes stated in separate letters that it took place at their home (Symmes to Silas Condict, 28 Feb. 1796, *Intimate Letters*, 103; Susan Livingston Symmes to Sarah Livingston Jay, 13 Mar. 1796, John Jay Papers, Columbia University), but they were not present.

21. Susan Livingston Symmes to Sarah Livingston Jay, 13 Mar. 1796, John Jay Papers, Columbia University; John Cleves Symmes to Robert Morris, 4 Nov., 16 Dec. 1795, in Bond, *Intimate Letters*, 100, 101; WHH to Susan Livingston Symmes, 13 Dec. 1795, WHH Papers, IHS. The tea service, incidentally, was ordered before the Harrisons' wedding—another indication that the "run away wedding" was something of a charade. Symmes's letter of 16 December is evidence that he had cooled down by that time. James Wilkinson to WHH, 13 Apr. 1796, WHH Papers, LC; Green, *William Henry Harrison*, 59.

22. Kohn, *Eagle and Sword*, 185–87; Richard Allison to Anthony Wayne, 16 July 1796; John M. Scott to Anthony Wayne, 28 July 1796; and John Thorp to Anthony Wayne, 18 Aug. 1795, all in Anthony Wayne Papers, HSP; William E. Foley, *Wilderness Journey: The Life of William Clark* (Columbia, Mo.: Univ. of Missouri Press, 2004), 40 ("Though to his way of thinking he had performed his duties ably and always acquitted himself honorably, his superiors had failed to award him the recognition he coveted and expected."); WHH to James Wilkinson, 13 May 1796, WHH Papers, IHS.

23. WHH to Wayne, 11 July 1796, WHH Papers, LC.

24. Wayne's letter to WHH, 1 Aug. 1795 (Anthony Wayne Papers, HSP), ends in a tone very different from his usual stiff formality ("My best & kindest wishes to Mrs. Harrison to Mrs, & Judge Symmes, and all our mutual friends"), which suggests that the general had recently seen the judge and his wife in a social setting. On Cincinnati society, see, for example, the recollections and letters of Charlotte Chambers Ludlow, a genteel young Pennsylvanian who arrived there in 1797 as the bride of surveyor Israel Ludlow. Susan Symmes and Anna Harrison (together) were among the first women who called on her; she found the latter "delicate in her person," with manners that indicated "sweetness of disposition." Lewis H. Garrard, *Memoir of Charlotte Chambers* (Philadelphia: privately printed, 1856), 22, 29, 35. On laundry service, see R. R. Jones, *Fort Washington*, 19. On WHH as commandant, see WHH to Anthony Wayne, 30 June 1796, Anthony Wayne Papers, HSP.

25. Burnet, *Notes*, 32–33. On Burnet, see J. Jefferson Looney and Ruth L. Woodward, *Princetonians, 1791–1794* (Princeton, N.J.: Princeton Univ. Press, 1991), 14–22; and Green, *William Henry Harrison*, 58–59.

26. Victor Collot, *A Journey in North America*. . . . (Paris: Arthur Blanchard, 1826), 132; WHH to Wayne, 30 June 1796, Anthony Wayne Papers, HSP;

Kohn, *Eagle and Sword,* 174–75; R. R. Jones, *Fort Washington,* 55, 58; Nelson, *Anthony Wayne,* 299–300.

27. Heiser (*West to Ohio,* 44–45, 56–57, 61) clearly refers to the same distillery mentioned in R. R. Jones, *Fort Washington,* 56. WHH to John Tipton, 6 Dec. 1833, in *Messages and Letters,* 2:749.

28. Ford and Ford, *Hamilton County,* 49. For the background, see Arthur P. Whitaker, *The Mississippi Question, 1795–1803* (New York: D. Appleton-Century Co., 1934), especially 58. On WHH's reading, see Smith and Findlay account books, 1796–1797, Torrance Papers CHS. On Sargent's hopes, see Samuel Hodgdon to Sargent, 13 June 1797, Sargent Papers, MHS.

29. Note from Thomas Jefferson to James Madison, 19 Apr. 1798, in *Papers of Thomas Jefferson,* 30:281n. For background, see Whitaker, *The Mississippi Question,* 65, and note, 282. On recommendatory letters, see Winthrop Sargent to Timothy Pickering, 21 May 1798, *Mississippi Territory Archives,* 1:16; and WHH to Robert Goodloe Harper, 26 May 1798, in Goebel, *William Henry Harrison,* 38–40. The statement is often made (e.g., Cleaves, *Old Tippecanoe,* 26) that WHH took over the "land office" when he resigned his commission, but this is impossible in the literal sense: the federal land office in Cincinnati was not set up until 1801, under an act sponsored by WHH himself. George W. Knepper, *The Official Ohio Lands Book* (Columbus, Ohio: State Auditor, 2003), 35. The nearest equivalent before that time would be Symmes's sales office, usually handled by his nephew Daniel, a lawyer about WHH's age (Heiser, *West to Ohio,* 23).

Afterword

1. Daniel A. Cohen, "Arthur Mervyn and His Elders: The Ambivalence of Youth in the Early Republic," *William and Mary Quarterly,* 3rd series, 43 (July 1986): 303. More broadly, Andrew Cayton, in discussing both the Harrison household and that of Harrison's bride, Anna Tuthill Symmes, links them to the "rearrangement of family relationships in the United States at the end of the eighteenth century." Andrew R. L. Cayton, *Frontier Indiana* (Bloomington, Ind.: Indiana Univ. Press, 1996), 169–71.

2. Roy Harvey Pearce, *Savagism and Civilization: A Study of the Indian and the American Mind* (Baltimore, Md.: Johns Hopkins Press, 1965), especially chapters 4 and 5.

3. Robert M. Owens's statement (*Mr. Jefferson's Hammer,* 41ff.) that WHH was driven by an obsessive quest for recognition as a gentleman is, I think, correct with just a little tweaking: WHH had no personal insecurity at all—quite the reverse—but he had a strong desire that his family receive social recognition and financial security.

Bibliography

Primary Sources

Manuscript Collections

Barton, Benjamin Smith. Papers, 1778–1813. HSP, Philadelphia, Pa.

Byrd, Charles Willing. Papers, 1794–1881. Lilly Library, Indiana University, Bloomington, Ind.

Charles City County. Will Book, 1789–1808. VSL, Richmond, Va.

Coxe, Tench. Papers. HSP Philadelphia, Pa.

Draper, Lyman C. Manuscripts. State Historical Society of Wisconsin, Madison, Wis.

Dreer, Ferdinand Julius. Collection, 1492–1925. HSP, Philadelphia, Pa.

Duer, William. Papers. NYHS, N.Y.

Farley, Elizabeth. Letter to Thomas T. Byrd, 25 June 1783. Miscellaneous Manuscripts. NYHS, N.Y.

Gratz Collection. HSP, Philadelphia, Pa.

Green, James A. Papers. CHS, Cincinnati, Ohio

Harrison, Benjamin [V], Letter to Robert Morris, 5 Sept. 1776. Emmet, Thomas Addis. Collection, 1483–1876 (bulk: 1700–1800). NYPL, New York, N.Y.

Harrison, Benjamin VI. Account Book. VHS, Richmond, Va.

——. Letter Book, July 1787–Sept. 1789. Harrison, Benjamin, Mss. Collection, Patricia D. Klingenstein Library, NYHS, N.Y.

Harrison, Nathaniel. Diary (microfilm). Robert Alonzo Brock Collection. Henry M. Huntington Library, San Marino, Calif.

Harrison, William Henry. Letter to Erastus Brooks, 20 July 1839. William Henry Harrison Correspondence, 1802–1815 and 1836–1841. NYHS, New York, N.Y.

——. Papers, 1800–1815. IHS, Indianapolis, Ind.

——. Papers, 1734–1939 (bulk: 1796–1841). Manuscript Division, LC, Washington, D.C.

Hubard Family. Papers, 1741–1907. SHC, University of North Carolina, Chapel Hill, N.C.

Innes, Harry. Papers, 1754–1900 (bulk: 1780–1850). Manuscript Division, LC, Washington, D.C.

Jay, John. Papers, 1668–[ca. 1862]. Rare Book & Manuscript Library, CU, New York, N.Y.

Jefferson, Thomas. Papers. Albert and Shirley Small Special Collections Library, UVa

Knox, Henry. Papers, 1736–1823. MHS, Boston, Mass.

Lee, Richard Henry. Papers. Manuscript Division, LC, Washington, D.C.

Mettauer, John Peter. Papers. H-SC, Hampden-Sydney, Va.

Morris, Gouverneur. Papers, 1768–1816. Rare Book & Manuscript Library, CU, New York, N.Y.

O'Reilly Collection. NYHS, N.Y.

Pleasants, Robert. Letter Book. Valentine Museum, Richmond, Va.

Post Revolutionary War Collection, National Archives, Washington, D.C.

Powel Family. Papers, 1681–1938. HSP, Philadelphia, Pa.

Pratt, John. Papers, 1778–1824. CSL, Hartford, Conn.

Richmond Common Hall Records. VSL, Richmond, Va.

Richmond Personal Property Tax Lists, 1789–1798. VSL, Richmond, Va.

St. Clair, Arthur. Papers, 1746–1882. Ohio Historical Society, Columbus, Ohio.

Sargent, Winthrop. Papers, 1771–1948 (bulk: 1785–1801). MHS, Boston, Mass.

———. Papers, 1776–1865. Ohio Historical Society, Columbus, Ohio.

Shippen Family Papers, 1671–1936. Manuscript Division, LC, Washington, D.C.

Shirley Plantation Collection, 1650–1989. CW, Williamsburg, Va.

Society Collection, HSP, Philadelphia, Pa.

Spencer, William. Diary, 24 Apr.–29 May; 4 June–1 Aug., 1790. CW, Williamsburg, Va.

Strong Family. Papers. CHS, Cincinnati, Ohio.

Trumbull, Joseph. Papers. CSL, Hartford, Conn.

Wayne, Anthony. Papers, 1765–1890. HSP, Philadelphia, Pa.

Wilkinson, James. Letters, Chicago Historical Society, Chicago, Ill.

Printed Primary Sources

Adams, Abigail. *New Letters of Abigail Adams.* Edited by Stewart Mitchell. Boston, Mass.: Houghton Mifflin, 1947.

Alder, Jonathan. *A History of Jonathan Alder: His Life and Captivity with the Indians.* Edited by Larry Nelson. Akron, Ohio: Univ. of Akron Press, 2002.

American State Papers: Indian Affairs. 4 vols. Washington, D.C.: Gales and Seaton, 1832.

"An Eighteenth-Century Recruiting Poster," edited by Julian P. Boyd. *Pennsylvania Magazine of History and Biography* (hereafter, *PMHB*) 60 (Apr. 1936): 186–88.

Appleby, Joyce, ed. *Recollections of the Early Republic: Selected Autobiographies.* Boston, Mass.: Northeastern Univ. Press, 1997.

Armes, Ethel, ed. *Nancy Shippen: Her Journal Book.* Philadelphia, Pa.: J. B. Lippincott, 1935.

Bailey, Robert. *The Life and Adventures of Robert Bailey....* Richmond, Va.: J. and G. Cochran, 1822.

Baily, Francis. *Journal of a Tour in Unsettled Parts of North America in 1796 and 1797.* Edited by Jack D. L. Holmes. Carbondale, Ill.: Southern Illinois University, 1969.

Balch, Thomas Willing. *Willing Letters and Papers.* Philadelphia, Pa.: Allen, Lane, and Scott, 1922.

Bayard, Ferdinand-Marie. *Travels of a Frenchman in Maryland and Virginia. ...* Edited and translated by Ben C. McCary. Ann Arbor, Mich.: Edwards Brothers, 1950.

Beatty, Joseph M., Jr., ed. "Letters of the Four Beatty Brothers of the Continental Army, 1774–1794," *PMHB* 44 (July 1920): 193–263.

"Biographical Memoirs of Major General William Henry Harrison." *Port Folio,* 3rd series, 5 (Apr. 1815).

[Bland, Theodorick]. *The Bland Papers, Being a Selection from the Manuscripts of Colonel Theodorick Bland, Jr., of Prince George County, Virginia.* 2 vols. Petersburg, Va.: Edmund and Julian C. Ruffin, 1841–43.

Bonney, Catharina V. R. *A Legacy of Historical Gleanings.* 2 vols. Albany, N.Y.: J. Munsell, 1875.

Brackenridge, Henry M. *Recollections of Persons and Places in the West.* Philadelphia, Pa.: James Kay, Jun., and Brother, 1834.

Bradley, Daniel. *Journal of Capt. Daniel Bradley.* Edited by Frazer E. Wilson. Greenville, Ohio: Frank H. Jobes and Son, 1935.

Breck, Samuel. *Recollections of Samuel Breck.* Edited by H. E. Scudder. London: Sampson Low, Marston, Searle, and Rivington, 1877.

Brissot de Warville, J.-P. *New Travels in North America.* Edited and translated by Durand Echeverria. Cambridge, Mass.: Belknap Press of Harvard University, 1964.

Bunn, Matthew. *A Journal of the Adventures of Matthew Bunn.* Providence, R.I.: Matthew Bunn, 1796.

Burnett, Edmund C. *Letters of Members of the Continental Congress.* 8 vols. Washington, D.C.: Carnegie Institution of Washington, 1921–36.

Burton, Clarence M., ed. "General Wayne's Orderly Book." *Michigan Pioneer and Historical Collections* 34 (1904): 341–733.

Byrd, William S. *Letters from a Young Shaker.* Edited by Stephen J. Stein. Lexington, Ky.: Univ. Press of Kentucky, 1985.

Caldwell, Charles. *Autobiography.* Edited by Harriot W. Warner. Philadelphia, Pa.: Lippincott, Grambo, and Co., 1855.

Carrington, Elizabeth J. Ambler. "An Old Virginia Correspondence." *Atlantic Monthly* 84 (Oct. 1899): 535–49.

Carter, Clarence E., ed. *The Territorial Papers of the United States*. Vols. 2–3, *Northwest Territory, North of the Ohio, 1787–1803*. Washington, D.C.: GPO, 1934.

Carter, Landon. *The Diary of Landon Carter of Sabine Hall, 1752–1778*. Edited by Jack P. Greene. 2 vols. Charlottesville, Va.: Univ. Press of Virginia, 1965.

Castiglioni, Luigi. *Viaggio negli Stati Uniti dall' America Settentrionale fatto negli anni 1785, 1786, e 1787*. Milano: Stamperia di Giuseppe Marelli, 1790.

Celebration of the Forty-fifth Anniversary of the First Settlement of Cincinnati and the Miami Country, on the 26th Day of December, 1833, by Natives of Ohio. Cincinnati, Ohio: Shreve and Co., 1834.

Chapman, Thomas. "Journal of a Journey through the United States, 1795–96." *The Historical Magazine* 5 (June 1869): 357–69.

Chastellux, Francois-Jean (marquis de). *Travels in North America in the Years 1780, 1781 and 1782*. 2 vols. Chapel Hill, N.C.: Univ. of North Carolina Press, 1963.

Chateaubriand, François Auguste René (vicomte de). *Travels in America*. Translated by Richard Switzer. Lexington, Ky.: Univ. of Kentucky Press, 1969.

Cist, Charles. *The Cincinnati Miscellany*. 2 vols. Cincinnati, Ohio: C. Clark, Printer, 1845–46.

———. *Sketches and Statistics of Cincinnati in 1859*. Cincinnati, Ohio: N.p., 1859.

Clark, William. *Dear Brother: Letters of William Clark to Jonathan Clark*. Edited by James J. Holmberg. New Haven, Conn.: Yale Univ. Press, 2002.

———. "William Clark's Journal of General Wayne's Campaign." *Mississippi Valley Historical Review* 1 (1915): 418–44.

Clarke, Robert. *The Pre-Historic Remains Which Were Found on the Site of the City of Cincinnati, Ohio. . . .* Cincinnati, Ohio: Robert Clarke, 1876.

Coke, Thomas. *Extracts of the Journals of the Rev. Dr. Coke*. London: G. Paramore, 1793.

Collot, Victor. *A Journey in North America. . . .* Paris: Arthur Blanchard, 1826.

Condict, Lewis. "Journal of a Trip to Kentucky in 1795." *Proceedings of the New Jersey Historical Society*, n.s., 4 (1919): 108–27.

Cooke, John. "General Wayne's Campaign in 1794 & 1795." *American Historical Record* 2:311–16.

Craig, Isaac. "Major Isaac Craig: Extracts from His Letter-Books while Quartermaster at Fort Pitt, 1791–1804." Vols. 1–2, *Historical Register: Notes and Queries, Historical and Genealogical. . . .* Harrisburg, Pa.: L. S. Hart, 1883–84.

Cutler, William P., and Julia P. Cutler. *Life, Journals and Correspondence of Rev. Manasseh Cutler, LL.D.* 2 vols. Cincinnati, Ohio: Robert Clarke and Co., 1888.

Davies, Benjamin. *Some Account of the City of Philadelphia*. Philadelphia, Pa.: Richard Folwell, 1794.

Dewees, Mary. "Mrs. Mary Dewees's Journal from Philadelphia to Kentucky, 1787–1788." *PMHB* 28 (Apr. 1904): 182–98.

Drake, Daniel. *Discourses Delivered by Appointment before the Cincinnati Medical Association. . . .* Cincinnati, Ohio: Moore and Anderson, 1852.

——. "Dr. Daniel Drake's Memoir of the Miami Country, 1779–1794 (An Unfinished Manuscript)." Edited by Beverley W. Bond. *Ohio Historical and Philosophical Society Quarterly* 18 (Apr. 1923): 155–71.

——. *Notices Concerning Cincinnati.* Cincinnati, Ohio: John W. Browne and Co., 1810.

Elliot, James. *The Poetical and Miscellaneous Works of James Elliot.* Greenfield, Mass.: Thomas Dickman, 1798.

Farrand, Max, ed. *The Records of the Federal Convention of 1787.* rev. ed. 4 vols. New Haven, Conn.: Yale Univ. Press, 1966.

Fithian, Philip V. *Journal & Letters of Philip Vickers Fithian, 1773–1774.* Edited by Hunter D. Farish. Williamsburg, Va.: Colonial Williamsburg, 1943.

Garrard, Lewis H. *Memoir of Charlotte Chambers.* Philadelphia, Pa.: privately printed, 1856.

Hamilton, Alexander. *The Papers of Alexander Hamilton.* Edited by Harold C. Syrett et al. 27 vols. New York: Columbia Univ. Press, 1961–87.

Harrison, William Henry. *Discourse on the Aborigines of the Ohio Valley. . . .* Cincinnati, Ohio: Printed at the Cincinnati Express, 1838.

——. Letter to A. B. Howell. *Cincinnati Daily Gazette,* 7 Apr. 1838.

——. Letter to Thomas P. Chilton, 17 Feb. 1834. Printed in the *Cincinnati Daily Gazette,* 10 May 1834.

——. *Messages and Letters of William Henry Harrison.* Edited by Logan Esarey. 2 vols. Indiana Historical Collections, 8–9. Indianapolis, Ind.: Indiana Historical Commission, 1922.

Harrower, John. *The Journal of John Harrower.* Edited by Edward Miles Riley. Williamsburg, Va.: Colonial Williamsburg, 1963.

[Hatchett, John]. *Prince Edward County, Virginia: A Short Narrative of the Life of John Hatchett.* Edited by Joseph D. Eggleston. Farmville, Va.: N.p., n. d.

Heads of Families at the First Census of the United States: Virginia. Washington, D.C.: GPO, 1908.

Heise, John. Catalogue #2467. n.d., American Antiquarian Society.

Hill, William. *Autobiographical Sketches of Dr. William Hill. . . .* Historical Transcripts, 4. Richmond, Va.: Union Theological Seminary in Virginia, 1968.

Hopkinson, Francis. *The Miscellaneous Essays and Occasional Writings of Francis Hopkinson, Esq.* Philadelphia, Pa.: T. Dobson, 1792.

Hunter, Robert, Jr. *Quebec to Carolina in 1785–1786.* Edited by Louis B. Wright and Marion Tinling. San Marino, Calif.: Huntington Library, 1943.

Jefferson, Thomas. *Notes on the State of Virginia.* New York: W. W. Norton and Co., 1954. First published 1785.

——. *The Papers of Thomas Jefferson*. Edited by Julian P. Boyd et al. 24 vols. to date. Princeton, N.J.: Princeton Univ. Press, 1950–.

Johnston, Charles. *A Narrative of the Incidents Attending the Capture, Detention, and Ransom of Charles Johnston....* New York: J. and J. Harper, 1827.

Jordan, John W. "Notes of a Journey from Philadelphia to New Madrid, Tennessee, 1790." *PMHB* 36, no. 2 (1912): 209–16.

Knepper, George W. *The Official Ohio Lands Book*. Columbus, Ohio: State Auditor, 2003.

Knopf, Richard C., ed. *Anthony Wayne: A Name in Arms*. Pittsburgh, Pa.: Univ. of Pittsburgh Press, 1960.

——, ed. "A Precise Journal of General Wayne's Last Campaign." *Proceedings of the American Antiquarian Society* 64 (1955): 273–302.

——, ed. "A Surgeon's Mate at Fort Defiance: The Journal of Joseph Gardner Andrews for the Year 1795." *Ohio Archeological and Historical Quarterly* 66 (Jan. 1957): 55–86.

——, ed. "Two Journals of the Kentucky Volunteers, 1793 and 1794." *Filson Club History Quarterly* 27 (July 1953): 247–81.

Latrobe, Benjamin H. *The Virginia Journals of Benjamin Henry Latrobe*. Edited by Edward C. Carter II. 2 vols. New Haven, Conn.: Yale Univ. Press, 1977.

"Letters of John Dandridge to John Hopkins." *WMQ*, 1st series, 20 (Jan. 1912): 146–67.

"Letters of the Byrd Family." *VMHB* 38 (Jan. 1930): 51–63.

Maclay, William. *The Journal of William Maclay*. Edited by Kenneth R. Bowling and Helen E. Veit. Baltimore, Md.: Johns Hopkins Univ. Press, 1988.

Madison, James. *The Papers of James Madison*. Edited by Robert A. Rutland et al. 17 vols. Chapel Hill, N.C.: Univ. of North Carolina Press, 1974–.

Marshall, John. *The Papers of John Marshall*. Edited by Herbert A. Johnson et al. 7 vols. to date. Chapel Hill, N.C.: Univ. of North Carolina Press, 1974–.

May, John. "Journal of Colonel John May, of Boston, relative to a Journey to the Ohio Country, 1789." *PMHB* 45 (Apr. 1921): 101–79.

McBride, James. *Pioneer Biography*. 2 vols. Ohio Valley Historical Series, no. 4. Cincinnati, Ohio: Robert Clarke and Co., 1869.

Mease, James. *The Picture of Philadelphia*. Philadelphia, Pa.: B. and E. Kite, 1811.

Memorials Presented to the Congress of the United States of America, by the Different Societies Instituted for Promoting the Abolition of Slavery, &c., &c. Philadelphia, Pa.: Francis Bailey, 1792.

Mordecai, Samuel. *Richmond in By-Gone Days*. Richmond, Va.: George M. West, 1856.

Moreau de St. Méry. *Moreau de St. Méry's American Journey, 1793–1798*. Edited by Kenneth Roberts and Anna M. Roberts. Garden City, N.Y.: Doubleday and Co., 1947.

Morris, Robert. *Catalogue No. 1183: The Confidential Correspondence of Robert Morris....* Philadelphia, Pa.: Stan. V. Henkels, n.d.

Morrison, Alfred J. *The College of Hampden-Sydney—Calendar of Board Minutes, 1776–1876.* Richmond, Va.: Hermitage Press, 1912.

Morrow, Josiah, ed. "Tours into Kentucky and the Northwest Territory: Three Journals by the Rev. James Smith of Powhatan County, Va., 1783–1795–1797." *Ohio Historical and Archeological Quarterly* 16 (1907): 318–401.

Nall, Charles T., ed. "A Letter from Petersburg, Virginia, January 10, 1789." *VMHB* 82 (Apr. 1974): 144–49.

Newman, Samuel. "A Picture of the First United States Army: The Journal of Captain Samuel Newman." Edited by Milo M. Quaife. *Wisconsin Magazine of History* 2 (Sept. 1918): 40–73.

Niles, William Ogden, comp. *The Tippecanoe Text-Book.* Baltimore, Md.: Duff Green, 1840.

Parry, Needham. "John D. Shane's Copy of Needham Parry's Diary of Trip [*sic*] Westward in 1794." Edited by Lucien Beckner. *The Filson Club History Quarterly* 22 (Oct. 1948): 227–47.

Pendleton, Edmund. *The Letters and Papers of Edmund Pendleton.* Edited by David J. Mays. Virginia Historical Society Documents, vols. 7–8. 2 vols. Charlottesville, Va.: Univ. of Virginia Press, 1967.

Pope, John. *A Tour through the Southern and Western Territories of the United States ...* Richmond, Va.: John Dixon, 1792.

Priest, Josiah. *American Antiquities and Discoveries in the West.* 4th ed. Albany, N.Y.: Hoffman and White, 1834.

Rollin, Charles. *The Ancient History of the Egyptians....* 8 vols. New York: Evert Duyckinck, 1812.

Rowland, Dunbar, ed. *The Mississippi Territorial Archives, 1798–1803.* 2 vols. Nashville, Tenn.: Press of Brandon Printing Co., 1905.

Rush, Benjamin. *The Autobiography of Benjamin Rush.* Edited by George W. Corner. Memoirs of the American Philosophical Society, vol. 25. Princeton, N.J.: Princeton Univ. Press, 1948.

——. Letter to Elizabeth Rush, 25 July 1791. *The Collector* 72, no. 685 (June 1949).

——. *Letters of Benjamin Rush.* Edited by L. H. Butterfield. 2 vols. Princeton, N.J.: Princeton Univ. Press, 1951.

Sargent, Winthrop. "A Letter from Colonel Winthrop Sargent, to Dr. Benjamin Smith Barton, accompanying Drawings and some Account of certain Articles, which were taken out of an ancient Tumulus, or Grave, in the Western-Country." *Transactions of the American Philosophical Society* 4 (1799): 177–81.

Saugrain de Vigni, Antoine François. "Dr. Saugrain's Note-Books, 1788. . . ." Edited by Eugene F. Bliss. *Proceedings of the American Antiquarian Society*, n.s., 19 (1908): 222–38.

Schoepf, Johann D. *Travels in the Confederation*. Edited by Alfred J. Morrison. 2 vols. Philadelphia, Pa.: W. J. Campbell, 1911.

Schreiner-Yantis, Netti, and Florene Speakman Love, comp. *The 1787 Census of Virginia*. 3 vols. Springfield, Va.: Genealogical Books in Print, 1987.

Shaw, John Robert. *An Autobiography of Thirty Years, 1777–1807*. Edited by Orissa W. Teagarden. Athens, Ohio: Ohio Univ. Press, 1992.

Smith, Dwight L., ed. "From Greene Ville to Fallen Timbers." *Indiana Historical Society Publications* 16, no. 3 (1952): 249–326.

——. *With Captain Edward Miller in the Wayne Campaign in 1794*. Ann Arbor, Mich.: William L. Clements Library, 1965.

Smith, William Henry, comp. *The St. Clair Papers*. 2 vols. New York: Da Capo Press, 1971. First published 1882.

Smith, William Loughton. "The Journal of William Loughton Smith, 1790–1791." *Proceedings of the Massachusetts Historical Society* 51 (1917–18): 20–75.

Spencer, Oliver M. *The Indian Captivity of O. M. Spencer.* Edited by Milo M. Quaife. The Lakeside Classics, vol. 15. Chicago: R. R. Donnelley and Sons, 1917.

Stanley, William. "The Diary of Major William Stanley, 1790–1810." Edited by L. Belle Hamlin. *Ohio Historical and Philosophical Society Quarterly* 14 (Apr.–July 1919): 19–32.

Sugden, John. *Blue Jacket: Warrior of the Shawnees*. Lincoln, Neb.: Univ. of Nebraska Press, 2000.

Symmes, John Cleves. *The Correspondence of John Cleves Symmes*. Edited by Beverley W. Bond. New York: Macmillan, 1926.

——. *Intimate Letters of John Cleves Symmes*. Edited by Beverley W. Bond. Cincinnati, Ohio: Historical and Philosophical Society of Ohio, 1956.

Thrift, Minton. *Memoir of the Rev. Jesse Lee*. New York: N. Bangs and T. Mason, 1823.

Toulmin, Harry. *The Western Country in 1793*. Edited by Marion Tinling and Geoffrey Davies. San Marino, Calif.: Henry E. Huntington Library, 1948.

Tucker, George. *The Valley of Shenandoah*. 2 vols. New York: Charles Wiley, 1824.

Turner, Charles W., ed. "Letters (1790–1800) of John Johnston, Rockbridge Medical Student and Doctor." *Journal of the History of Medicine* 14 (Apr. 1959): 191–96.

Turner, George. "Memoir on the Extraneous Fossils, Denominated Mammoth Bones: Principally Designed to Shew, That They Are the Remains of More than One Species of Non-Descript Animal." *Transactions of the American Philosophical Society* 4 (1799): 510–18.

Tyler, Lyon G. *Letters and Times of the Tylers*. 2 vols. Richmond, Va.: Whittet and Shepperson, 1884.

Van Cleve, Benjamin. "Memoirs of Benjamin Van Cleve." Edited by Beverley

W. Bond. *Ohio Historical and Philosophical Society Publications* 17 (Jan. 1922): 1–71.

Von Closen, Ludwig. *The Revolutionary Journal of Baron Ludwig Von Closen, 1780–1783*. Edited by Evelyn M. Acomb. Chapel Hill, N.C.: Univ. of North Carolina Press, 1958.

Washington, George. *The Papers of George Washington: Presidential Series.* Edited by W. W. Abbot et al. 12 vols. to date. Charlottesville, Va.: Univ. Press of Virginia, 1987–.

Wilkinson, James. "General James Wilkinson's Narrative of the Fallen Timbers Campaign." Edited by M. M. Quaife. *Mississippi Valley Historical Review* 16 (June 1929): 81–90.

"Will of Colonel William Byrd 3rd." *VMHB* 9 (July 1901): 80–88.

Newspapers and Periodicals

American Historical Record
American Museum
American Pioneer
Bulletin of the Virginia Historical Society
Centinel of the North-West Territory
Cincinnati Daily Gazette
Cincinnati Philanthropist
Cist's Advertiser
Northwest Ohio Quarterly
Ohio Historical and Philosophical Society Publications
Pennsylvania Gazette
Pennsylvania Magazine of History and Biography
Quarterly Publication of the Historical and Philosophical Society of Ohio
Virginia Gazette
Virginia Independent Chronicle
Virginia Magazine of History and Biography
William and Mary Quarterly

Secondary Sources

Books and Articles

Alberts, Robert C. *The Golden Voyage: The Life and Times of William Bingham, 1752–1804*. Boston, Mass.: Houghton Mifflin Co., 1969.

American Philosophical Society. *Historic Philadelphia.* Transactions of the American Philosophical Society, vol. 43, pt. 1. Philadelphia, Pa.: American Philosophical Society, 1953.

Baine, Rodney M. *Robert Mumford: America's First Comic Dramatist.* Athens, Ga.: Univ. of Georgia Press, 1967.

Bakeless, John. *Lewis and Clark.* New York: William Morrow and Co., 1947.

Barbier, C. P. *Samuel Rogers and William Gilpin.* London: Oxford Univ. Press, 1959.

Barr, Lockwood. "Joseph Strong, M.D., Yale 1788: Army Surgeon, Inventor, Practitioner of Physic." *Yale Journal of Biology and Medicine* 13 (Mar. 1941): 429–50.

Baumeister, Roy F. *Identity: Cultural Change and the Struggle for the Self.* New York: Oxford Univ. Press, 1986.

Binger, Carl. *Revolutionary Doctor: Benjamin Rush, 1746–1813.* New York: W. W. Norton and Co., 1966.

Blanton, Wyndham D. B. *Medicine in Virginia in the Eighteenth Century.* Richmond, Va.: Garrett and Massie, 1931.

Bond, Beverley W. *The Civilization of the Old Northwest.* New York: Macmillan Co., 1934.

Borer, Alan. "William Henry Harrison and the Rhetoric of History." *Northwest Ohio Quarterly* 68 (1996): 116–32.

Boyd, Thomas. *Light-horse Harry Lee.* New York: Charles Scribner's Sons, 1931.

Bradshaw, Herbert C. *History of Hampden-Sydney College.* Durham, N.C.: Privately printed, 1976.

Breen, T. H. *Tobacco Culture: The Mentality of the Great Tidewater Planters on the Eve of Revolution.* Princeton, N.J.: Princeton Univ. Press, 1985.

Brettschneider, Carl A. "Some of the Personalities and Problems of Supply Affecting the Indian Campaign of 1792–1794." *Bulletin of the Historical and Philosophical Society of Ohio* 9 (Oct. 1951): 299–318.

Brinkley, John Luster. *On This Hill.* Hampden-Sydney, Va.: Hampden-Sydney College, 1995.

Brockett, F. L. *The Lodge of Washington.* Alexandria, Va.: G. H. Ramey and Son, 1899.

Brown, Ralph H. *Mirror for Americans.* New York: Da Capo Press, 1968. First published 1943.

Bruce, William Cabell. *John Randolph of Roanoke.* 2 vols. New York: G. P. Putnam's Sons, 1922.

Brydon, G. McLaren. "The Wealth of the Clergy in Virginia in 1791." *Historical Magazine of the Protestant Episcopal Church* 22 (Mar. 1953): 91–98.

Burnet, Jacob. "Letters Relating to the Early Settlement of the Northwestern Territory." *Transactions of the Historical and Philosophical Society of Ohio,* part 2, 1. Cincinnati, Ohio: George W. Bradbury and Co., 1839.

——. *Notes on the Early Settlement of the Northwestern Territory.* 8 vols. Cincinnati, Ohio: Derby, Bradley, and Co., 1847.

Burr, S. J. *The Life and Times of William Henry Harrison.* New York: L. W. Ransom, 1840.

Burton, Clarence M., ed. "General Wayne's Orderly Book." *Michigan Pioneer and Historical Collections* 34 (1904): 341–733.

Bushman, Richard L. *The Refinement of America: Persons, Houses, Cities.* New York: Vintage Books, 1992.

Caldwell, Norman W. "The Enlisted Soldier at the Frontier Post, 1790–1814." *Mid-America: An Historical Review* 37 (Oct. 1955): 195–204.

Carson, Jane. *Colonial Virginians at Play.* Williamsburg, Va.: Colonial Williamsburg, 1965.

Carson, Joseph. *A History of the Medical Department of the University of Pennsylvania. . . .* Philadelphia, Pa.: Lindsay and Blakiston, 1869.

Carter, Harvey Lewis. *The Life and Times of Little Turtle: First Sagamore of the Wabash.* Urbana, Ill.: Univ. of Illinois Press, 1987.

Casper, Scott E. *Constructing American Lives: Biography and Culture in Nineteenth-Century America.* Chapel Hill, N.C.: Univ. of North Carolina Press, 1999.

Cayton, Andrew R. L. *Frontier Indiana.* Bloomington, Ind.: Indiana Univ. Press, 1996.

———. "'Noble Actors' upon 'the Theatre of Honour': Power and Civility in the Treaty of Greenville." In *Contact Points: American Frontiers from the Mohawk Valley to the Mississippi, 1750–1830,* edited by Andrew R. L. Cayton and Fredrika J. Teute, 235–69. Chapel Hill, N.C.: Univ. of North Carolina Press, 1998.

Cheshire, Joseph B., ed. *Sketches of Church History in North Carolina.* Wilmington, N.C.: L. DeRosset Jr., 1892.

Church, Randolph W. "James Markham Marshall." *Virginia Cavalcade* 13 (Spring 1964): 22–29.

"Cincinnati Pioneers." *Bulletin of the Ohio Historical and Philosophical Society* 20 (Apr. 1962): 148–49.

Cleaves, Freeman. *Old Tippecanoe.* Garden City, N.Y.: Doubleday and Co., 1939.

College of William and Mary. *A Provisional List of Alumni, Grammar School Students, Members of the Faculty, and Members of the Board of Visitors of the College of William and Mary in Virginia, from 1693 to 1888.* Richmond, Va.: Division of Purchase and Printing, 1941.

Cooper, William. "Notices of Big Bone Lick." *The Monthly American Journal of Geology and Natural Science* 1 (Sept. 1831): 159–61.

Cox, Joseph W. *Champion of Southern Federalism: Robert Goodloe Harper of South Carolina.* Port Washington, N.Y.: Kennikat Press, 1972.

Craig, Isaac. "Fort Lafayette at Pittsburgh." *American Historical Record* 2 (1873): 497–503.

Craig, Neville B. *The History of Pittsburgh.* Pittsburgh, Pa.: John H. Mellor, 1851.

Crawford, Alan Pell. *Unwise Passions.* New York: Simon and Schuster, 2000.

Dandridge, Danske. *George Michael Bedinger: A Kentucky Pioneer.* Charlottesville, Va.: Michie Co., 1909.

Davis, David Brion. *The Problem of Slavery in Western Culture.* Ithaca, N.Y.: Cornell Univ. Press, 1966.

Davis, Richard B. *Intellectual Life in Jefferson's Virginia, 1790–1830*. Chapel Hill, N.C.: Univ. of North Carolina Press, 1964.

Dawidoff, Robert. *The Education of John Randolph*. New York: W. W. Norton and Co., 1978.

Dowdey, Clifford. *The Great Plantation*. New York: Rinehart and Co., 1957.

Dunbar, Seymour. *A History of Travel in America*. 2 vols. Indianapolis, Ind.: Bobbs-Merrill Co., 1915.

Evans, Nelson W. "Charles Willing Byrd." *The "Old Northwest" Genealogical Quarterly* 11 (Jan. 1908): 1–6.

Fischer, David Hackett. *Albion's Seed: Four British Folkways in North America*. New York: Oxford Univ. Press, 1989.

Fliegelman, Jay. *Prodigals & Pilgrims: The American Revolution against Patriarchal Authority, 1750–1800*. Cambridge, UK: Cambridge Univ. Press, 1982.

Foley, William E. *Wilderness Journey: The Life of William Clark*. Columbia, Mo.: Univ. of Missouri Press, 2004.

Foote, William H. *Sketches of Virginia Historical and Biographical*. 2 vols. Philadelphia, Pa.: W. S. Martien, 1850–55.

Ford, Henry A., and Kate B. Ford. *History of Hamilton County, Ohio*. Cleveland, Ohio: L. A. Williams and Co., 1881.

Fox, Dixon Ryan. "Culture in Knapsacks." *Quarterly Journal of the New York State Historical Association* 11 (Jan. 1930): 31–52.

Gaff, Alan D. *Bayonets in the Wilderness: Anthony Wayne's Legion in the Old Northwest*. Norman, Okla.: Univ. of Oklahoma Press, 2004.

Gardner, A. B. "The Uniforms of the American Army." *Magazine of American History* 1 (Aug. 1877): 461–92.

Garland, Hugh A. *The Life of John Randolph of Roanoke*. New York: Johnson Reprint Corporation, 1968. First published 1855.

General Catalogue of the Officers & Students of Hampden-Sidney College, Virginia, 1776–1906. Richmond, Va.: Whittet and Shepperson, 1908.

Gewehr, Wesley M. *The Great Awakening in Virginia, 1740–1790*. Gloucester, Mass.: Peter Smith, 1965. First published 1930.

Goss, Charles F. *Cincinnati, The Queen City, 1788–1912*. 4 vols. Cincinnati, Ohio: S. J. Clarke Publishing Co., 1912.

Gray, Lewis C. *History of Agriculture in the Southern United States to 1860*. 2 vols. Gloucester, Mass.: Peter Smith, 1958. First published 1932.

Green, James A. *William Henry Harrison: His Life and Times*. Richmond, Va.: Garret and Massie, 1941.

Greve, Charles T. *Centennial History of Cincinnati and Representative Citizens*. Chicago, Ill.: Biographical Publishing Co., 1904.

Gribbin, William. "Rollin's Histories and American Republicanism." *WMQ*, 3rd series, 29 (Oct. 1972): 611–22.

Griswold, Rufus B. *The Republican Court, or American Society in the Days of Washington*. New York: D. Appleton and Co., 1854.

Gunderson, Robert G. "William Henry Harrison: Apprentice in Arms." *Northwest Ohio Quarterly* 65 (Winter 1993): 3–29.

Hall, David D. "Books and Reading in Eighteenth-Century America." In *Of Consuming Interests: The Style of Life in the Eighteenth Century*, edited by Cary Carson, Ronald Hoffman, and Peter J. Albert, 354–72. Perspectives on the American Revolution. Charlottesville, Va.: Univ. Press of Virginia, 1994.

Hall, Virginius C. "Richard Allison, Surgeon to the Legion." *Bulletin of the Historical and Philosophical Society of Ohio* 9 (Oct. 1951): 266–98.

Hamilton, Phillip. *The Making and Unmaking of a Revolutionary Family.* Charlottesville, Va.: Univ. of Virginia Press, 2003.

Hamlin, L. Belle. "Peyton Short." *Ohio Historical and Philosophical Society Quarterly* 5 (Jan.–Mar. 1907): 3.

Hawke, David Freeman. *Benjamin Rush: Revolutionary Gadfly.* Indianapolis, Ind.: Bobbs-Merrill, 1971.

Hay, Thomas R., and M. R. Werner. *The Admirable Trumpeter: A Biography of General James Wilkinson.* Garden City, N.Y.: Doubleday, Doran and Co., 1941.

Hedeen, Stanley. *Big Bone Lick: The Cradle of American Paleontology.* Lexington, Ky.: Univ. Press of Kentucky, 2008.

Heiser, Alta H. *West to Ohio.* Yellow Springs, Ohio: Antioch Press, 1954.

Heitman, Francis B. *Historical Register and Dictionary of the United States Army.* 2 vols. Washington, D.C.: GPO, 1903.

Hildreth, Samuel. *Pioneer History.* Cincinnati, Ohio: H. W. Derby and Co., 1848.

*History of Van Wert and Mercer Counties, Ohio.*Wapakoneta, Ohio: R. Sutton and Co., 1882.

Horsman, Reginald. "William Henry Harrison: Virginia Gentleman in the Old Northwest." *Indiana Magazine of History* 96 (2000): 125–50.

Howe, Daniel Walker. *Making the American Self: Jonathan Edwards to Abraham Lincoln.* Cambridge, Mass.: Harvard Univ. Press, 1997.

Howe, Henry. *Historical Collections of Ohio.* Cincinnati, Ohio: Henry Howe, 1852.

Hulbert, Archer B. *Historic Highways of America.* Vol. 12, *Pioneer Roads and Experiences of Travelers.* Cleveland, Ohio: Arthur H. Clark Co., 1904.

——. *The Ohio River.* New York: G. P. Putnam's Sons, 1906.

Hurt, R. Douglas. *The Ohio Frontier: Crucible of the Old Northwest, 1720–1830.* Bloomington, Ind.: Indiana Univ. Press, 1996.

Hutton, Paul A. "William Wells: Frontier Scout and Indian Agent." *Indiana Magazine of History* 74 (Sept. 1978): 183–222.

Isaac, Rhys. "Stories and Constructions of Identity: Folk Tellings and Diary Inscriptions in Revolutionary Virginia." In *Through a Glass Darkly: Reflections on Personal Identity in Early America*, edited by Ronald Hoffman, Mechal Sobel, and Fredrika Teute, 206–37. Chapel Hill, N.C.: Univ. of North Carolina Press, 1997.

——. *The Transformation of Virginia, 1740–1790*. Chapel Hill, N.C.: Univ. of North Carolina Press, 1982.

[Jackson, Isaac R.]. *The Life of William Henry Harrison (of Ohio)*. . . . Philadelphia, Pa.: W. Marshall and Co., 1840.

Jacobs, James R. *The Beginning of the U.S. Army, 1783–1812*. Princeton, N.J.: Princeton Univ. Press, 1947.

——. *Tarnished Warrior: Major-General James Wilkinson*. New York: Macmillan Co., 1938.

James, C. L. R. *The Black Jacobins*. New York: Vintage Books, 1963.

Jillson, Willard R. "The Big Bones of Northern Kentucky." *Register of the Kentucky State Historical Society* 33 (July 1935): 181–90.

Jones, A. E. *Extracts from the History of Cincinnati*. . . . Cincinnati, Ohio: Cohen and Co., 1888.

Jones, Robert E. "Portraits of Dr. Benjamin Rush, M.D., by His Contemporaries." *Antiques* 108 (July 1975): 94–113.

Jones, Robert R. *Fort Washington at Cincinnati, Ohio*. Cincinnati, Ohio: Society of Colonial Wars in the State of Ohio, 1902.

Jordan, Winthrop D. *White over Black: American Attitudes toward the Negro, 1550–1812*. Chapel Hill, N.C.: Univ. of North Carolina Press, 1968.

Katzenberger, George A. *Major David Ziegler*. Columbus, Ohio: F. J. Heer Printing Co., 1912.

Kett, Joseph F. *Rites of Passage*. New York: Basic Books, 1977.

Kett, Joseph F., and Patricia A. McClung. "Book Culture in Post-Revolutionary Virginia." *Proceedings of the American Antiquarian Society* 94 (1984): 97–147.

Kierner, Cynthia A. *Scandal at Bizarre*. New York: Palgrave Macmillan, 2004.

Knopf, Richard C. "Crime and Punishment in the Legion, 1792–1793." *Bulletin of the Historical and Philosophical Society of Ohio* 14 (July 1965): 232–38.

Kohn, Richard H. *Eagle and Sword*. New York: Free Press, 1975.

Kulikoff, Allen. *Tobacco and Slaves: The Development of Southern Cultures in the Chesapeake, 1680–1800*. Chapel Hill, N.C.: Univ. of North Carolina Press, 1986.

Looney, J. Jefferson, and Ruth L. Woodward. *Princetonians, 1791–1794*. Princeton, N.J.: Princeton Univ. Press, 1991.

Ludwig, Arnold M. *How Do We Know Who We Are? A Biography of the Self*. New York: Oxford Univ. Press, 1997.

Lumpkin, H. Henry. *From Savannah to Yorktown*. Columbia, S.C.: Univ. of South Carolina Press, 1981.

Lyerly, Cynthia L. *Methodism and the Southern Mind, 1770–1810*. New York: Oxford Univ. Press, 2006.

Main, Jackson T. "The One Hundred." *WMQ*, 3rd series, 11 (July 1964): 354–84.

Malone, Dumas. *Jefferson the Virginian*. Boston, Mass.: Little, Brown and Co., 1948.

Marx, Rudolph. *The Health of the Presidents.* New York: G. P. Putnam's Sons, 1960.

Mastromarino, Mark A. "'The Horrid Disposition of the Times': Charles City County, Virginia, and the American Revolution." In *Charles City County, Virginia: An Official History,* edited by James P. Whittenburg and John M. Coski, 45–51. Salem, W.V.: Don Mills, 1989.

Mayo, Bernard. "Lexington: Frontier Metropolis." In *Historiography and Urbanization: Essays in American History in Honor of W. Stull Holt,* edited by Eric F. Goldman, 21–42. Port Washington, N.Y.: Kennikat Press, 1968. First published 1941.

McCabe, W. Gordon. *Virginia Schools before and after the Revolution.* Charlottesville, Va.: Society of the Alumni of the University of Virginia, 1890.

McColley, Robert. *Slavery and Jeffersonian Virginia.* Urbana, Ill.: Univ. of Illinois Press, 1964.

McDonald, Forrest. *Alexander Hamilton.* New York: W. W. Norton and Co., 1979.

McLean, John. *Sketch of Rev. Philip Gatch.* Cincinnati, Ohio: Swormstedt and Poe, 1854.

Meade, William. *Old Churches, Ministers, and Families of Virginia.* 2 vols. Philadelphia, Pa.: J. B. Lippincott and Co., 1857.

Meyer, Balthasar H., et al. *History of Transportation in the United States before 1860.* Gloucester, Mass.: Peter Smith, 1948. First published 1917.

Montgomery, Henry. *The Life of Major-General William Henry Harrison.* Philadelphia: Porter and Coates, 1852.

Morgan, Edmund. *Virginians at Home: Family Life in the Eighteenth Century.* Williamsburg, Va.: Colonial Williamsburg, 1952.

Morrison, Alfred J. *College of Hampden-Sidney—Dictionary of Biography, 1776–1825.* Hampden-Sydney, Va.: Hampden-Sydney College, 1921.

Mullin, Gerald W. *Flight and Rebellion: Slave Resistance in Eighteenth-Century Virginia.* New York: Oxford Univ. Press, 1972.

Murray, Iain. *Revival and Revivalism: The Making and Meaning of American Evangelicalism, 1750–1858.* Edinburgh: Banner of Truth Trust, 1994.

Nash, Gary B., and Jean R. Soderlund. *Freedom by Degrees: Emancipation in Pennsylvania and Its Aftermath.* New York: Oxford Univ. Press, 1991.

Nelson, Paul David. *Anthony Wayne: Soldier of the Early Republic.* Bloomington, Ind.: Indiana Univ. Press, 1985.

Niven, John. *Martin Van Buren and the Romantic Age of American Politics.* New York: Oxford Univ. Press, 1983.

Norfleet, Fillmore. *Saint-Memin in Virginia: Portraits and Biographies.* Richmond, Va.: Dietz Press, 1942.

Oberholtzer, Ellis P. *Robert Morris: Patriot and Financier.* New York: Macmillan Co., 1903.

Odom, William O. "Destined for Defeat: An Analysis of the St. Clair Expedition of 1791." *Northwest Ohio Quarterly* 65 (Spring 1993): 68–77.

Owens, Robert M. *Mr. Jefferson's Hammer: William Henry Harrison and the Origins of American Indian Policy.* Norman, Okla.: Univ. of Oklahoma Press, 2007.

Pace, F. "Daingerfield Family." *WMQ,* 1st series, 8, no. 2 (Oct. 1899): 96–100.

Pershing, B. H. "Winthrop Sargent." *Ohio Archeological and Historical Quarterly* 35 (Oct. 1926): 583–602.

Porter, Dorothy, and Roy Porter. *Patient's Progress: Doctors and Doctoring in Eighteenth-Century England.* Cambridge, UK: Polity Press, 1989.

Posey, John Thornton. *General Thomas Posey: Son of the American Revolution.* East Lansing, Mich.: Michigan State Univ. Press, 1992.

Powell, John H. *Bring Out Your Dead.* Philadelphia, Pa.: Univ. of Pennsylvania Press, 1949.

Prentiss, Charles. *The Life of the Late Gen. William Eaton.* Brookfield, Mass.: E. Merriam and Co., 1813.

Preston, John Hyde. *A Gentleman Rebel: The Exploits of Anthony Wayne.* New York: Farrar and Rinehart, 1930.

Proceedings of the 103d Annual Communication of the M. W. Grand Lodge of Ancient York Masons of Virginia. . . . Richmond, Va.: J. E. Goode, 1880.

Prucha, Francis Paul. *The Sword of the Republic: The United States Army on the Frontier, 1743–1846.* London: Collier-Macmillan Ltd., 1969.

Reinhold, Meyer, ed. *The Classick Pages: Classical Reading of Eighteenth-Century Americans.* University Park, Pa.: American Philological Association, 1975.

Riling, Joseph R. *Baron Von Steuben and His Regulations.* Philadelphia, Pa.: Ray Riling Arms Book Co., 1966.

Risch, Erna. *Quartermaster Support of the Army: A History of the Corps, 1775–1939.* Washington, D.C.: Office of the Quartermaster General, 1962.

Rothman, Ellen K. *Hands and Hearts: A History of Courtship in America.* Cambridge, Mass.: Harvard Univ. Press, 1987.

Rowland, Kate M. *Life of George Mason.* 2 vols. New York: G. P. Putnam's Sons, 1892.

Royster, Charles. *Light-Horse Harry Lee and the Legacy of the American Revolution.* New York: Alfred A. Knopf, 1981.

Rusche, Timothy M. "Treachery within the United States Army." *Pennsylvania History,* 65 (Autumn 1998): 478–91.

Sanderson's Biography of the Signers of the Declaration of Independence. Edited by Robert T. Conrad. Philadelphia, Pa.: Thomas, Cowperthwait and Co., 1848.

Scharf, J. T., and Thompson Westcott. *The History of Philadelphia.* 3 vols. Philadelphia, Pa.: L. H. Everts and Co., 1884.

Sellers, Charles Grier. "John Blair Smith." *Journal of the Presbyterian Historical Society* 34 (Dec. 1956): 201–25.

Shafer, Henry B. *The American Medical Profession, 1783 to 1850.* Studies in History, Economics, and Public Law, no. 417. New York: Columbia Univ. Press, 1936.

Silverberg, Robert. *Mound Builders of Ancient America: The Archeology of a Myth.* Greenwich, Conn.: New York Graphic Society, 1968.

Simmons, David A. *The Forts of Anthony Wayne.* Fort Wayne, Ind.: Historic Fort Wayne, 1977.

Skelton, William B. *An American Profession of Arms: The Army Officer Corps, 1784–1861.* Modern War Studies. Lawrence, Ks.: Univ. Press of Kansas, 1992.

Smith, Billy G. *The "Lower Sort": Philadelphia's Laboring People, 1750–1800.* Ithaca, N.Y.: Cornell Univ. Press, 1980.

Smith, Daniel Blake. *Inside the Great House.* Ithaca, N.Y.: Cornell Univ. Press, 1980.

Smith, Howard W. *Benjamin Harrison and the American Revolution.* Williamsburg, Va.: Virginia Independence Bicentennial Commission, 1978.

Speed, Thomas. *The Wilderness Road.* Filson Club Publications, no. 2. Louisville, Ky.: John P. Morton and Co., 1886.

[Stanard, W. G.]. "Harrison of James River." *VMHB,* 30:408–12; 31:83–87, 180–82, 277, 283, 361–80; 32:97–104, 199–202, 298–304, 404–10; 33:97–103, 205–8, 312–16, 410–16; 34:84–92, 183–87, 285–87, 384–88; 35:89–93, 207–11, 302–9, 451–55; 36:97, 199–206, 271–72, 385, 386; 39:173–77, 270–71; 40:95–96, 289–93, 377–79; 41:87, 162–66.

Staples, Charles. *The History of Pioneer Lexington, 1779–1806.* Lexington, Ky.: Univ. Press of Kentucky, 1996. First published 1939.

Stein, Stephen J. "The Conversion of Charles Willing Byrd to Shakerism." *Filson Club History Quarterly* 56 (Oct. 1982): 395–414.

Stilgoe, John R. *Borderlands: Origins of the American Suburb, 1820–1939.* New Haven, Conn.: Yale Univ. Press, 1988.

Sword, Wiley. *President Washington's Indian Wars.* Norman, Okla.: Univ. of Oklahoma Press, 1975.

Tate, Thad W., Jr. *The Negro in Eighteenth-Century Williamsburg.* Williamsburg Research Studies. Williamsburg, Va.: Colonial Williamsburg, 1965.

Todd, Charles S., and Benjamin Drake. *Sketches of the Civil and Military Services of William Henry Harrison.* Cincinnati, Ohio: U. P. James, 1840.

Truman, Ben C. *The Field of Honor.* New York: Fords, Howard, and Hulbert, 1884.

Tucker, Glenn. *Mad Anthony Wayne and the New Nation.* Harrisburg, Pa.: Stackpole Books, 1973.

Van Every, Dale. *Ark of Empire.* New York: William Morrow and Co., 1963.

Ver Steeg, Clarence L. *Robert Morris, Revolutionary Financier.* Philadelphia, Pa.: Univ. of Pennsylvania Press, 1954.

Wallace, Paul A. W. *Thirty Thousand Miles with John Heckewelder.* Pittsburgh, Pa.: Univ. of Pittsburgh Press, 1958.

Ward, Harry M. *Charles Scott and the "Spirit of '76."* Charlottesville, Va.: Univ. Press of Virginia, 1988.

Ward, Harry M., and Harold E. Greer Jr. *Richmond during the Revolution, 1775–1783.* Charlottesville, Va.: Univ. Press of Virginia, 1977.

Weeks, Stephen B. *Southern Quakers and Slavery.* Johns Hopkins University Studies in History and Political Science, extra volume, 15. Baltimore, Md.: Johns Hopkins Press, 1896.

Weslager, C. A. *The Delaware Indian Westward Migration.* Wallingford, Pa.: Middle Atlantic Press, 1978.

Whitaker, Arthur P. *The Mississippi Question, 1795–1803.* New York: D. Appleton-Century Co., 1934.

White, Richard. *The Middle Ground: Indians, Empires, and Republics in the Great Lakes Region, 1650–1815.* Cambridge, UK: Cambridge Univ. Press, 1991.

Wildes, Harry Emerson. *Anthony Wayne.* New York: Harcourt, Brace, and Co., 1941.

Wilson, Frazer E. *Around the Council Fire.* Mt. Vernon, Ind.: Windmill Publications, 1990. First published 1945.

———. *History of Darke County, Ohio. . . .* 2 vols. Milford, Ohio: Hobart Publishing Co., 1914.

Wilson, Paul C., Jr. *A Forgotten Mission to the Indians: William Smalley's Adventures among the Delaware Indians of Ohio.* Galveston, Tex.: privately published, 1965.

Wilstach, Paul. *Tidewater Virginia.* Indianapolis, Ind.: Bobbs-Merrill, 1929.

Worrall, Jay, Jr. *The Friendly Virginians: America's First Quakers.* Athens, Ga.: Iberian Publishing Co., 1994.

Wright, Louis B. *The First Gentlemen of Virginia: Intellectual Qualities of the Early Colonial Ruling Class.* Charlottesville, Va.: Dominion Books, 1964. First published 1940.

Young, Eleanor M. *Forgotten Patriot: Robert Morris.* New York: Macmillan Co., 1950.

Index